PRAISE FOR *THE BUDDHA AND THE BEE* SERIES

"Life is an adventure. Cory Mortensen has captured the fun, wisdom, and sense of accomplishment gained from keeping your heart and mind open to life's gifts."

—Rob Angel, Creator of *Pictionary*
WSJ Bestselling Author of *Game Changer*

"This book gave me the refreshment I needed; to put it more precisely, it was a short vacation from everything that I was reading and living. While reading this memoir, I went through the myriads of experiences with the author and lived the lives and places I have no connections with. It triggered some suppressed desires that I'd buried deep down in my mind and compelled those emotions that were just too surreal."

—*The Lectorem & Books*

"At times, *The Buddha and the Bee* series feels like what would happen if Jeff Spicoli, Sean Penn's iconic anti-hero from *Fast Times at Ridgemont High* had taken up biking and set his sights on San Francisco. Dude."

"*The Buddha and the Bee* book series sort of turns the idea of the inspirational memoir upside down, a few obscenities here and there joined at the hip by an occasional joint and near daily rural roadside Chinese dinners and overnight stays in forgotten America's roadside motels."

—*Devon Street Review*

"The only thing I didn't like about this book was that it ended. It's not just for bikers. It speaks to the heart of anyone who's ever wondered if their life is going in the right direction. Every page is a reminder that life is meant to be lived, not spent wishing for something to change. At best, this book will change your life. At worst, you'll be left hoping Saturn returns for you."

—Lisa T.

"Humorously written books that prove life isn't about the destination, but about the journey and all the beauty that unfolds if you simply allow life to come to you... with some effort of course.

"These books are page turners. I found myself lying in bed at night laughing aloud at the situations the author experienced while biking across the country. And at the same time, distilling life lessons that we all encounter into compassionate and simple statements that remind us that we're all human, living life and wanting to be happy and smile... even when hardships come our way."

—F. Schilling

"Cory takes the reader on a journey into the vast landscapes of the American West and into his deepest thoughts. Told from an honest, emotional, funny, self-deprecating perspective, it gives the reader pause to reflect on their own life and perhaps light a fire or at least stir some dormant embers of a quest for adventure. If you are a fan of *Blue Highways, Fear and Loathing in Las Vegas, On the Road, Into the Wild, A Walk In the Woods* or other similar tomes, then you should put *The Buddha and the Bee* books on your reading list."

—John H.

"This guy is crazy, someone who you don't want planning a trip for you, but who you'd probably love to have beers with or read a book by. A great storyteller with tons of asides and background info. If you have any interest in biking cross country, reading this will either convince yourself to do it or never try such a thing. Hopefully if you decide to, you'll plan it out better than he did."

—E.W. Bertram

"This books are engaging, humorous, and a great escape [especially during a pandemic]. Interesting facts and trivia about the landscape and cities Mortensen travels through are an added bonus. This series is a gift to the reader to examine our own lives and reveal our adventurous spirit!"

—Joyce E.

"I was in just the right mood to read a book like this. Different from my usual fiction, mysteries, etc., *The Buddha and the Bee* is the story of Cory Mortensen, who decides to make his way by bicycle from Minnesota to California with almost no supplies, no helmet, and practically no plan. Along the way, he meets his share of characters, eats a ton of Subway Italian sandwiches and Chinese food, stays in some of the country's sleaziest motels and takes in the sights in every town he visits—like the giant stuffed polar bear—The White King in Elko, Nevada. His bike breaks down multiple times, but he finally makes it to California.

"Cory Mortensen is a true free spirit. I have never done anything like he's done and I am envious. I hope he continues to have adventures and write about them! This book was a great change of pace for me from my normal reads and I enjoyed it immensely."

—Eileen

"Cory Mortensen writes about his journey biking from Minnesota to California. I 'oh, no'ed' every time a car pulled up. And, I had a mini-anxiety response every time he blew out a tyre! What really caught my attention were the historical aspects of the towns he went through. Interesting, engaging, entertaining! Well written and witty."

—Angie

"Can't put it down good! We all at some point in our lives catch the wanderlust itch. Most of us try try to scratch it with a week or two of vacation from our 9 to 5 existence. Cory, on the other hand, went all in by quitting his job and restructuring his life to undertake a cycling adventure followed by a South American trekking journey. Read part I, *The Buddha and The Bee* first. The adventuring flows in a free form manner, loosely planned with maximum opportunities for fun and fellowship. This is an extremely well written narrative with plenty of historical facts and side stories for context."

— Kenneth
Wanderlust Adventure

"*UNLOST* continues Cory's journey after his epic bike ride in *The Buddha and the Bee*. From immigration and border crossing issues to forty-hour bus rides, Cory's sense of humor guides us through his hitchhiking journey along the Pacific Coast Highway.

"I really enjoyed reading this 2nd installment of Cory's life changing adventure."

—Urbangirluk

"We read, in his first book, *The Buddha and the Bee*, about the author's bike ride from Minnesota to California. At that point, he made what, in my opinion, was the best decision of his life—he quit his job and kept traveling. I found *UNLOST* more casual and with many more interesting friends and scenery descriptions. Amazing how many young people travel freelance like this, and the temporary but strong bonds they form."

—Gypsy Grandmum

"There is nothing pretentious about this book. Rather it is like having a friendly catch up chat with a buddy: informal yet informative. So pull up your favorite chair, grab a beer, and enjoy the repartee."

— mlh

MIDDLE MILES

BOOKS BY CORY MORTENSEN

The Buddha and the Bee:
Biking Through America's Forgotten Roadways
On an Accidental Journey Of Discovery

UNLOST:
Roaming Through South America on a Spontaneous Journey

Embracing Bewilderment:
A Reluctant Entrepreneur's Journey—
An Unconventional European Summer Twisting into a
Mind-Bending Excursion Through Southeast Asia

Middle Miles:
Cycling From Canada To Mexico Along the Pacific Coast
Highway

MIDDLE MILES

CYCLING FROM CANADA TO
MEXICO ALONG
THE PACIFIC COAST HIGHWAY

CORY MORTENSEN

WHITE
CONDOR

MIDDLE MILES: CYCLING FROM CANADA TO MEXICO

ALONG THE PACIFIC COAST HIGHWAY

Published by White Condor LLC

www.White-Condor.com
Hardcover: 978-1-7354981-4-0
Paperback: 978-1-7354981-0-2

Library of Congress Control Number: 2025911807

Cataloging in publication on file with the publisher

Publishing and Production by Concierge Marketing Inc.

Printed in the United States of America

10 9 8 7 6 5 4 3 2 1

Dedicated to:
Kevin Flanders & his daughter Adia Flanders,
for their words of encouragement.

Eddie Karow for support and endless positivity.

Todd LeGare for the thirty years of friendship,
see you on the flip side.

"EVERY MAN IS THE SUM TOTAL OF HIS REACTIONS TO EXPERIENCE. AS YOUR EXPERIENCES DIFFER AND MULTIPLY, YOU BECOME A DIFFERENT MAN, AND HENCE YOUR PERSPECTIVE CHANGES. THIS GOES ON AND ON... SO IT WOULD SEEM FOOLISH, WOULD IT NOT, TO ADJUST OUR LIVES TO THE DEMANDS OF A GOAL WE SEE FROM A DIFFERENT ANGLE EVERY DAY? HOW COULD WE EVER HOPE TO ACCOMPLISH ANYTHING... THE ANSWER, THEN, MUST NOT DEAL WITH GOALS AT ALL...WE DO NOT STRIVE TO BE FIREMEN, WE DO NOT STRIVE TO BE BANKERS, NOR POLICEMEN, NOR DOCTORS. WE STRIVE TO BE OURSELVES. BUT DON'T MISUNDERSTAND ME. I DON'T MEAN THAT WE CAN'T BE FIREMEN, BANKERS, OR DOCTORS...BUT THAT WE MUST MAKE THE GOAL CONFORM TO THE INDIVIDUAL, RATHER THAN MAKE THE INDIVIDUAL CONFORM TO THE GOAL...BEWARE OF LOOKING FOR GOALS: LOOK FOR A WAY OF LIFE. DECIDE HOW YOU WANT TO LIVE AND THEN SEE WHAT YOU CAN DO TO MAKE A LIVING WITHIN THAT WAY OF LIFE."

—*Hunter S. Thompson*

CONTENTS

Day 1: Peace Arch Park, Canadian Border to Burlington, Washington 1

Day 2: Burlington, Washington to Port Townsend, Washington 23

Day 3: Port Townsend, Washington to Shelton, Washington 39

Day 4: Shelton, Washington to Raymond, Washington 51

Day 5: Raymond, Washington to Seaside, Oregon 59

Day 6: Seaside, Oregon to Pacific City, Oregon 71

Day 7: Pacific City, Oregon to Newport, Oregon 81

Day 8: Newport, Oregon to Florence, Oregon 91

Day 9: Florence, Oregon to Bandon, Oregon 101

Day 10: Bandon, Oregon to Gold Beach, Oregon 115

Day 11: Gold Beach, Oregon to Requa, California 123

Day 12: Requa, California to Eureka, California 139

Day 13: Eureka, California to Garberville, California 149

Day 14: Garberville, California to Fort Bragg, California 159

Day 15: Fort Bragg, California to Gualala, California 167

Day 16: Gualala, California to Petaluma, California 173

Day 17: Petaluma, California to San Francisco, California.....................179

Day 18: San Francisco, California to Santa Cruz, California....................185

Day 19: Santa Cruz, California to Carmel, California 193

Day 20: Carmel, California to Big Sur, California 203

Day 21: Big Sur, California to Paul's Landslide a.k.a. Lucia, California 215

       Paso Robles, California to San Simeon, California 215

Day 22: San Simeon, California to Santa Maria, California 221

Day 23: Santa Maria, California to Santa Barbara, California 229

Day 24: Santa Barbara, California to Malibu, California 235

Day 25: Malibu, California to Huntington Beach, California 243

Day 26: Huntington Beach, California to Carlsbad, California 249

Day 27: Carlsbad, California to Tijuana, The Border 253

Afterword 263

We made it! 265

About the Author 267

CALIFORNIA
1
PACIFIC COAST HIGHWAY

DAY 1

Peace Arch
Burlington
Port Townsend
Shelton
Raymond

WASHINGTON

Seaside
Pacific City
Newport
Florence

OREGON

Bandon
Gold Beach

Redwood National
and State Park
Requa
Eureka
Garberville
Fort Bragg
Gualala
Petaluma
San Francisco
Santa Cruz
Carmel
Big Sur
Lucia
San Simeon
Paso Robles
Santa Maria
Santa Barbara
Malibu
Huntington Beach
Carlsbad
Tijuana

DAY 1 - JULY 6, 2023

Peace Arch Park, Canadian Border to Burlington, Washington

49 MILES: 1,324' ELEVATION GAIN

We begin this trip on a small patch of grass, a place that blurs the line between the United States and Canada—Peace Arch Park. The road I will ride along is aptly named "Adventure, Uncertainty, and Everything in Between, Next Stop: the Twilight Zone." Or perhaps, "Final Stop: Mexico."

Every adventure starts with a gaze into the unknown. Experience has taught me that plans rarely survive the road. Flat tyres, arthritic knees, mechanical failures, unpredictable weather, and loneliness all lurk along the way. These challenges are not surprises; they are tests of resolve. So, while not every detail has been meticulously thought out, I have created a simple plan that can be modified as needed. I packed light, trusted in my abilities, and embraced the bewilderment ahead.

Why undertake this journey? This question often arises from a concerned parent or during that first torrential downpour while battling a headwind up a steep climb. For me, this ride represents how I choose to spend my fifty-third summer—twenty-three more if I'm fortunate. This journey is more than just an adventure; it is a fight against time, a rebellion against the physical process of aging.

In my mind, I'm the avatar of the scrappy kid I used to be, weighing one hundred nineteen pounds, with long, thick blond hair, hardly able to pinch an inch of skin on my toned body, blissfully unaware that I would someday grow old. Today, I am a fifty-three-year-old man with bags under my eyes, lines on my face, gray stubble, nose and ear hair, and a receding hairline. When I look in the mirror, I don't ask, "Mirror, mirror, on the wall, who is the fairest of them all?" The mirror is always honest; instead, I ask myself, *Who is that old man looking back at me?*

My avatar possesses the memory of a goldfish; he ignores my aches, pains, and the extra hundred pounds. He feels youthful, and so do I—young enough to embark on another biking adventure, travel without constraints or planning, and cling to a level of immaturity that still allows me to tap my niece's arm and say, "Tag, you're it."

Cory's Three Rules for Staying Young:

- Avoid mirrors.

- Convince yourself that all your friends are older than you.

- Ride your bike.

Today, I trade comfort and ease for uncertainty, danger, unpredictability, and isolation. Today marks another test to push myself further. Adapt, overcome, quit, or die trying. I ponder at what age I should set aside these youthful pursuits, settle down, and acknowledge my limitations. These four men have shown me the answer:

- Dale Sanders paddled the Mississippi River at age 87.

- M.J. "Nimblewill Nomad" Eberhart hiked the Appalachian Trail at the young age of 83.

- Dermot Higgins was 56 when he set the world record for biking around the globe.

- Yuichiro Miura summited Mount Everest at 80.

Tick-tock, tick-tock, tick-tock.

Disclaimer: While I stand by the quote I include in all my books—*"I hope this book guides you in some way, but this is not a guidebook"*—if you're reading this for guidance as you plan your own Pacific Coast adventure, you'll likely find some of the information useful. That said, I still recommend combining it with your own research. No two journeys are the same; part of the fun is figuring it out as you go.

This trip came together last minute. A few months earlier, my brother called to tell me that my nephews wanted to run a marathon with me as their Christmas present. To be honest, I wasn't thrilled about the idea of running a marathon. I was out of shape, and the thought of covering 26.2 miles felt like a nightmare—one I had already experienced sixteen times. I had originally aimed to run a marathon in all fifty states, but it occurred to me that aiming for seven continents might be a smarter goal. Having completed marathons in North and South America, Europe, Asia, and Antarctica, I just had Australia and Africa left to check off that list.

The marathon they chose was just outside of Portland, Oregon, held on July 4th, 2023, called "The Flats." In the end, I ran the half marathon with Micah, who was 16, while Elijah completed his first full marathon at 17.

I was touched that they wanted to spend time with their "funcle" (that's "fun uncle" for anyone who doesn't know), and it was a great opportunity to reconnect. I had only seen them a handful of times over the years since they were born and grew up on the island of Saipan. I'd flown out once to surprise them for Christmas. I saw them again when my dad passed away. Later they moved to Oahu, where Kate and I visited. The last time I saw them was in Columbus, GA, where they dared me to eat a Carolina Reaper—a fiery experience.

Now, they were older, their personalities more defined, and their curiosity about the world greater than ever. I took them up to Mount Hood, and we visited the Stanley Hotel. They'd never heard of *The Shining*, so I tried to share the movie's storyline, but they were more interested in watching the snowboarders enjoy the late snowfall. We hiked for about an hour, during which I recounted the story of the time their funcle almost got taken out by an avalanche while attempting to summit Mount Hood back in 1995. We celebrated our running accomplishments with a steak dinner at Jack's Grill in downtown Portland. Tomorrow, they would return home, and I would head north.

On the marriage front, Kate was in Norway for three weeks in June. She had performed for the King of Norway in the '90s when she sang with the St. Olaf Choir in college. The graduates from St. Olaf formed a group called Magnum Chorum choir with whom she performed with for over a decade, and now, as a board member, she was chaperoning the next generation of singers as they toured Norway.

While on a training run for the marathon, my mind started wandering, and I thought that if I brought my bike to Portland, I could take the train to Canada and then spend the month of July biking the Pacific Coast to Mexico.

I sent Kate a text:

"Hey babe, hope you're having a great time in Norway. Happy anniversary! Just wanted to let you know I've decided to bike from Canada to Mexico along the Pacific Coast Highway. Should be home by August 3rd."

Her reply came quickly:

"Yes, having a great time. That sounds fun; have a great ride. Thank you for the wonderful gift. Love you."

Kate was away for our tenth anniversary, and I had arranged for one of her friends to give her a necklace made by Amy Schilling, an internationally renowned artist—and my cousin. We don't like to keep score, but I'm pretty sure I scored some major points with that one.

My 19,416th day began with an unwelcome case of diarrhea, which struck me during the witching hour. It was brought on by the overpriced, microwaved hamburger I bought in the Amtrak commissary—not out of hunger, but as an excuse to leave my assigned seat. A seat that was right in front of two kids playing games on their iThings—with the volume on, naturally.

There are things that make us a society:

- You don't clip your toenails on a plane.

- You corral your grocery cart.

- You don't use the express lane with more than twelve items.

- You hold the door open for people behind you.

- You keep your kids in check in public. In this case, volume off on their damn iThings.

The Cascades line, marketed as "European-style," took me from Portland to Vancouver. East European-style might be more accurate—having experienced both, you can see what Amtrak wants to be, just as I want to be twenty-four again.

I found a place called Below the Botanist Bar, just a couple of blocks from Union Station, was the perfect place to kill some time as I waited for my European-style train ride north. I had a martini and made some small talk with the bartender, who had just returned from Guatemala. She showed off her fresh tattoo applied by a Mayan artist in Antigua—so she was told—she felt she was now one with the locals. The symbol? Something that meant something and nothing at all. "No one makes Pepián like they do in Antigua," she said, as she poured another cocktail.

I wanted to share my months roaming Central America, smuggling myself into Guatemala on a fisherman's boat and then sneaking back into Belize. Or my tattoo done by a guy in Chile that holds no cultural meaning, no significance—hell, it's not even finished. Just a weird line on my shoulder, $5 well spent.

The second drink always seems a little fuller. Maybe it's to encourage a bigger tip. My pen scratches notes in the Moleskine—thoughts flow faster now, and the pen seems to move of its own accord… but I know it's just the distilled wheat.

I watched a young couple take a seat at the bar. It seemed to be a first date. They ordered drinks, and she placed her hand on his leg. Her eyes were glued to him; his were glued to the game. For our first date, Kate and I went to *Les Misérables*. We started with a glass of wine, which quickly turned into a bottle. It was December, so I ordered the Beaujolais Nouveau to impress her. We then sat for three hours in the theater—no phones, just a brief chat during intermission, followed by mediocre egg rolls at an Irish bar. I'm still not sure how I scored a second date. Maybe she was moved by my sensitive side when I cried after Gavroche was shot.

"One more?" the Mayan bartender asks.

"Yes, no olives this time."

With my passport in my pocket, I was ready for the regulatory process at the northern border. Entering Canada had always been simple—just a wave and a smile, eh? Getting back into the States, however, was a bit more conversational. I'd been detained twice, once for "lying" to a customs agent. When asked, "Did you buy anything in Canada?" I answered, "No, just drove from Buffalo to Detroit—it was faster than going around Lake Erie."

"That a Tim Horton's wrapper?"

"Yeah, I had a burger on the way."

"You said you didn't buy anything in Canada."

"Food? I thought you meant something to declare."

"Please proceed to the left for further inspection."

The other time? That was my stupid nineteen-year-old self.

Sipping my cocktail, I started thinking about tomorrow—my first day on the bike. What time did I want to start? Looking at my maps app, I began to question my destination for the day. Should I pay three times more for a hotel room in Vancouver, or opt for a cheaper one in Bellingham? Did I want to arrive in Vancouver at midnight or Bellingham at 8 p.m.?

Bellingham was only twenty-five miles south of the Canadian border—less than a marathon. A distance that would stew in my head for the next twenty-something days if I started that far from the border. I couldn't say I rode from Canada to Mexico—it'd be from Bellingham to Mexico. And who's ever heard of Bellingham, Washington? Canada is an entire country. Country to country, across another country—that's something. Unless you're European, where 100 miles is far, then it's an epic trek.

Thanks to Steve Jobs, I used my iPhone and learned that the Whatcom[1] Transportation Authority (WTA) had a bus that could take me from Bellingham to the border town of Blaine, Washington—"Where America Begins," as their slogan goes.

In case you were wondering where America's *day* begins: Guam originally claimed that badge with its slogan, "Where America's Day Begins." However, having worked on Wake Island for a few months, I learned its slogan holds true: "Where America's Day Really Begins." Both are west of the International Date Line, but Wake wins by 1,302 miles.

Let's get back to the Marriott in Bellingham. After a few explosive trips to the hotel bathroom, going back to bed wasn't an option. I was wide awake. The usual Marriott amenities were in the room, but it was the coffee maker that was most important. The TV was on for companionship; the world was awaiting Sweden's NATO induction while Russia was shooting down American drones in Syria. And while it didn't make the news, here in Bellingham, I unpacked my bags and reviewed the inventory I was already so familiar with.

This wasn't my first long-distance bike ride. My first was almost as poorly planned as Charles Bedaux's 1934 "Champagne Safari" across Alaska, which included limousines, Citroën half-tracks, 130

---

1   From the Lummi people's word Xwot'qom, which means "noisy, rumbling water"

horses, a film crew, his wife, a butler, caviar, his Italian mistress, and, of course, cases of champagne. My first "safari" was a bike ride from Minneapolis to California, with nothing more than a tent, sleeping bag, change of clothes, debit card, bike pump, four spare tubes, and a solid sense of direction.

I documented the trip in *The Buddha and the Bee*. (Shameless plug.)

I did that ride in 2001. Back then, connecting with friends and family meant sending a random email when I found a library with a computer. No GPS, just a stack of Rand McNally maps. The most advanced technology I had was a cycling computer displaying speed and distance, based on a magnet attached to a spoke that passed a sensor on the fork—the faster the wheel spun, the faster I was going, and the miles ticked off. Brilliant and rudimentary.

Since then, I've done several long-distance rides, and I think I know what to bring and what not to bring. I still overpack and forget little things. In fact, my toothbrush and fingernail clippers were sitting in my bathroom at home. Pobody's nerfect.

Older and wiser, I heeded my Grandfather Heckenlaible's words, "Why would I want to sleep on the ground when there is a perfectly good hotel to be had?" My camping days were not entirely behind me; this was a "credit card ride." Towns, cities, and country markets provided drinks, snacks, and shelter if, by chance, I encountered a bit of rain. Each day's distance and destination dictated by the next town with an available hotel or motel, all pre-booked. Carrying food on a trip like this wasn't even part of the equation. Would I find myself in remote country? Yes, but would it be so remote that I might have to live off grubs to survive? There is always a solution. No, it would just be a couple of power bars for emergencies in case I started to fade from hunger in some remote landscape.

It was July. I was on vacation, which, by definition, is perfect. I packed for sunny days, blissful views, and transcendental musings—what awaited me for the next twenty-plus days. Aside from any unforeseen road closures, this Pacific Coast Highway was simply a point-to-point journey starting at the Canadian border and finishing at the Mexican border, with a couple of hills and turns along the way. Easy peasy lemon squeezy.

My rationale for pre-booking was based on the assumption that, now with COVID behind us, the Pacific Coast would be a traffic jam of cars and RVs—people crawling along the coast after years of forced isolation, in search of migrating whales, ice cream shops, and parents attempting to corral their disinterested kids for photo ops in front of the Pacific, Chinese tourists cutting in line, and motorcycle groups with matching leather jackets, beers in hand.

Pre-booked accommodations allowed me to pack light.

Handlebar Bag:

- Two T-shirts
- Two pair of shorts
- Extra set of bibs
- Extra set of socks
- Extra cycling jersey
- Flip-flops
- Cycling jacket
- Gloves

Frame Bag:

- iPad w/Bluetooth keyboard (to write the wisdom attained from each day on the road)
- Notebook and pen
- Four bottles of Stan's sealant—used to seal any tyre punctures as I was running tubeless
- Two tubes, as backup in case I can't get punctures to seal
- Knife, to fend off lions and tigers and bears
- Bike lock

- Bag full of charging cables for all the electronic devices
- Topeak Road Morph hand pump, with a built-in pressure gauge capable of reaching 160 psi, and a fold-out foot pad to help hold the pump steady for better leverage. This pump is the same one I had over twenty years ago when I did my first cross-country bike ride, and I still praise its awesomeness with the same exuberance Ralphie Parker had when talking about his Red Ryder carbine action, 200-shot, range model air rifle
- Bill Thorness's book, *Cycling the Pacific Coast: The Complete Guide from Canada to Mexico*

Cockpit Bag:

- Chain links, in case chain breaks – from experience
- Tyre glider (a superior tool in lieu of tyre irons)
- Tyre
- Plug repair kit
- Bike multi-tool
- Wallet
- iPhone

What I would be wearing each day:

- Pair of bibs
- Cycling jersey
- Socks
- Helmet
- Shokz headphones
- Sunglasses
- Heart rate strap
- Hoka running shoes

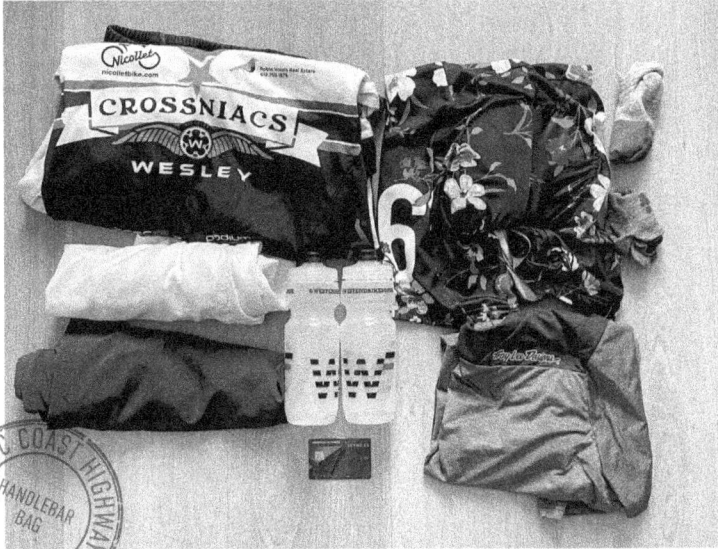

PACIFIC COAST HIGHWAY
JULY 6, 2023
READY TO GO

Thinking I would be doing some sort of exercise regime after a 5-6-7 hour bike ride, I opted for deck pedals instead of my usually preferred clipless pedals. This way, I wouldn't need to carry an extra pair of shoes. In hindsight, I should have stuck with clipless.

This brings us to the bike. Originally, I planned to take my Canyon Ultimate CF SLX 8 road bike, which is so fast it sends postcards back to the peloton while sipping a cappuccino. However, after visiting my local bike shop to stock up on spare tubes—because, as past experience has taught me, you can never have too many tubes—I changed my mind.

Greg, the shop owner, was showing his Pivot Vault gravel bike to the Pivot sales rep when I joined the conversation.

"Now that's the bike I should be taking on my trip. Tubeless tyres, off and on road toughness…able to leap tall buildings in a single bound."

"Throw your leg over it," he said.

I took it for a spin. "How much?"

"Well, I just built this for myself, but how about… [for the sake of my marriage, this information has been redacted]."

I handed him my credit card and never looked back. To this day, this is hands down my favorite bike, which I named Oceanus after Oceanus Hopkins. He is the only person born on the Mayflower, with no country of origin—just the open sea. This bike will have no home, no borders; it was built to roam, and roam it shall.

Mounted on the handlebars is the crown jewel: a Garmin 1040 cycling computer, a marvel of modern cycling technology. Each day of my ride was planned out using the Map My Ride website, downloaded into its electronic brain. If I were to get lost between Canada and Mexico, it would be because I worked hard at doing so. I could have chosen other technology, but when it comes to fitness gadgets, I pray at the Church of Garmin. The 1040, much like HAL 9000, occasionally develops a mind of its own, but it remains one of the best cycling computers I've ever used. Mornings began with a sip of coffee and a simple press of the *Start Route* button, followed by hours of mindlessly chasing the little arrow for as many miles as I had assigned myself that day. If I missed a turn—and I have and will—the 1040 will ask if I want to reroute or backtrack to my original course. I sometimes waited for it to say, "I'm sorry, Dave. I'm afraid I can't do that." That's when I know I'm lost.

Looking back at my first ride twenty-three years ago, using the Garmin felt like cheating; my old Rand McNally maps now seem as outdated as a sextant.

1

As I threw my bike onto the front rack of the bus at the Whatcom Transportation Authority Bellingham, WA station, the driver looked at me and said, "One dollar." I happily paid the fee and then glanced at the fee chart. $1.00 was the senior citizen rate.

"Senior Citizen." I looked at my reflection in the window of the bus. *Well, Cory, you skipped mid-life and jumped right into Senior Citizen.*

At Peace Arch Park, a lone U.S. Border Patrol truck sat in the lot. Between me and Canada stretched fifty yards—or fifty meters, to comply with the metric system the entire civilized world uses—of open grass, with one border patrol officer standing guard against the impending invasion from the land of Anne Murray, Tim Hortons, and millions of people who pledge allegiance to a maple leaf, eh.

The agent chatted with me for about ten minutes, sharing stories from his career in the Army—he was an Airborne Ranger. I asked if he knew my brother. "I know the name," he said. My brother Ryan, also an Airborne Ranger, is one of the rare few who serve as both a Ranger and a Chaplain. He has since climbed the ranks to Major.

"You probably want to get started on your ride," the agent said. "If you want to see the Arch, just follow that sidewalk, and you'll find the memorial. You'll be in an official no man's land between Canada and the United States. Go make the start official."

Flowers lined the paved path that led to a large, perfectly manicured field where a 67-foot-tall white marble arch stood in this undefended plot of land. The southern section of Peace Arch Park is maintained by Washington State Parks; the northern section is maintained by British Columbia Parks.

Built in honor of the treaty between the U.S. and Britain after the War of 1812, the Canadian and U.S. flags hung atop the arch without favoritism. Three inscriptions adorned the monument. On the United States side, it reads, "Children of a common mother," a nod to the British Empire. On the Canadian side, the inscription reads, "Brethren dwelling together in unity." Inscribed in the middle of the arch is the phrase: "May these gates never be closed."

With those fine words of unity and brotherly love set for all to see, on the very day I was born, May 9, 1970, four hundred and fifty Canadians invaded the United States, ripping down the inscription "May these gates never be closed." They scrawled "Amerika at War With the Earth," "Power to the People," "Free Bobby Seale," and various other slogans popular during the anti-Vietnam War era on the arch. The invaders made their way into Blaine, damaging buildings and cars, ripping down American flags from government buildings and the veterans' memorial.

"We'll have none of that," I assume the people of Blaine said, and began to fight back, pushing the Canadians back across the border. After the dust settled, Canada's House of Commons Member George Muir responded to the situation, calling it "a disgraceful invasion by a large group of hoodlums, queers, and just plain fools from the Canadian side of the border who tore down the American flag and engaged in insurrection."

Maybe it was good the border patrol was keeping an eye on things.

Ceremoniously, I took a photo of my bike against the arch to share with my social media followers, gave the flags a salute, and started my trip. The journey to Mexico had begun, a web of interconnected roads now leading me south, through new landscapes, unfamiliar scents, unexpected encounters, and the unpredictable joys of the open road. It's that mix of unknown experiences that keeps me loading up my gear, strapping on my helmet, and making that first pedal stroke.

With the border in the rearview, 1850+/- miles of bituminous companionship stretched ahead. Today, I found myself on a flat country road with a generous shoulder; traffic opted for Interstate 5, which ran parallel to Portal Way Road.

After Blaine came Custer, Washington. At fifteen, Loretta Lynn married Oliver Lynn, and he immediately moved her to Custer. During her fourteen years there, she not only wrote "I'm a Honky Tonk Girl," but she also embraced her secret skill—being a ribbon-winning favorite at the Northwest Washington Fair for her canning skills. Today, Custer is little more than a handful of buildings, a few homes, and 518 residents. In 1890, the town was relocated to its current location to accommodate the railroad; one hundred and thirty years later, a train derailment spilled 30,000 gallons of oil. Cause of the accident? Sabotage.

Next stop: Ferndale. Originally named Jam due to a mile-long log jam on the Nooksack River so old that trees and shrubs were growing on it. In 1876, local resident Phoebe Judson had had enough. She raised $450 and paid a group of men to clear the obstruction. A year later, the jam was no more.

While the town was known as Jam, it was never officially registered. The name Ferndale came about when Alice Eldridge, the first schoolteacher in the area, was writing a letter to her father. She asked her mother, "How shall I head this letter? I don't know where I am." Before her mother could respond, she said, "Oh, I know. I'll call it Ferndale because there are so many ferns around the schoolhouse."

Back in Bellingham, I took time to enjoy a bit of its downtown. A ride along Harris Ave, named after an eccentric smuggler by the name of Dirty Dan Harris, led me past a series of randomly placed inscribed stones highlighting peculiar bits of this port city's history:

SITE OF FIRE WAGON AND HAY BARN 1904

CHINESE DEADLINE NO CHINESE ALLOWED BEYOND THIS POINT 1898-1903 / MAYOR APOLOGIZES TO CHINESE COMMUNITY 2011

HERE IS WHERE MATHEW WAS CUT IN TWO BY A STREETCAR 1891

POLICEMAN PHIL DeFRIES SHOT AT 23 TIMES 1899-1905
(NOT SURE IF HE WAS SHOT AT 23 TIMES BETWEEN THESE DATES OR 23 TIMES ON EACH OF THESE DATES. SOMEONE CLEARLY DIDN'T LIKE HIM.)

SITE OF AM LOW'S OPIUM DEN 1904

CHINESE MAFIA ATTEMPT ASSASSINATION HERE 1909

SITE OF CITY DROWNING POOL DOGS ONLY 1891

The last one caught my attention. Drowning pools were originally put into use in 1057 by Scottish King Canmore as a gentler way to execute women instead of hanging, which was considered a violent death reserved for men. The practice ended in 1685 when Scottish Episcopalians executed two Scottish Covenanters found guilty of being rebels. The French continued the practice until 1793. Bellingham? They kept the practice going for another hundred years, reserved only for unwanted dogs.

The most fascinating legend associated with this area is known as the Spanish Massacre, which, if true, would suggest that Europeans were present as early as the 1600s. According to the legend, the Spanish arrived, built a fort, and began mistreating the local Indigenous people. The Indians quickly decided they would not tolerate this, and attacked and slaughtered the four hundred Spaniards. What makes this story particularly intriguing is that historical records indicate the Spanish did not arrive until the 1790s. So who were those four hundred individuals that arrived and died here two hundred years earlier?

South of Bellingham was a lookout station watching for marauding Indians. In 1857, settlers stationed two men to stand watch. While on duty, they drank whiskey, became intoxicated, and were subsequently killed by, you guessed it, marauding Indians, which led to the name Dead Man's Point.

Thanks to Charles Larrabee, the world gets to enjoy Chuckanut[2] Drive. Nicknamed "Washington's Big Sur," this 24-mile ribbon of asphalt winds along the edge of the Cascade Mountains. Built by thousands of convicts, it overlooks Samish Bay, the San Juan Islands, and Chuckanut Bay. For cyclists, it offers no shoulder whatsoever. It is, in fact, one of the most beautiful rides I have ever experienced. Aside from two logging trucks that nearly hit me on a blind curve, most traffic was patient and tolerant of my slow pace and waited for an opportunity to pass.

I pulled into the first scenic overlook to catch my breath and enjoy the view. I watched ferries and other boat traffic slowly move east, west, north, and south. This was my first long climb in a while, albeit a gentle ascent surrounded by dense forest and plenty of big trucks to provide some adrenaline for good measure.

For his generosity, Governor Ernest Lister named Washington's first state park after him: Larrabee State Park.

Just past the park was the Samish Shellfish Market & Oyster Bar, where a sign read "FRESH OYSTERS." With names like Oyster Creek, Oyster Creek Lane, and Oyster Dome Trail, there is no doubt that oysters have been part of the Pacific Northwest since time immemorial.

Burlington was my goal for the day. Once there, I picked up a few items: a fingernail clipper, water, a couple of ramen noodle bowls, and, for whatever reason, $20 worth of lottery tickets. I decided not to replace the Elmo child's toothbrush my nephews bought me in Portland

---

2   "Long beach far from a narrow entrance," Translation from the Nooksack language

after I realized I had forgotten my toothbrush. Elmo was now part of the journey.

Let me revisit and share a few features of the Garmin 1040, as there may or may not be references to it later. It is just a tad smaller than an iPhone, which means it has a nice large screen and gathers a tremendous amount of information. I probably use only 15% of its capabilities and rarely, if ever, review the data I collect. I do love that I can see my speed, heart rate, time of day, distance, distance to destination, grade percentage, and average speed all on one screen. All of these data points can be adjusted, including Grade, Time of Day, Average Speed, etc. If I swipe the screen, I can see a detailed map with an elevation profile; another swipe takes me to a screen with a compass, and more screens can be added and customized if I choose.

I only use two of the screens: the one displaying the seven bits of information and the one showing the map.

The map features a unique element: the Virtual Partner (VP), represented as a second arrow. One arrow represents me, while the other represents my virtual nemesis—my younger, fitter self, a ghost from past rides stored in the memory of my Garmin. The VP allows me to race against myself, serving as a moving benchmark of previous efforts. It's significantly faster than I am on the climbs. Or perhaps I was once faster than I am now on the climbs?

Matrix-level thoughts began to creep in. No matter—today, my Virtual Partner (VP) beat me. Handsomely.

CORY: 0
VP: 1

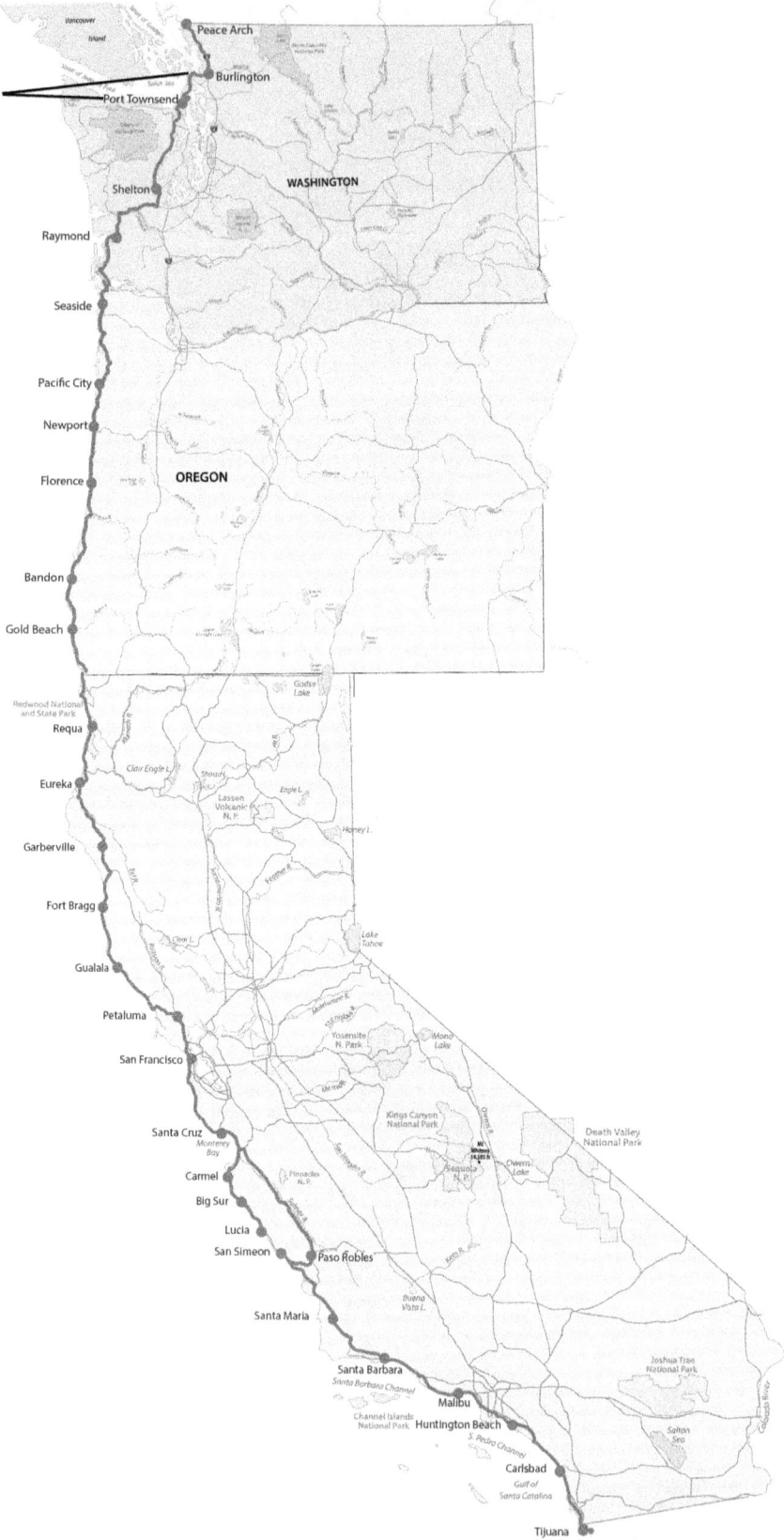

DAY 2

Peace Arch
Burlington
Port Townsend
Shelton
Raymond
Seaside
Pacific City
Newport
Florence
Bandon
Gold Beach
Requa
Eureka
Garberville
Fort Bragg
Gualala
Petaluma
San Francisco
Santa Cruz
Carmel
Big Sur
Lucia
San Simeon
Paso Robles
Santa Maria
Santa Barbara
Malibu
Huntington Beach
Carlsbad
Tijuana

WASHINGTON

OREGON

DAY 2 - JULY 7, 2023

Burlington, Washington to Port Townsend, Washington

54 MILES: 1,630' ELEVATION GAIN

During my first cross-country solo ride, by day two I found myself in a state of depression brought on by loneliness. I was also experiencing significant pain due to a lack of training. After day five, following hours of convincing myself to quit while riding through vast cornfields, I broke through the depression, and the physical pain began to dissipate, thanks to some sort of mind-body truce. When the mind declares that you are done, exhausted, and wiped out, the body often has more energy than you realize. Out here, the world became smaller. My focus narrowed to survival—getting through the day, proving to myself that I could reach point B, regardless of the obstacles, whether physical or mental. I knew where I had been—a life unwanted. Now, my eyes were opening with a liberating clarity.

By day six, my perspective on being alone had changed. By day twelve—to paraphrase Joan Didion—I had lost touch with a couple of the people I used to be and started becoming the person I was meant to be. Alone and free from distractions, I could finally see myself clearly.

By day twenty, I was entirely different. By then, I was in the desert, and the desert has a transformative effect. It strips everything down until you are nothing more than part of it. You don't conquer it—you survive it. I was no longer interested in being part of society; I had become part of my surroundings.

In the final two days, depression set in again—not from loneliness, but from knowing the end was near. On day one, I had wanted the trip to be over before it even started. By the final days, I didn't want it to end. And in a way, it never did.

That ride marked the beginning of something else. Instead of heading home, I left my bike in California and spent the next two years
traveling the world. Eventually, I started a company, sold it ten years
later, got married to Kate a month after that, fulfilled a two-year contract, and in 2015, along with Kate, we sold everything and spent two
years traveling, volunteering, trekking, and exploring South America.

Now, I embark on this journey—shorter, but no less meaningful. A
trip to scratch the itch to move, to grow, to embrace the unknown. If
only for this month of July.

Today's weather was a far cry from yesterday's sunny, 75-degree
perfection—a light drizzle paired with a brisk 50 degrees. Cars and
trucks disappeared into a low-hanging cloud.

By comparison, my last ride was in Phoenix, where it was 112 degrees. Now, I was downright frozen. I patted myself on the back for
bringing my jacket and gloves—packed on the off chance it might be
cold for a day or two on this little July ride down the Pacific Coast.
Turns out, I'd be wearing them all the way to Santa Barbara.

Throwing my leg over the bike, I settled in. A few pedal strokes, and
I disappeared into the mist.

The Swinomish Channel Bridge carried me onto Fidalgo Island. In
1493, Spain claimed exclusive rights to colonize the entire Western
Hemisphere—except Brazil, which was handed to Portugal, and is why
Brazil is the only country in South America that speaks Portuguese.

With whom did the Spanish negotiate these exclusive rights? The
Russians? The Africans? The Chinese? No matter. The claim was made,
and 300 years later, Spaniard Salvador Fidalgo arrived to explore the
region known as New Spain.

By the 1700s, Britain and Russia had established fur trading posts
in the Pacific Northwest, infringing on Spain's claim to *New Spain* (try
saying that ten times fast). In 1819, the signing of the Adams-Onís

Treaty handed over all Spanish-claimed lands—including California and Florida—to the United States. So, the next time you're sipping mojitos and dancing merengue in South Beach or hanging ten off your favorite California beach, you can thank the sixth President of the United States, John Quincy Adams.

Before all these white people showed up and crashed the party, the land belonged to the Samish—*"People who are there/who exist"*—and the Swinomish—*"People by the water"*—who had been living peacefully, enjoying island life, for thousands of years.

At Pass Lake, I stopped to take in the glass-like water wrapped in low clouds. *"Smoke on the water, fire in the sky."*

I took a photo. One that will eventually be deleted because—let's be honest—who but me will ever care about it? My dad was an amateur photographer who had a darkroom and loved making photos, which is why we have stacks of photo albums. Now, images are stored in the cloud, one forgotten password away from being lost forever in a world of ones and zeros.

The photo album of the future: strangers' images stored in a cloud, waiting to be repurposed to generate random AI images for other strangers.

Sorry friends, the machines have won.

A calendar reminder popped up. I sent a text. Today was my buddy Todd's fifty-second birthday.

"Happy birthday, handsome."

"Thanks, Cory. Woke up to this… pretty solid start."

He sent a picture from inside his tent, the sun creeping over the trees.

I wanted to send him a picture of my bike leaning against the Peace Arch, to tell him where I was and what I was doing—but it was his birthday. And a damn good one. His doctor had just informed him he'd beaten pancreatic cancer, miraculously catching it at stage two.

The last time Todd and I hung out was a year ago. Along with his brother Mike, we picked up right where we left off, just as we always had. That was our friendship—solid, nonjudgmental, loving, respectful, timeless.

I met Todd at a party in Winona, MN. Not long after, I got him a job at the architecture firm where I was working in Minneapolis, and we became roommates. The day he moved in, we bungee-strapped his mattress to the top of my Bronco II. Without thinking, I jumped onto the interstate. That's when the straps snapped, and his mattress took flight, landing in the middle lane of the highway. As we watched it soar through the air, I looked at him and said, "So, you're sleeping on the couch?"—which he did. For six months.

Todd had dreams of moving to San Francisco, chasing the Silicon Valley boom. It didn't take much for me, Ric, and Adam to make sure he got there. Todd in his 1986 Honda Prelude—sans air conditioning—Ric in his 1995 Saturn SL1, and all of us armed with a VHS tape recorder, no plan, just an arrival date. We headed west. The Badlands of South Dakota. Wall Drug. Mount Rushmore. Racing cars on the Bonneville Salt Flats. Sleeping at roadside rest stops.

Todd settled into his new place in San Francisco. Adam, Ric, and I made the executive decision to go to Tijuana. The rest of that story… I'll leave to your imagination.

Years later, over a couple of whiskeys, Todd and I caught up on life—the present, before drifting into the past. Old loves, bad decisions, motorcycle trips, and the kind of adventures that stack up over two decades of friendship. As the night ended, we made plans to reconnect the following summer. Two years was too long.

The cosmos had different plans.

Three months after this text exchange, the cancer was back. This time, the doctor gave him four months.

"Hey buddy, I'm on the next flight whenever you're ready. Love you, Todd. You are beyond special."

"Thanks, Cory…Love you too."

I made two trips to see him, but the cancer advanced too quickly. 118 days after this birthday text exchange, he was gone.

It had been a tough couple of years. I lost my buddy Shawn—forty-eight summers old. Ric and Tony—both just forty-nine summers. Marc—gone by his own hand. And my dad—69 summers, over a decade ago now.

When you lose friends—the kind you have history with, the kind who know the best and worst of you—there's a part of you that resists making new ones. Because you know you'll lose them, too. I try to live my life in honor of theirs.

Losing my dad was hard—it happened so fast. To lose a parent is surreal. It took me months to even accept it. Then one day, I was in my office, picked up a notebook, and saw his handwriting. Beautiful, distinct, familiar. That's when it hit me.

But losing Todd—that hit the hardest. When he left the game, I realized I was just one of a handful of pieces still on the board, playing a game with no reset.

It'd be nice to think that when the game is over, the game master reassigns us—same players, different game. Maybe that explains why some of us are born with natural talents—skills carried over from a previous life. Why, when we meet certain people, it feels like we've known them forever.

Because maybe…we have.

"Every existing thing is born without reason, prolongs itself out of weakness, and dies by chance."
—*Jean-Paul Sartre*

①

Just west of Pass Lake stood the totem of *Maiden of Deception Pass*, a homage to the Samish maiden Ko-kwal-alwoot. While walking along the shore one day, she met a handsome sea creature and fell in love. In exchange for her hand, the sea creature promised the Samish that the sea would always provide them a full bounty. The totem depicts her life as she lived on the land on one side and her life as she lived in the sea on the other.

This duality theme is seen in all mythology: good and evil, light and darkness, life and death, death and resurrection—in this case, land and sea.

Spaniard Manuel Quimper was the first European to chart the area he named Deception Pass, *Boca de Flon*, in 1790, believing it to be just a bay. Two years later, Joseph Whidbey, a member of the Royal Navy, took a deeper dive into exploring the area. He circumnavigated what is now called Whidbey Island, referring to the pass as "Deception," as it had deceived the Spanish into thinking it was merely a bay. Captain George Vancouver honored him by naming the island Whidbey. The Salishan people, who had been gathering nuts, berries, and roots, and fishing in the area for over ten thousand years, were likely unaware of the Spanish claim to the entire region. They already knew it was an island, which they called Tscha-kole-chy.

Deception Pass Bridge is a 1,487-foot-long steel bridge suspended 180 feet above the water, built by the Civilian Conservation Corps (CCC) in 1934 and completed in 1935. The CCC was part of Franklin D. Roosevelt's New Deal, which provided work projects during the Depression for young unmarried men. The program lasted from 1933 until the Japanese bombed Pearl Harbor in 1942, diverting funds used for the CCC to the war effort. Notable participants in the CCC included Raymond Burr, Robert Mitchum, Walter Matthau, and Chuck Yeager.

From the bridge, I descended onto Whidbey Island, taking full advantage of gravity and shifting my gears to see how fast I could go. That's when the chain dropped off the rear cassette, wedging itself between the cassette and the frame. At that moment, I thought my ride was over, and I hate to admit it, but the thought of the ride ending gave me a sense of relief, which I quickly squashed.

A quick yank freed the chain, and I shifted the gears to ensure everything was functioning properly. I was back on the horse, heading to the Coupeville Ferry Terminal. It was 11:45 a.m., and I had 24 miles to cover to catch the 1:15 p.m. ferry. If I missed it, the next ferry was at 2:45 p.m.

The Blue Fox Drive-In Theatre opened in 1959, debuting with the film *April Love*. Legend has it, a story I have heard more times than I can count, that the name Blue Fox came about when the owner contacted a sign company said, "I've got a deal for you if you're not picky about your name. You know the old Blue Fox Drive-In restaurant? I repossessed one of the signs; if you want it, it's a heck of a deal."

After missing the 1:15 p.m. ferry and shivering from the cold, I found refuge at Callen's, a ma and pa restaurant next to the dock that offered some wonderful clam chowder and tea.

As the ferry approached, I grabbed my bike and queued up. A woman with her dog struck up a conversation, commenting on my bike bibs, which had a floral print. She then proceeded to share the best pot dispensaries to stop at while in Oregon. She was retired and had been exploring the San Juan Islands, now on her way home to Port Angeles.

When she asked what I did, I replied, "I'm an author."

After I wrote my first book, Kate congratulated me on becoming an author. "No," I told her. "Anyone can write one book. I'm not an author until I write two."

When I finished my second book, she congratulated me again. "Now you're an author."

"Nope, it still doesn't feel right. I think I need to write a third. Then I can call myself an author."

I finished that third book in 2022. This was the first time a stranger had asked me what I did, and I said, "I'm an author."

She opened her Amazon app. "There, I just bought all three."

"Thank you. That just paid for the ferry ride. Hope you enjoy them."

She headed to the upper deck, which was enclosed and warm. I stayed on the bow of the vehicle deck, watching the ferry, boats, and ships move through Puget Sound, keeping an eye out for whales. Summer is the best time to see humpbacks, grays, and minke, but the one that has always eluded me is the orca.

A retired couple approached and stood next to me. The husband asked, "How far are you going?"

I love that question when I'm on a long-distance ride. It usually elicits one of two responses:

"Oh, I wish I had done that."

"You're riding alone?! How long will it take you?"

Sometimes, you get the unexpected:

"My wife and I rode our bikes from Alaska to Panama in 1977."

Or:

"I used to race with Greg LeMond in the '80s."

One of my favorites happened on a flight to Montana. An older gentleman—70s, maybe 80s—sat next to me. I was working on a crossword puzzle, earbuds in. Everything about my body language said, *I don't want to talk.*

"So, I see you're doing a crossword puzzle," he said.

"Yup."

"Using a pen. My first wife used to use a pen when she did crossword puzzles."

"That's nice."

The flight attendant came by, and we both ordered Scotch. She filled the glasses to the rim, and when she handed him his, he smiled and said, "Well, that's a real humdinger."

I laughed. We toasted, and just like that, I found myself in one of the most fascinating conversations I've ever had.

"I was a pilot in World War II."

"Were you a pilot when you enlisted?"

He gave me a sideways glance and smirked. "I was seventeen. My mom lied for me. I had never even been in a plane. My first solo flight, the instructor said, 'Point to the stick.' I pointed. 'Point to the instruments.' I pointed. He handed me a pair of headphones, patted me on the back, wished me luck, and then spent the next thirty minutes yelling instructions at me while I flew around the base. Once I was qualified, they sent me to New Guinea."

"What did you fly?"

"P-38s."

"No way. You flew P-38s?! Those are amazing."

The P-38 Lightning was one of the most iconic planes of WWII, known for its twin tails and sleek design.

He grinned. "On leave, I'd tell the ladies at the bar that I could handle two tails at a time."

"Did that line ever work?"

"Not once." He took a sip of his Scotch.

"What was a normal day like?"

"Every morning, we woke up, ate breakfast, then jumped in our planes and strafed[3] the Japanese base on the other side of the island. Came back, refueled, rearmed, had lunch—then strafed them again. Most of my time was in New Guinea. As the U.S. moved closer to Japan, I was stationed in Vietnam, then Hong Kong. That's where I was when they dropped Little Boy on Hiroshima. Three days later, Fat Man on Nagasaki. A month later, the war was over."

"Was that the end of your military career?"

"Oh no. In 1948, I was part of the Berlin Airlift. Flew Gooney Birds."

---

3   Attack repeatedly with bombs or machine-gun fire from low-flying aircraft

"C-47s? My dad flew DC-10s when he started as a pilot and had little Gooney Bird statuettes."

I took a sip. "Man, you need to write a book. You are American history."

He shrugged. "Then I flew troops in and out of Korea. Qualified to pilot Air Force One but decided I wanted a family."

"Amazing. What brings you to Bozeman?"

"Hiking."

"Alone?"

He smiled and finished his scotch. "Nobody else wanted to go with me."

This guy was the real-life Allan Karlsson[4].

The couple I met on the ferry were taking their RV down the coast. He had built multi-million-dollar custom homes in the San Francisco Bay Area and recently sold the business to his employees. Their daughter had spent the past decade teaching English abroad—South Korea, Ghana, Mexico City, and now San José, Costa Rica.

"I wish she would just come home and settle down," her mother sighed. "But we know that's not who she is. She should live the life that suits her, so we support her."

First stop in town: The Broken Spoke bike shop.

On my first long-distance ride, I broke a spoke in Wendover, Nevada—a town with no bike shops. I had to ride 107 miles wobbling across the desert before finding, by some miracle, a bike shop in Elko. So, The Broken Spoke seemed a fitting name. Hopefully not an omen.

I hate skipping the line, but when I'm riding long-distance and have a mechanical issue, I don't hesitate to let the shop know. Nine times out of ten, they'll throw my bike on the stand immediately. The derailleur was ghost-shifting, so while the mechanic worked his magic, I discussed my route with the owner.

---

4   Main character who at 100 escapes his retirement home to embark on a new adventure in *The 100-Year-Old Man Who Climbed Out the Window and Disappeared*, novel by Jonas Jonasson

From Port Townsend, riders face two options:

Option 1: West around the Olympic Peninsula. More remote, fewer places to stay. I wasn't carrying a tent, so I ruled it out.

Option 2: South along the Hood Canal. More services, more places to sleep. This was my pick.

I had already decided on Option 2 due to the lack of motels on Option 1. The bike shop owner shook his head. "That route's dangerous. Windy, lots of traffic, no shoulder."

Not what I wanted—or needed—to hear.

I have a thing about people telling me what I can't or shouldn't do. Nine times out of ten, the people dishing out these warnings have never done the thing they're warning against. But this guy had. He lived here. He'd ridden it.

I took his words under advisement, but I had no intention of changing my route.

Next stop: Siren's Pub, with its inviting sign—*"Be a local – Come on up!"*

I locked my bike, climbed the creaky wooden stairs, and stepped into my favorite bar in Port Townsend.

When Kate and I returned from South America, I took a consulting job with a guy who headquartered his company here. I'd been to Port Townsend at least a dozen times, and each time, I made it a point to stop at Siren's.

Bellying up to the bar, I ordered food, logged into the Wi-Fi, checked emails, and posted an update on my Facebook author page.

I followed a Pacific Coast Bike Route Facebook group—great for connecting with other riders, asking questions, and sharing updates. Riders often offered their couches to those passing through.

Today, someone posted a sobering update: Bradley Stark, age fifty-seven, was killed riding his bike along Highway 101 by a logging truck near Lincoln Beach, Oregon.

I closed my eyes. The trucks had been merciless back on Chuckanut Drive. That *could* have been me. I try not to dwell on it—what would happen if I got hit? Does Kate have all the passwords? Does she know the safe combination?

I've had cars turn in front of me, drivers try to run me off the road—but I've never been hit. Yet.

In 2022, 928 cyclists were killed by motor vehicles in the U.S.

June 17, 2017, a friend of mine was killed riding his bike by a sixteen-year-old girl who was texting and driving. She got a slap on the wrist. He was fifty-six and left behind a wife and daughter. It was his birthday.

Thinking about Bradley—and the bike shop owner's words about the road ahead—I decided I'd leave at first light to beat the traffic.

Until then, I could only enjoy the rest of the day.

My final stop—for the night, at least—was The Palace Hotel in Port Townsend, picked specifically because it's haunted.

I used to travel a lot for work and made it a point to stay in haunted hotels. They didn't offer the same amenities as my preferred Marriott, but they added a little spice to the trip. Plus, they were great conversation starters when breaking the ice with new clients.

A few favorites:

- Holiday Inn Express, Grand Island, Buffalo, NY – Home to
  Tanya, a little girl who reportedly runs through the hallways
  and has a particular fondness for Room 412. One night, I
  heard a child laughing and running down the hall. I opened
  the door—empty hallway. Imagination is powerful.

- Biltmore, Coral Gables, Miami, Florida – A strange place. Hosts a few ghosts, most notably Thomas "Fatty" Walsh, a mobster shot dead on—wait for it—the 13th floor. There's also a woman in a white dress who supposedly killed herself after being jilted at the altar. The one time I stayed there, they gave me a room on the 13th floor. Just before the witching hour, I called the front desk:

  "I'd like to change rooms."

  "I'm sorry, sir. Why?"

  "I'm on the 13th floor. I think you know why."

  A brief pause.

  "Certainly, sir. We'll move you to the 11th floor."

  Not saying weird stuff happened. Not saying it didn't. Just saying… switching floors was the right move.

- Hassayampa Inn, Prescott, Arizona – Home to Faith, a young bride who committed suicide after her husband disappeared on their honeymoon. Kate and I stayed there. No ghosts, no incidents.

- Whitehall Mansion Inn, Mystic, Connecticut – Hands down, my favorite haunted place to stay. I've booked Lucy's room multiple times. The first time, I left to grab a glass of wine. The room's lock requires a key to turn the bolt. I left the door unlocked and had the key. Came back five minutes later—it was locked. The second time, I tossed a pile of clothes onto the bed while searching for something to wear. I left the room for a few minutes, came back—all my clothes were neatly folded. Apparently, Lucy enjoys tidying up.

- The Palace Hotel, once a brothel nicknamed *The Palace of Sweets*, is said to be haunted by a few of the working girls who never left. The most famous? Claire, the Lady in Blue. According to the guy at check-in, she's been known to make her presence felt in Room 4. A painting of her hangs near the staircase. If she's missing from the painting, she's wandering the halls. When I checked, she was in the painting.

The only experience I had was a restless night with very little sleep.

Maybe it was Claire. Maybe it was my imagination. Maybe I was just anxious.

Whatever the reason, by the time I finally started drifting off, the sun was coming up.

CORY: 1
VP: 1

CALIFORNIA
1
PACIFIC COAST HIGHWAY

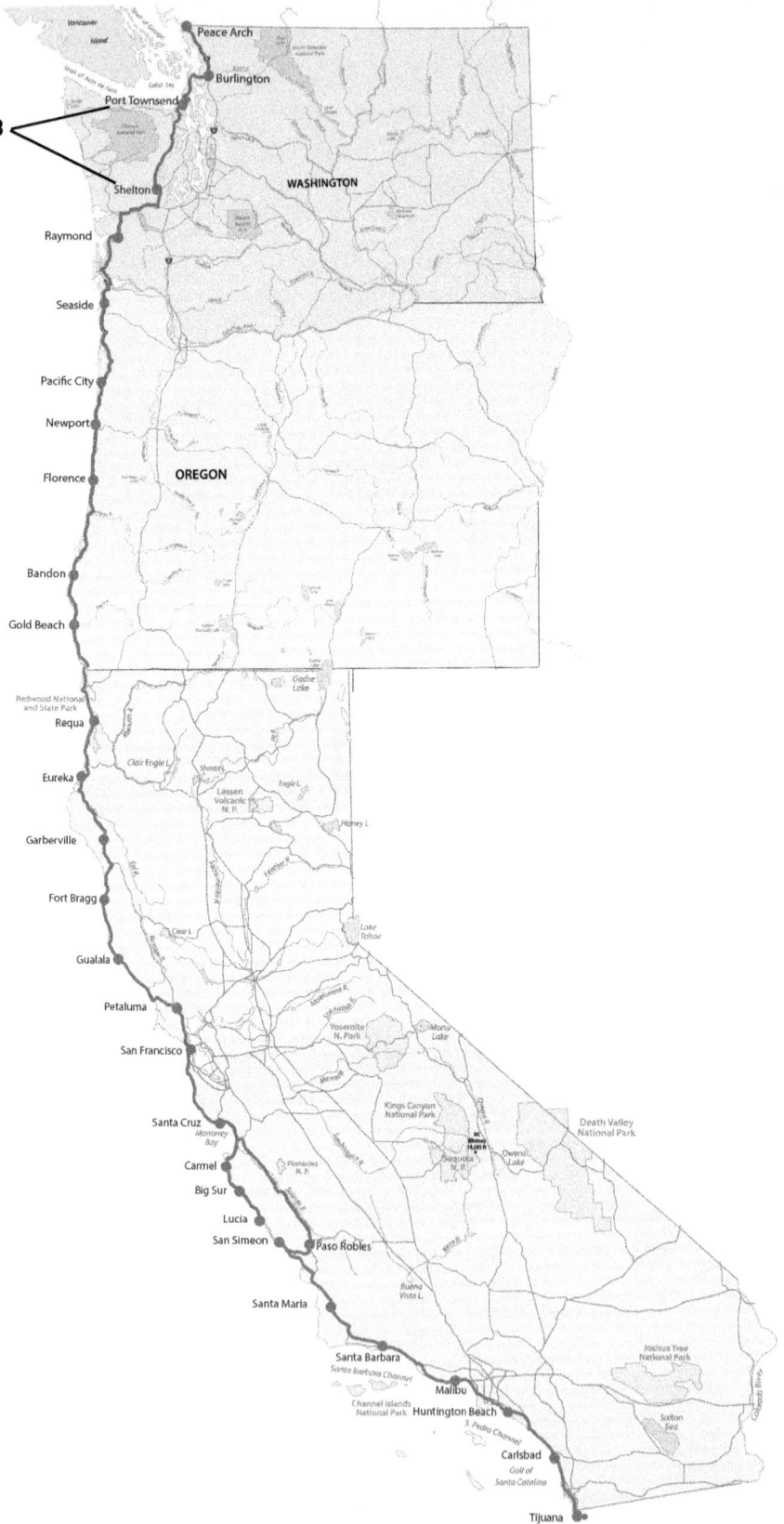

DAY 3

Peace Arch
Burlington
Port Townsend
Shelton
Raymond
Seaside
Pacific City
Newport
Florence
Bandon
Gold Beach
Requa
Eureka
Garberville
Fort Bragg
Gualala
Petaluma
San Francisco
Santa Cruz
Carmel
Big Sur
Lucia
San Simeon
Paso Robles
Santa Maria
Santa Barbara
Malibu
Huntington Beach
Carlsbad
Tijuana

WASHINGTON

OREGON

DAY 3 - JULY 8, 2023

Port Townsend, Washington to Shelton, Washington

78 MILES: 3,005' ELEVATION GAIN

Too tired to sleep, I stepped out into the crisp morning air at 5 a.m., letting it wake me up better than any cup of coffee could. I wandered over to Adam's State Park, the world still quiet, the streets empty.

Looking east, Puget Sound stretched out before me, a hazy sunrise trailing behind. The day hadn't yet decided if it wanted to be sunny or cloudy—so long as it wasn't rainy, I'd take either.

I snapped a photo, one that, like so many before it, would soon be deleted.

Scrolling through Spotify, I landed on the perfect song to start the day—*5 a.m.* by The Millennium.

In the real world, I'm not much of a morning person. But when I travel, I rise with the sun. There's something about being the only one awake in a strange place—whether it's a foreign country or, like today, the open road, riding through the cool morning mist. In those moments, it feels like I'm the only person on Earth.

The older I get, the more I appreciate solitude. It's when ideas come, when words string themselves into sentences, sentences grow into paragraphs, and paragraphs mature into pages—only for me to forget all of it somewhere between mile five and mile forty.

I jumped onto the Pacific Northwest Trail, bouncing along its pothole-ridden, cracked pavement. The peaceful four-mile stretch followed the coast, cut through dense woods, and eventually spit me out onto County Road 20. Between the quiet morning, the great music, and my head full of ideas, I completely missed my turnoff for Highway 101. Instead, I unknowingly stayed south on Center Road.

The Garmin recalculated—21 extra miles until I'd reconnect with the 101 at Quilcene.

The first shot at breakfast was Chimacum, named after an extinct tribe that once lived here for thousands of years. Their land is now home to a Chevron station, a cannabis dispensary, a handful of homes, and The Keg and I—a taproom that hosts trivia every Wednesday and punk music on the last Thursday of the month.

Nothing was open.

Moving on.

Next up: Quilcene. Population 598. A booming metropolis compared to Chimacum. Big enough to have its own coffee shop—Catkin Coffee. But like everything else this morning, it was closed.

I pictured myself inside, sipping an Americano, nibbling on some homemade pastry, listening in on local conversations, maybe chatting up the barista. Instead, my stomach growled as I reconnected with Highway 101 and hit my second climb of the trip: 5 miles long, 725 feet of elevation gain, steady 5% grade.

Not the hardest climb, but steady enough. For all my dislike of climbing, this one was actually enjoyable. A nice wide shoulder carried me into Olympic National Park.

Teddy Roosevelt first designated this area Mount Olympus National Monument in 1909. In 1938, his fifth cousin, Franklin D. Roosevelt, turned it into Olympic National Park. Then, in 1976, it became a UNESCO site for its biodiversity.

And, because who doesn't love a little Roosevelt family gossip—Eleanor Roosevelt was Teddy's niece, which means her maiden name was Roosevelt and her husband, Franklin (FDR) was her fifth cousin once removed.

Descending into the valley, I spotted a Cove RV Park and Country Store. My stomach growled. A sign read: Closed.

A quarter mile down the road—another general store. Also closed.

It didn't matter anymore. I was beyond tired and beyond hungry. I focused instead on the gift of riding along the Hood Canal.

①

Captain George Vancouver originally named this waterway Hood's Channel after Lord Samuel Hood. However, when he drew his map, he mistakenly wrote Hood's Canal. Instead of correcting the error, the United States Board of Geographic Names just went with it.

Looking at a map of Northwest Washington is like revisiting a sixth-grade geography quiz, with its bays, sounds, canals, channels, inlets, straits, and coves—so, class, let's refresh:

Canal: Man-made waterway linking two bodies of water
Channel: Natural waterway linking two bodies of water
Strait: Natural narrow body of water linking two larger bodies of water
Sound: Large body of water connected to the sea or ocean
Inlet: Long, narrow indentation of shoreline leading to an enclosed body of water
Bay: Recessed coastal body of water connected to a larger body of water
Cove: Small bay
Gulf: Large bay

We all caught up? Great.

Three miles south was Brinnon, where again, the general store was closed.

A sign pointed toward Camp Parsons, the oldest continuously running Boy Scout camp west of the Mississippi. As an Eagle Scout, I look back on my time in scouting fondly. The guys in my troop were the same ones I played little league with.

Scouting has taken a hit in recent years. Just like most things, one bad apple ruins the bunch. We can all thank bad apple Richard Covin Reid (the shoe bomber) for requiring us to remove our shoes at airport security.

Hidden in plain sight, I found myself surrounded by the legends and myths of the Twana—a group of nine tribes who had lived here for thousands of years before the Europeans and Russians arrived to trap, hunt, and colonize the land.

I crossed the Dosewallips River, which, according to Twana myth, flows because of a great chief who sacrificed himself for his people. He transformed into a mountain so that the water would always reach them.

These kinds of stories fascinate me—reminders that magic is everywhere if we just take the time to notice.

In Australia, they call them Songlines—oral maps that connect celestial patterns with geographical landmarks, used by Aboriginal Australians to navigate their country.

In New Zealand, Mount Taranaki is considered to be an ancestor by the Mori and is recognized as a legal person, granted all the rights and responsibilities of a human being.

The Point No Point Treaty, signed in 1855 between the United States government and the Twana tribes, required the tribes to free all their slaves—a bit ironic, considering the United States wouldn't abolish slavery for another ten years. It also required them to cede all their land to the U.S. government.

In exchange, the nine Twana tribes were relegated to the 8.2-square-mile Skokomish Indian Reservation, receiving $60,000—trading their ancestral lands for the Lucky Dog Casino and eight miles of shoreline for fishing.

Brinnon was where the shoulder disappeared—just as the bike shop owner had warned me. I had twenty-five miles before it would return in Hoodsport.

Twelve miles after Brinnon, I came across the Eldon Country Store. To my surprise, it was open.

A wanted poster hung in the window:

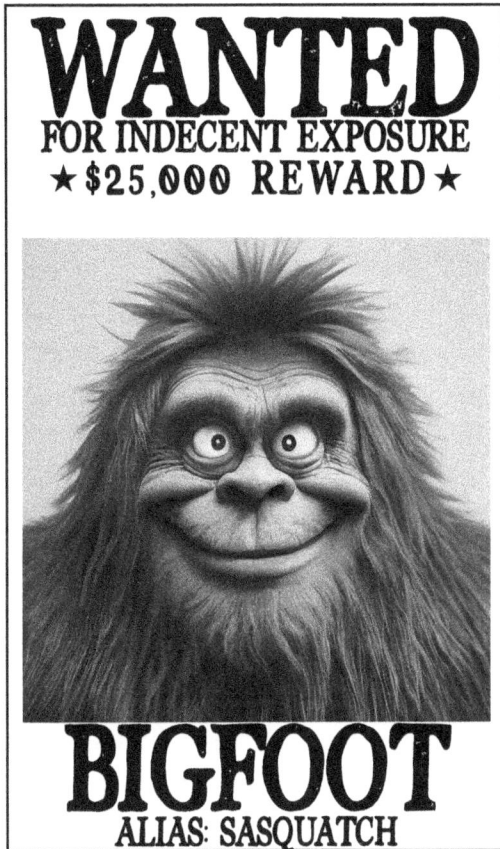

WANTED
FOR INDECENT EXPOSURE
★ **$25,000** REWARD ★

BIGFOOT
ALIAS: SASQUATCH

My first stop of the day. At 11 a.m., fifty miles behind me, it was time to grab a Gatorade, and while I passed on the prepackaged sandwiches, I told myself I'd find a place in Hoodsport to relax.

A Jeep Wrangler rolled up—doors off, top down. Two young guys in surf shorts and tank tops, and two young women in bikini tops and Daisy Dukes. They piled out, walked into the store with a mission, and emerged minutes later with two cases of beer and a bottle of tequila.

Was I ever that cool?

Hell yeah, I was.

Cooler.

Proof of that can be found in all my high school yearbooks—messages from classmates reminding me to "stay cool this summer."

Yeah, no doubt about it. I was cooler than cool. Still am—for an old guy.

Hoodsport was buzzing with tourists from Seattle, Tacoma, and Olympia flooding in for a day of boating, jet skiing, fishing, skydiving, and wine tasting at the local vineyards.

I found refuge in the Model T Pub and Eatery, a poorly lit establishment where I plopped into a corner booth, ordered two big glasses of carbonated water with a splash of grapefruit juice, and stared out at the tourist chaos.

That's when I noticed the dive shop across the street.

"People dive around here?" I asked the waitress.

"Oh, yes. It's really popular. People come from all over the world to see the Giant Octopus and Wolf Eels. There's a bunch of other stuff too—I'm not a diver, but my boyfriend is, and he says those are the biggest draws. Be back with your order—another water?"

I pulled out my phone. Google: Wolf Eel. Seven feet long. Forty pounds. A terrifying-looking creature.

Now, the Giant Pacific Octopus—that's something I'd love to see. Twenty feet long. Over 100 pounds.

Octopuses fascinate me. They're proof of alien life on this planet. If we ever make contact with extraterrestrial life, my money's on octopuses being the first to say, "Oh, hey, what took you guys so long?"

I've never seen an octopus while diving, but I have come across cuttlefish in Saipan. Both are cephalopods[5], both are masters of deception. Octopuses have eight arms. Cuttlefish have ten. Octopuses don't have shells or skeletons at all. They are completely soft

---

5   A member of the molluscan class, such as squid, octopus, cuttlefish or nautilus.

other than a small beak which means they can do some absolutely mind-blowing things.

- They can squeeze through any hole bigger than their beak.

- They can regrow lost tentacles.

- They can solve complex problems.

- And best of all? They can shapeshift—mimicking textures, colors, even other creatures.

Turns out, they have another talent. Allow me to introduce you to Paul the Octopus.

Paul lived in the Sea Life Centre in Oberhausen, Germany. In 2010, he accurately predicted the outcome of the FIFA World Cup semi-finals.

Match	Prediction	Outcome
Germany vs. Australia	Germany	Correct
Germany vs. Serbia	Serbia	Correct
Ghana vs. Germany	Germany	Correct
Germany vs. England	Germany	Correct
Argentina vs. Germany	Germany	Correct
Germany vs. Spain	Spain	Correct
Uruguay vs. Germany	Germany	Correct
Netherlands vs. Spain	Spain	Correct

By comparison, Lean the porcupine, Petty the pygmy hippopotamus, and Anton the tamarin did not fare as well in their predictions.

Mani the parakeet got seven correct, sparking the "Octopus-versus-parakeet showdown of 2010."

Rabio the Octopus correctly predicted all matches in the 2018 FIFA World Cup and was rewarded by being served up as dinner on July 2, 2018.

1

I didn't expect much from the motel I reserved; therefore I was not disappointed by how crappy it was. Options in Shelton were limited, and for sixty bucks, this checked all the boxes: bed, shower, desk with chair, and TV. The office was locked, with a phone number written on the glass door. When I called, a man with a Chinese accent answered.

"Herro."

"Checking in?"

"Check-in four o'clock."

I looked at the parking lot; there was one car in it. I was sure the room was ready; there was no sign of any maid service going on.

"Is there an early check-in?"

"Check-in four!" Click.

Another couple pulled in with the same hope of an early check-in. The man responded with the same answer, "Check-in 4 p.m.!"

I decided to roll down Railroad Ave, where I came across Railroad Tap Station, a beer and pizza spot that welcomed me in.

I was feeling pretty good. Had I not already prepaid for the motel, I might have convinced myself to keep going. But eighty miles was a solid effort, so I decided to relax—have a slice of pizza, chat with the bartender, catch up on email and social media, and do some writing. In the grand scheme of things, I was right on time.

I locked my bike to a post, reached for my phone… and then—

Where was my wallet?

Checked my top tube bag. Not there.

Maybe I put it in my frame bag when I grabbed my charging cable at The Model T? Nope.

Jacket pockets? Empty.

Son of a…

I had it in Hoodsport—I paid for my meal there. I didn't stop anywhere between Hoodsport and Shelton. Could it have fallen out of my pocket? I inspected my jacket. No holes.

Where did I eat in Hoodsport? The Model T.

I called them up.

"Hey, I was there about an hour ago, sat in the corner, ordered the soda water with grapefruit. Did you happen to find a wallet?"

"Oh, I am so glad you called. I was thinking, I don't have his number—how am I going to tell him he left his wallet?"

"So, you have it?"

"Yes, we have it."

"Okay, awesome. I'll get there as soon as I can."

I could have ridden back—adding thirty more miles to the day. My big talk about how I *could* have kept going if I hadn't prepaid for the motel? Muted.

Could I have done it? Yes.

Did I have time? *Check-in 4 p.m.* So, yes.

Instead, I found the only taxi in Shelton. The driver picked me up in his family car and, in exchange for $100, drove me to Hoodsport and back.

Back in Shelton, the motel owner had clearly had enough of people loitering in his parking lot, calling to see if they could check-in early. By 3 p.m., I was checked in, showered, and grabbing deli pasta at Safeway. I should have grabbed a couple of slices at the Railroad Tap Station.

After a nap, I strolled around town and came across a statue of a lumberjack, the plaque reading:

DEDICATED TO THE MEN AND
WOMEN OF THE
WOODWORKING INDUSTRY
WHO HAVE CARVED THEIR
COMMUNITIES AND LIVING OUT OF
THE FOREST...SOMETIMES AT THE
COST OF THEIR OWN LIVES.
SEPTEMBER 8, 1990

Just down the street from the statue was The Tollie 7—a locomotive engine and caboose displayed in front of the post office.

Listed on the National Register of Historic Places, Washington's Tollie 7 was built in 1924, hauling logs, supplies, and people to and from Shelton for forty-one years.

Now, it sits here on Railroad Ave—a monument to itself.

CORY: 2
VP: 1

POP QUIZ: Match the word with the description

1.	Inlet	a.	Small bay
2.	Cove	b.	Large bay
3.	Gulf	c.	Natural narrow body of water linking two larger bodies of water
4.	Sound	d.	Man-made waterway linking two bodies of water
5.	Canal	e.	Long, narrow indentation of shore line leading to a body of water
6.	Bay	f.	Recessed coastal body of water connected to a larger body of water
7.	Channel	g.	Large body of water connected to the sea or ocean
8.	Strait	h.	Natural waterway linking two bodies of water

DAY 4

Peace Arch
Burlington
Port Townsend
Shelton
Raymond
Seaside
Pacific City
Newport
Florence
Bandon
Gold Beach
Requa
Eureka
Garberville
Fort Bragg
Gualala
Petaluma
San Francisco
Santa Cruz
Carmel
Big Sur
Lucia
San Simeon
Santa Maria
Santa Barbara
Malibu
Huntington Beach
Carlsbad
Tijuana

WASHINGTON

OREGON

Paso Robles

Redwood National and State Park

Lassen Volcanic N. P.

Yosemite N. Park

Kings Canyon National Park

Sequoia N. P.

Death Valley National Park

Joshua Tree National Park

Channel Islands National Park

Salton Sea

Monterey Bay

Lake Tahoe

Vancouver Island

DAY 4 - JULY 9, 2023
Shelton, Washington to Raymond, Washington

62 MILES : 1,915' ELEVATION GAIN

A t one a.m., the digital clock shattered the silence with a relentless beep. What the…?! Who sets an alarm for one a.m.? In the darkness, I instinctively slammed my hand down on the nightstand—only to discover the clock wasn't there at all, but perched mockingly on the dresser.

Seriously, who puts an alarm clock on the dresser? I fumbled in the dark, half-assuming I'd hit snooze, flipping a few switches, uncertain if I'd even silenced the chaos. Ten minutes later, that infernal alarm returned. With a frustrated yank, I ripped the cord from the wall and tossed the clock into the closet. Problem solved, right? Six hours remained before departure, and sleep was my only salvation.

At six a.m., my phone dinged. Kevin's[6] text came through—a link to AC/DC's "Highway to Hell" accompanied by: "¡Venga! ¡Venga! ¡Venga! ¡Venga!"[7]

In 2008, Kevin and I signed up for the Trans Rockies, a seven-day mountain bike stage race in the Canadian Rockies. Each day started with AC/DC's "Highway to Hell," and it became our anthem leading us into battle at all future mountain bike events.

I dumped my gear onto the bed—unpacking wasn't really necessary; all I needed was to slip on my cycling kit and ride. Still, there was a certain Zen to the ritual: checking every charging cable and ensuring each electronic lifeline was ready for the long haul. "¡Venga! ¡Venga! ¡Venga! ¡Venga!"

---

6   The same Kevin from *The Buddha and the Bee*, and the reason I spell tyre with a 'y', just to annoy him. His rebuttal is always the same, a link to the "Siege of Tyre" where Alexander the Great defeated the Persians in 332 BC.

7   Spanish, it can mean "Come on" or "Let's go." Commonly said in the international cycling community to motivate and encourage riders.

Having not yet cracked it open, I sat on the bed and decided to take a look at Bill Thorness's book *Cycling the Pacific Coast: The Complete Guide from Canada to Mexico.*

My plan was to make this ride a book, the very one you are reading now. I hope you are enjoying the ride. I bought Bill's book as a source of inspiration, wanting to read other authors' thoughts and experiences along the way—what they overcame and how they did it.

The book has a well-deserved 4.7 out of 5 stars on Amazon. It is intensely detailed and an excellent resource for someone who has never ridden a bike any distance at all or for someone who likes to have every mile of their trip laid out. In one early paragraph, he discusses hills as follows:

> "Hills: Uphill climbs hold safety problems, as your speed is reduced
> to a crawl. On steep sections, train yourself not to veer back and
> forth in an S pattern, as you might if you were switchbacking on a
> steep trail."— Bill Thorness, *Cycling the Pacific Coast*

These are perfectly fine instructions for someone planning to ride the PCH with zero experience. I celebrate this, as when I did my first long-distance ride, I was that person with no experience. What I sought from this book, or any book for that matter, was motivation to ride and to write about the experience. Did I need motivation? In a way, I did.

I wanted to read about the author's thoughts. It had been a year since I published my last book, and I was looking for a new voice, to hear how someone else described the same places and events, and then compare their experiences with my own. What was important to them? Where did they struggle (physically and mentally), and how did they overcome those struggles? What did they find fascinating? Which routes did they take? Did they share the history of the places they passed through or offer more contemporary descriptions? Did they converse with others? If so, what were those conversations about?

Did they pay attention to the moon phases? Was the weather a focus? I was simply curious about what others found intriguing.

Reading Thorness's list of safety recommendations, packing tips, and advice on finding lodging or campsites just wasn't what I needed, so I decided to leave it behind at the motel in Shelton, hoping it would motivate someone else to take on the trip or remind someone of the importance of locking their bike.

Before leaving, I started reading another book about a guy who rode the PCH alone. Unlike Bill's methodical narrative, this author jumped from Astoria to Crescent City, and then suddenly found himself in San Francisco—without details of towns, conversations, struggles, or coastal views. Instead, the chapters focused on his strained relationship with his parents. After all, solo riding is a kind of therapy—a time to confront your demons while reconnecting with your true self.

Maybe I am too wordy or not wordy enough. Do I share too much random historical trivia or not enough? As an author, every word is scrutinized and every detail researched.

Peddling out of Shelton along Cloquallum Road—a name shared as a nod to Bill Thorness's ultra-detailed turn-by-turn instructions—I passed Tuggs & Chuggs, a fine name for either a biker bar or a full-service strip club.

Cloquallum Road didn't offer much of a shoulder, but aside from a one-mile-long, 250-foot climb, it provided a nice flat ride through some of the most beautiful countryside Washington state has to offer.

Soon, I reached Elma—a tiny town I had no intention of revisiting—and decided to indulge in a modern convenience: Starbucks. Nestled between the Rusty Tractor Restaurant and The Church of Jesus Christ of Latter-Day Saints, it was a brief pit stop.

The guy in front of me wore a shirt that read "Montana," so I ventured, "Are you from Montana?" His curt, almost indignant "No" was as brief as small talk can be.

Armed with an Americano and a 290-calorie feta egg wrap, I refueled for the road ahead. Besides reaching Mexico, one of my personal goals was to shed a few pounds. I recalled Angus Barbieri—a man who, at 456 pounds, embarked on a 382-day fast and dropped 180 pounds, subsisting on nothing but tea, coffee, sparkling water, and vitamins. I wasn't fasting, but I had my own plan: abstain from alcohol for a month (or at least a couple of weeks), eat smarter, and ride anywhere from five to seven hours a day. Not your typical "How to Lose 20 Pounds in 30 Days" plan, yet perhaps it could be.

How to Lose 20 Pounds in 30 Days
By Cory Mortensen

- Ride your bike for six hours or more every day for 30 days.

- Eat healthy, in modest portions.

- Stay hydrated.

- Abstain from alcohol.

- Get six hours of sleep a night.

There it is—two for one: a journey down the Pacific Coast Highway and a weight loss guide, intertwined.

South of Elma, I encountered Satstop—a relic of one of America's most ambitious nuclear power plant projects. Mismanagement and cost overruns left behind two concrete cooling towers, now repurposed as a quirky business park.

Rejoining Highway 101—a road I hadn't seen since Hoodsport—I found myself at a lonely intersection deep within Washington's dense woods. Just south lay Artic Bar & RV Park, promising Live Music Sunday at 3 p.m. Three fifth-wheels were parked on a modest lot beside the bar. The local post office, established in 1887 and named "Arta" after the postmaster's wife, was misregistered as "Artic" due to a clerical error in Washington, DC. Although the post office closed in 1907, the bar endures. I pulled into the dusty lot and checked my GPS—sixteen miles remained. Hills? A mere 800 feet of elevation; no problem.

And tomorrow, what does tomorrow look like? Sixty-seven miles and a big climb to start the day.

"Never look at tomorrow's elevation when riding today's hills."
—*Cory Mortensen*

One hell of a metaphor for life.

With the final sixteen miles behind me, I descended into Raymond just after 1 p.m. Despite subsisting on nothing but that lonely feta egg wrap all day, I felt surprisingly strong. For a moment, I doubted my pre-paid hotel strategy—Astoria was only 55 miles away, with a 4 p.m. check-in. But this isn't a race; it's a ride. There's no medal, no T-shirt at the end—just the pure, unhurried pleasure of the journey. I soaked in the scenery, scribbled notes, and reminded myself to trust the plan.

The Pitchwood Inn, attached to the Pitchwood Alehouse, was a warm surprise—a far cry from the wild, woolly lumber mill town I'd anticipated. Now rebranded as "The City that Does Things," Raymond had shed its rugged past to become a quirky haven for marijuana startups and unexpected attractions. It even boasted the Northwest Carriage Museum, home to the Shelburne Landau carriage from *Gone with the Wind*. For the grunge fans among us, four miles south lies the site of Nirvana's first gig in 1987—sans Dave Grohl. And just beyond where Kurt Cobain once intoned, "Here we are now, entertain us," lies Willie Keil.

Willie was assigned to lead a wagon train west from Bethel, Missouri, to the promised land (the Oregon area) for a religious sect known as the Bethelites, a branch of the Jehovah's Witnesses. Before the group departed, Willie died of malaria. Because Willie was so eager to reach the promised land, it was decided that his body would be placed in a lead-lined box filled with 100-proof Golden Rule whiskey. At some point, tired of dragging a whiskey-soaked corpse, the group said, "This looks pretty much like the Promised Land," dug a hole, and buried him in a windswept field marked by a solitary stone.

WM. KEIL
Born: Jan 12, 1836
Died: May 19, 1855

Though my room was ready—confirmed by the ever-courteous bartender and hotel manager—she was quick to tell me that check-in wasn't until 4 p.m.

The Pitchwood Alehouse was bustling as Daniel Walker and his cover band, DNA, set up for tonight's entertainment. The space was rustic, with heavy timbers, wagon wheel chandeliers dangling from high ceilings, a balcony with worn couches, and decor ranging from bird heads to a moose mounted above the bar. Dollar bills were stapled to the beams, and the ambiance whispered tales of simpler times. The alehouse's sign welcomed guests: "When the sun shines, we pour."

I opted for the chicken noodle soup, perhaps the finest I'd had since my Grandma Heckenlaible's, whose secret ingredient was saffron—the spice more expensive than gold.

As the soup warmed me, my appetite slowly returned. I resisted the urge to devour everything on the menu; everything looked good, the sun was out, and I wanted a beer. My soda water with a splash of grapefruit juice held its own, and I decided to take advantage of the three for $8 Goose Point Oyster Shooters—fresh from Willapa Bay and served in a shot glass swimming in spicy cocktail sauce. I could have easily downed twenty.

While I enjoyed my oyster shots, a couple sat down next to me. His name was Craig; he was a cyclist, a retired professor, and an author. He asked about the oysters and my ride. It turned out we had several people in common in our professional lives. Coming from the athletic academic world—a world I spent over ten years selling to and presenting in across the country—we talked about fitness assessment. He shared his book with me, which I passed along to a few people I was still connected with in academia. I told him I was also an author and shared some information about my work.

The bartender, who also managed the hotel, came out to let me know that I could check into my room if I wanted to.

I thanked Craig and rolled my bike into my room, enjoying a well-deserved shower. If the Alehouse wasn't charming enough, this room was shockingly adorable. The bed—oh my God, the bed. And I paid only $40 for it. The soup and oyster shots were more expensive than the room. I could have stayed for a week. I was really enjoying the vibe of this little logging town, which would have never hit my radar had it not been for this bike trip.

That is really one of thousands of great things about traveling: the surprises. Good, bad… arriving someplace—a dot on the map—and having experiences you never thought were possible.

CORY: 3
VP: 1

Vancouver
Island

Peace Arch

Burlington

Port Townsend

WASHINGTON

Shelton

Raymond

DAY 5

Seaside

Pacific City

Newport

Florence

OREGON

Bandon

Gold Beach

Redwood National
and State Park

Requa

Eureka

Garberville

Fort Bragg

Gualala

Petaluma

San Francisco

Santa Cruz
Monterey
Bay

Carmel

Big Sur

Lucia

San Simeon
Paso Robles

Santa Maria

Santa Barbara
Santa Barbara Channel

Malibu

Channel Islands
National Park
Huntington Beach

Carlsbad

Gulf of
Santa Catalina

Tijuana

Death Valley
National Park

Kings Canyon
National Park

Sequoia
N. P.

Joshua Tree
National Park

Salton
Sea

Lassen
Volcanic
N. P.

Yosemite
N. P.

Lake
Tahoe

DAY 5 - JULY 10, 2023

Raymond, Washington to Seaside, Oregon

65 MILES : 2,484' ELEVATION GAIN

"The best thing one can do when it's raining is to let it rain."
— *Henry Wadsworth Longfellow*

I just wanted to lay in bed all day. I could hear and smell the rain coming down all night. Rain or no rain, there was still a job to do—chop chop. Seaside wasn't going to come to me. I got up and opened the door to assess the situation. Clouds hung low over the town, the rain was heavy, and it was cold. Everything about this day said, "stay in bed, grab some coffee, and watch hours of *Catfish* episodes."

I sat up, pulled on my shoes, and wrapped my hands around a steaming cup of coffee. It was the kind of day made for mindless TV marathons. I used to zone out to reruns of *Law and Order*—those classic episodes with Jerry Orbach and Chris Noth, where you didn't need to catch every word to follow the case. These days, *Catfish* had become my background noise of choice. It's a wild study of the human condition—half train wreck, half social experiment. The absurdity of it all: how someone could so easily scam another, and how someone else could so willingly fall for it.

I scrolled through social media between sips of coffee, half-heartedly posting an update. My buddy Kevin, forever off the grid, required what I called the "Kevin Flanders Specialized Status Update"—a daily text with Garmin routes and grainy photos to prove I was still alive.

Then, a Facebook memory pulled me back twelve years—to a solo ride from Minneapolis to Colorado, raising money for Mended Little Hearts.

Back then, I owned EKHO, a company I built from scratch. I had a full product line of heart rate monitors, pedometers, accelerometers, stopwatches, and pulse oximeters. One day, I started getting emails from a woman asking about the pulse oximeters. I only sold through distributors, so I directed her to a few of them. But she kept reaching out—email, LinkedIn, even Facebook.

Eventually, I called her. She told me about Mended Little Hearts, a national support group for families of children born with congenital heart defects (CHD)—the most common birth defect in the U.S., affecting one in every hundred children. She explained the financial burden CHD placed on families. Every time she took her child to the hospital to have their oxygen levels tested, it cost $175. I sold pulse oximeters for $125—a one-time purchase with unlimited use.

She urged me to attend the upcoming Mended Little Hearts conference in New Orleans. It was in two weeks.

I had already planned a month-long vacation. When you own a business, you don't take *real* vacations—you just step away for a bit. So, I adjusted my plans. I'd go to the conference, and I'd bring my bike. Instead of flying back, I'd ride home to Minneapolis.

Then, everything changed.

At the conference, I listened to story after story from parents whose children had CHD. Their struggles, their resilience—it hit me harder than I expected.

When I mentioned my plan to bike home, someone suggested something bigger: "What if you biked from your office in Minneapolis to our headquarters in Colorado Springs instead?" They'd turn it into a fundraiser.

I didn't hesitate. I scrapped my plans, reworked my route, and named the ride *Tour de Mended Little Hearts.*

By the time I arrived in Colorado Springs, the local paper, *The Gazette*, ran a story on it:

CEO wears heart on his sleeve during 900-mile bike ride. On Monday afternoon, Cory Mortensen, 41, was racing a child's tricycle amidst a pack of frenzied kids in Cottonwood Creek Park, and he was struggling to keep up. Every one of the children around him has heart disease or suffers from congenital heart defects—but that didn't slow them down.

Three weeks ago, Mortensen, who owns a heart monitor manufacturer, EKHO LLC, was inspired to take a bike trek to raise awareness about congenital heart defects and disease in children.

He rode 900 miles from Minneapolis to Colorado Springs, where he met with kids and parents of Mended Little Hearts, a local chapter of national The Mended Hearts, Inc., that provides support for families with children who have heart problems.

Mortensen met Berry and Koinzan at a conference in New Orleans last month and was inspired by the stories of their children. He decided to create a fundraiser in the form of a bike tour and dubbed it the Tour de Mended Little Hearts. The women got their local doctors from Pediatric Cardiology Associates to donate the first $500, and the rest Mortensen raised from friends and employees.

My phone dinged—a text with a link for a podcast from Kevin. My education and motivation for the day.

> (((🎙)))Podcast: THE REST IS HISTORY
> Episode: The American Revolution (Part 1)

Grabbing my coffee, I crawled back into bed and turned on an episode of *Catfish*. I didn't want to ride, so I looked up to see if there was a bus to Astoria. There was, and it was $4. As much as I wanted to jump on it, I didn't. I couldn't bring myself to do it. That was 55+ miles of cheating. It was rain, not hail. Not snow, no lightning. I just had to do what cyclists do when it rains…get wet.

At 9:10 a.m., I rolled out, the rain still heavy, and if you recall my list of things I brought with me, you'll remember rain gear was not on the list.

I took a few turns to connect with Highway 101. Along the way, the bus to Astoria rolled past me—my last chance to cheat. Instead, the bus hit a big puddle, covering me in cold, dirty water. *So, that's the kind of day this was going to be. Got it.*

Five miles west along 101, I came across the Robert E. Bush Park, which hosted a statue of the world's largest oyster and a memorial to a recipient of the Medal of Honor:

> For conspicuous gallantry and intrepidity at the risk of his life above and beyond the call of duty while serving as Medical Corpsman with a rifle company, in action against enemy Japanese forces on Okinawa Jima, Ryukyu Islands, 2 May 1945. Fearlessly braving the fury of artillery, mortar, and machine-gun fire from strongly entrenched hostile positions, Bush constantly and unhesitatingly moved from one casualty to another to attend the wounded falling under the enemy's murderous barrages. As the attack passed over a ridge top, Bush was advancing to administer blood

plasma to a marine officer lying wounded on the skyline when the Japanese launched a savage counterattack. In this perilously exposed position, he resolutely maintained the flow of life-giving plasma. With the bottle held high in one hand, Bush drew his pistol with the other and fired into the enemy's ranks until his ammunition was expended. Quickly seizing a discarded carbine, he trained his fire on the Japanese charging point blank over the hill, accounting for six of the enemy despite his own serious wounds and the loss of one eye suffered during his desperate battle in defense of the helpless man. With the hostile force finally routed, he calmly disregarded his own critical condition to complete his mission, valiantly refusing medical treatment for himself until his officer patient had been evacuated, and collapsing only after attempting to walk to the battle aid station. His daring initiative, great personal valor, and heroic spirit of self-sacrifice in service of others reflect great credit upon Bush and enhance the finest traditions of the U.S. Naval Service.

Reading his citation put a kibosh on any complaints I had about riding in the rain with 54-degree temperatures. Robert survived his wounds, dying of kidney cancer in 2005 at the age of 79.

My GPS told me to take a left up Willapa Ave. I could have stayed on 101 but decided to blindly follow HAL 9000.

Willapa Ave. quickly turned into a muddy, gravel logging road, kicking things off with a 531-foot climb. Had I stayed on 101, I would have had 11 miles of smooth pavement and just 120 feet of elevation gain. Instead, I got mud, rocks, and bumps—and was grateful I opted for the gravel bike.

I kept a sharp eye out for Bigfoot. According to what I'd learned back at the Eldon Country Store, there was a $25,000 reward for the elusive beast.

Rejoining 101, I followed the trail of salty air along Willapa Bay. The scent of the sea was thick, and oyster hunters were scattered across the exposed tide flats, taking full advantage of low tide. My craving for those little briny mollusks grew stronger with every mile.

I slipped into autopilot—just pedaling. Not thinking, not engaging, just moving.

At Naselle, WA, I veered off 101 and took Highway 4 to 401, shaving four miles off the route to Astoria. Naselle, home to the Finnish-American Folk Festival, marked a small fork in the road. No right or wrong way—just a choice.

Had I stayed on 101, I would have passed Cape Disappointment—the foggiest place in the United States. Bruno Heceta originally named it *Bahia de La Ascension*, but the name didn't stick. Hard to say whether that was an upgrade or not.

It wasn't long before the Columbia River came into view. Soon after, the Astoria-Megler Bridge emerged on the horizon—a four-mile stretch of steel spanning the water. The longest truss bridge in North America.

I had read that crossing this bridge on a bike was not ideal. The Adventure Cycling Association suggested an alternate route: crossing at Cathlamet via the Julia Butler Hansen Bridge.

But I was stubborn.

I stuck to my original course. After all, I had ridden a sketchy mountain bike down the forty-mile Yungas Road in Bolivia, known as the Death Road—what was a four-mile bridge by comparison?

Is riding across the Astoria-Megler Bridge for everyone? Heck ya, the bridge offered a small shoulder, and traffic moved slowly in waves due to a stoplight that regulated access onto the bridge.

One mile along the bridge, I came across another cyclist—not fast, not slow—but now we were two, and two is better than one. I drafted off him since there was no opportunity to pass, and frankly, I was in no hurry.

It was roughly 1 p.m.; Seaside, Oregon, was just 18 miles away, the rain had stopped, and the view from the bridge was epic.

If you do not like heights, the Astoria-Megler Bridge rises 200 feet over the water and quickly descends into Astoria on the south side, the elevated portion allowing for ship traffic. I am not a fan of heights, so I kept my eyes locked on the road, threw on my imaginary horse blinders, and pressed on.

Before tackling the mile-long New Youngs Bay Bridge over the Youngs River, I headed east along Lief Erikson Drive. While it is not a movie I look back on fondly, I felt drawn to find 368 38th St., the Goonies house.

Astoria is a treasure trove of oddities if you have time to explore—Shallon Winery (which specializes in whey wines, of all things), the Astoria Column, the Museum of Whimsy, the wreck of the *Peter Iredale*, and a replica of Fort Clatsop, where Lewis and Clark wintered in 1806.

How did Lewis and Clark convince their team to cut down trees and build a fort in the middle of nowhere? What kind of leadership does that take? How do you keep morale high and prevent men from losing it in the face of isolation, dwindling supplies, and the unknown? And then there's the human factor: keeping nerves in check when faced with native tribes, foreign landscapes, and no real certainty of survival.

Turns out, routine is key. Keep people busy—give them tasks and structure—so they don't dwell on their circumstances.

Astonishingly, Lewis and Clark's Corps of Discovery stayed together for the entire journey—nearly a year and a half, covering 8,000 miles of uncharted land. They lost only one man along the way: Sergeant Charles Floyd, just 21 years old, to a burst appendix.

His second-to-last journal entry: "I am very sick and have been for some time, but have recovered my health again." Then, he wrote on the day he died, "I am dull and heavy."

A few shouts from a passing car barely registered over the hum of my tyres as I rolled into Seaside. Here, at last, the rain had given way to sunshine. My bike chain, however, was less enthusiastic—grinding loudly, a not-so-subtle reminder that chain lube should've been on my packing list. It wasn't. But now, it had rocketed to the top of my priority list.

A's Bike Shop was surprisingly well-stocked. I have found whilst cycling cross-country, bike shops are not always fully equipped or are limited to a few bits and pieces. As a former business owner, I understand the reasoning behind that. No one wants to sit on a bunch of inventory that may or may not sell, and then you consider the cost of money and…well, that's for another book. As a cross-country cyclist, pulling into a bike shop that doesn't have all the "this and that's" you are looking for can be frustrating, but it's a reality.

As a friendly PSA to any cyclist reading this, here's some free advice: keep your setup simple, and bring extra "this and that's."

- Avoid lacing your wheels with unique spokes like DT Swiss Revolite Bladed Spokes, which no bike shop will have.

- If you go clipless, think SPD's, not Speedplay or Atec or the like. In the off chance your cleat breaks, you will never find a replacement cleat anywhere—this also happened to me.

Being that I forgot chain lube, God forbid I tell anyone how to pack for a long-distance ride.

Rolling my bike into the shop, the owner, a bit stoned, immediately engaged.

"Dude, that's a sweet bike. You riding the coast?"

"Yes, I left the Canadian border five days ago."

"Dude, you're making great time. I've only ridden the Oregon coast; how are the lumber trucks?"

"Brutal, especially between Raymond and Astoria. I heard a cyclist was killed the other day near Lincoln Beach."

"I heard, man, no bueno. Gotta be safe out there; those guys aren't always paying attention. What brings you in?"

"Lube, I need some chain lube." I pointed at the Giant Surly banner. "I have a single-speed Cross Check. Love that bike. Steel is real."

"Steel is real, bro; the Long Haul Trucker[8] is the number one bike on the PCH. They are indestroyable, bro."

Indestroyable? Is that a word? Probably, irregardless.

"Thanks for the lube; rubber side down and all that."

"Peace."

"Oh, one more thing, you seem like a guy who gets the munchies. Best pizza in Seaside?"

"Dude, Pizza Harbor! No question."

I was actually excited at the prospect of getting a pizza and saddened when I learned they were closed on Mondays, which today happened to be, so I headed straight over to the Coast River Inn.

The guy at the desk weighed no less than 350 lbs., greasy, unkempt, and uninterested in checking me in.

"Uh, yeah, so check-in isn't till three. It's only one-thirty, so…"

"Any chance I can check in early?"

He was confused by the question, as if no one had ever asked that and he didn't know what to do.

"Uh, so it's only one-thirty, so, yeah."

"Okay, no problem; can I leave my bike here in the office, back in the corner, so I can walk down to the beach?"

"Um." He adjusted his glasses and sat up in his chair, looking at the computer.

"What's your name?"

"Mortensen, last name Mortensen."

---

8   Surly is a bike brand, the Long Haul Trucker is one of their models.

"Oh, okay. Cory, is it? Yeah, okay, here, I'll give you a key so you can put your bike in your room."

"So I can check in early?"

"Well, just put your bike in your room and check-in at three."

"Are there any restaurants nearby?" He pointed northward.

I took the key for my room and never looked back.

Yellow Curry Cozy Thai called my name—exactly what I needed after 65 miles in the rain. Something spicy. Something warm.

The restaurant was tiny—just four small tables. A young girl, maybe fourteen, greeted me and asked if I knew what I wanted.

"I don't know," I said, "I haven't seen a menu."

She laughed, her smile lighting up the otherwise quiet space. Throughout my meal, she kept my water glass full and my tea hot, always appearing at just the right moment.

After my meal, I headed back to my motel. Technically, I hadn't even checked in yet—it wasn't quite 3 p.m.—but I grabbed my key, changed into a pair of shorts (which also doubled as swim trunks), and made my way to the hot tub.

The hot tub and pool were housed in a large building, shared with a couple who had exactly *zero* control over their four screaming kids. Times like this, I fully embrace W.C. Fields' sentiment: "I like children—fried."

It occurred to me that I hadn't actually spoken with Kate in a few days—just the occasional text. I sent her a quick update, let her know where I was, and then wandered down to the beach to catch the sunset.

A solid way to close out what would be the only rainy day of this trip.

CORY: 3
VP: 2

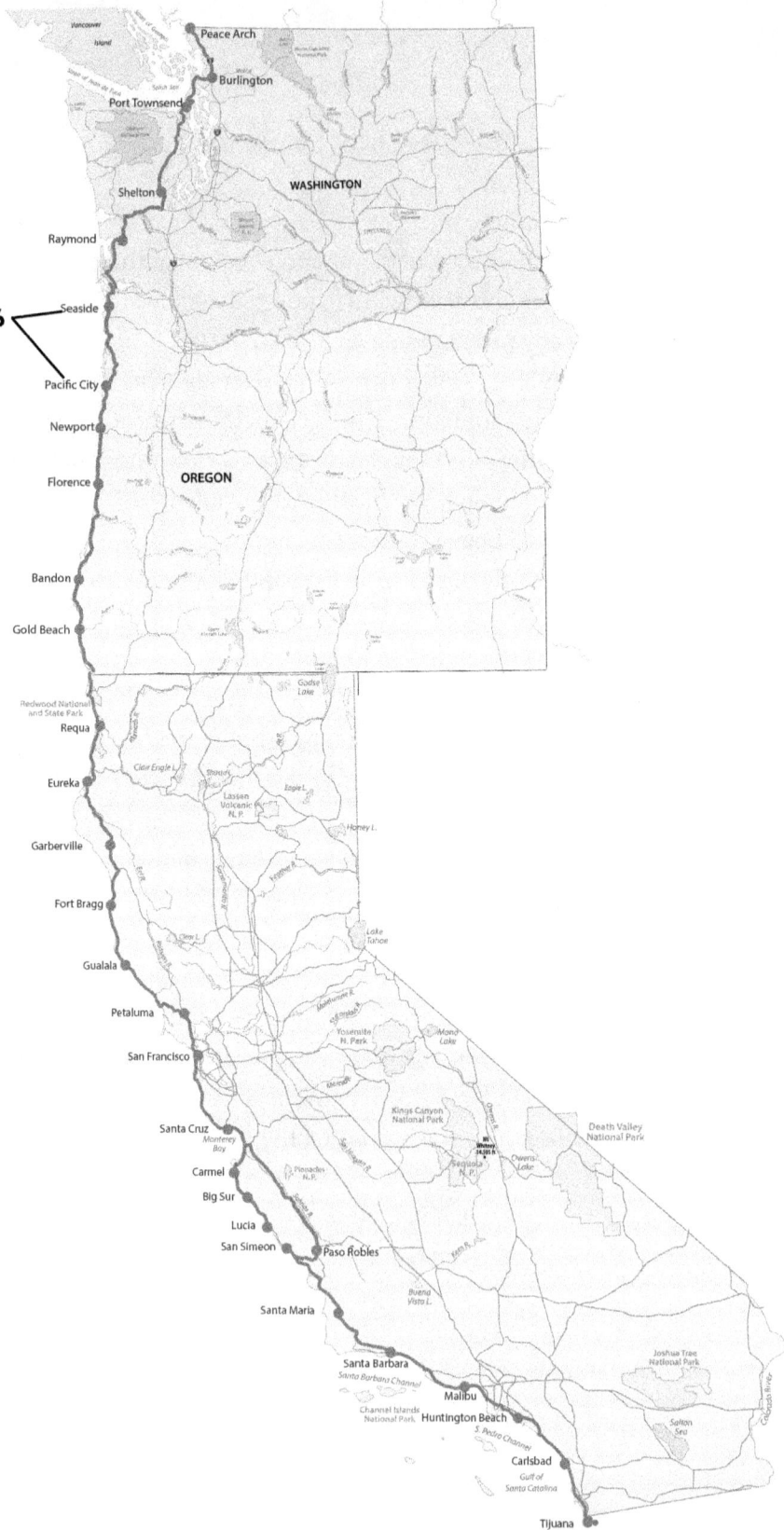

DAY 6

Peace Arch
Burlington
Port Townsend
Shelton
Raymond
Seaside
Pacific City
Newport
Florence
Bandon
Gold Beach
Requa
Eureka
Garberville
Fort Bragg
Gualala
Petaluma
San Francisco
Santa Cruz
Carmel
Big Sur
Lucia
San Simeon
Paso Robles
Santa Maria
Santa Barbara
Malibu
Huntington Beach
Carlsbad
Tijuana

WASHINGTON

OREGON

DAY 6 - JULY 11, 2023

Seaside, Oregon to Pacific City, Oregon

74 MILES : 4,452' ELEVATION GAIN

Instead of a text this morning, I got a voice message from Kevin—sent as an attachment via text. I didn't even know that was a thing.

To quote Groucho Marx:

"Of course, I understand this. Why, a four-year-old child could understand this. Run out and find me a four-year-old child—I can't make head nor tail out of it."

That's how I feel about technology. When I was a kid, I could swap out a car stereo or build a solar-powered toy car with parts from Radio Shack. Now? I have to call Kate just to figure out which remote turns on the TV.

Little did I know, Kevin's voice message wasn't a one-off. From here on out, he'd send me one every morning—a daily dose of motivation. Maybe it was also his way of being part of the trip, a trip he couldn't join because of family responsibilities.

We'd had our fair share of adventures—some legendary, some ending with us not speaking for weeks. Once, an entire year passed without a word between us. That's how friendships go.

But now, I wished he was here. Even if just for a few days.

"Good morning, Mr. D-Train. Hope you have a wonderful day planned. It is going to be a glorious day here in Minneapolis. It's going to be in the mid-70s. I hope your day goes well; it starts early, the coffee is good, and the bums stay strong. Anyway, great work; enjoy the day. Miss ya and looking forward to talking to you again."

I stopped at a Shell station to check the lottery tickets I'd bought in Burlington. Turns out, I won eight bucks. Unfortunately, since I bought them in Washington, Oregon wouldn't cash them out. So, I handed them off to a guy heading north and bought another twenty dollars' worth—I'd still be in Oregon when the next numbers were drawn.

I don't normally buy lottery tickets. I wasn't even sure why I was purchasing these, but since I wasn't spending money on beer or whiskey, I figured I might as well have a little fun. Gotta have *some* vice to keep life interesting. Besides, somebody's got to win, and it's always some random person from a town no one's ever heard of.

When was the last time you heard about *big* things happening in Seaside, Oregon?

There comes a point in a trip like this when the adventure loses its shine and starts to feel like work. You begin questioning why you're even doing it—especially when you're solo.

I hadn't hit that wall yet. Five days in, I was just settling into my groove. To keep myself engaged, I set small goals throughout the day:

- I'll make it to the top of that hill in eight minutes. Go!

- That barn looks about half a mile away. Go!

- *Let's see if the mileposts match my GPS.* (Spoiler: they usually don't. And sometimes, they're *way* off.)

During a podcast interview about my first book, the host made an interesting observation: "Those small goals essentially became your riding partner."

She was absolutely right.

Each goal, no matter how trivial, became my companion on the road. Over time, I've come to realize that long rides, treks, or multi-year journeys all follow a similar emotional arc:

1. **Excitement** – You're finally on your way.

2. **Apprehension** – You hit your first hiccup, and for a moment, you wonder what the hell you're doing.

3. **Loneliness or Solitude** – Your choice. As May Sarton put it: "Loneliness is the poverty of self, solitude is the richness of self."

4. **Immersion** – The journey and you become one. You stop resisting. You stop counting miles. You just *are*.

5. **Post-Trip Depression** – The adventure ends. Reality sets in. The bigger the trip, the worse the crash.

Had I known about the Tillamook Traverse Trail that followed the coast vs taking the 101, I would have taken it for no other reason that it would have given me a bit of diversity. I would have followed it. Instead, I traveled inland and stayed along the 101. Both routes ended in the same place, Cannon Beach.

Once called Elk Creek, Cannon Beach got its name thanks to the *USS Shark*, a U.S. Navy schooner that sank in 1846 while crossing what's known as the *Graveyard of the Pacific*—a brutal stretch of coast-line from Vancouver Island to Tillamook Bay, the final resting place for over 2,000 ships.

When debris from the *Shark* washed ashore, one of its cannons landed on the beach. (How a cannon washed up on a beach is a bit baffling to me, but that's the story.) In 1992, the town renamed itself Cannon Beach in its honor.

I stopped to take a photo of Chief Kiawanda Rock, the name given to it by the Nestugga Tribe. Later, it was renamed *Haystack Rock*—a 235-foot-tall, 17-million-year-old sea stack rising from the Pacific. It's a rock with a résumé: *The Goonies, Point Break*, and *Twilight* (which, I can proudly say, I've never seen).

When William Clark of the Lewis and Clark Expedition first laid eyes on Cannon Beach, he wrote:

"...the grandest and most pleasing prospects which my eyes ever surveyed, in front a boundless ocean..."

Just past Arch Cape came the Arch Cape Tunnel. Cyclists press a button at the entrance, triggering a flashing light to alert drivers that someone is inside—a simple, well-thought-out safety measure.

Once through the tunnel, the real work began—a six-mile, 580-foot climb.

At the top, I pulled over at the Neahkahnie South Viewpoint. Below, the waves crashed against Manzanita Beach, 500 feet down. It was one of the most stunning views of the entire trip.

PACIFIC COAST HIGHWAY
ON THE ROAD TO MANZANITA

Descending into Manzanita was fast—stupid fast. I hit over 50 MPH, ten miles over the posted speed limit.

Of course, there's always *that one guy* who has to ruin things.

This time, it was an RV driver who tailgated me the entire way down, honking as if I had any place to go. With no shoulder, I took the first pullout I could find, let him pass, and continued on. Only now—after blowing past me—he decided to obey the speed limit, presumably just to piss me off.

As if that wasn't enough to ruin a perfectly epic descent, a wasp flew straight into my mouth and stung the inside of my lower lip.

Over the years, I've had bees fly down my shirt, collided with birds, and even bunny-hopped over rattlesnakes. But a wasp in the mouth? That was a new one.

First, my face went numb. Then, it felt like my molars were going to explode. My lip swelled so much I probably looked like Donatella Versace.

Sucking on my lower lip with my mouth closed, I just kept pedaling—because what else can you do? Just keep on keeping on.

I don't think I need to tell anyone what comes to mind when you hear the name *Tillamook*.

Cheese.

Did I stop for some? No.

Instead, I pulled into a Safeway, grabbed a couple of prepackaged pasta meals, and found a spot to charge my phone—conveniently next to where they plugged in the store's electric carts. I sat down in one, ate my pasta, and enjoyed a little break from the road.

A man approached me while I was eating—he said he was a Royal Canadian Mounted Police officer traveling the coast with his wife. He was curious about my ride, asked a few questions, and seemed genuinely interested in the trip. His wife, however, had *zero* patience for our conversation. Before she dragged him away, I managed to convince him to download my audiobook and told him to reach out if he ever had questions about long-distance cycling.

Another couple, maybe ten years older than me, had also been riding the coast. Unlike the Mountie, they wanted nothing to do with a conversation. All I got out of them was that they started in Portland, were surprised by how much rain they'd encountered, and had only managed nine miles that day.

I had done twenty-eight. Winning!

From Tillamook, the road pulled away from the coast, heading directly south. Along the way, I passed *Hangar B*—the largest clear-span wooden structure in the world. Built during World War II to house dirigibles; it now holds over thirty aircraft, including an Aero-Spacelines *Mini Guppy*.

Ten miles east, at Cape Lookout, a quiet memorial stands, marking the site of a tragic crash that claimed the lives of ten men.

On a foggy night in 1943, a B-17 *Flying Fortress* met its end not in battle, but in the dense Oregon forest. Lost in heavy cloud cover, the pilot miscalculated his position, and at 200 miles per hour, the aircraft slammed into the mountainside.

Only one man survived. Bombardier Willie Perez was found 36 hours later, battered and exhausted. He had spent those hours trapped—suspended above a cliff, clinging to a mangled propeller. His crewmates, still alive but gravely wounded, cried out in agony. Helpless, he listened as their voices faded one by one, unable to do anything but hang there, waiting until rescuers reached the crash site.

For the next couple of hours, the ride was uneventful—aside from a long, sixteen-mile climb that topped out at 280 feet. A climb hardly worth mentioning. But I did. So, you're welcome.

To pass the time, I started Neil Peart's audiobook, *Ghost Rider: Travels on the Healing Road*. I didn't know much about Peart. Never a big Rush fan.

During the *Satanic Panic*, like many kids in the '80s, I was lead to believe that Rush was an acronym for *Rulers Under Satan's Hand*. KISS? That was *Knights in Satan's Service*, obviously. And if you played *Revolution 9* by The Beatles backward, it supposedly whispered, *Turn me on, dead man*.

Leaving Highway 101, I turned west onto Sandlake Road—right at the spot where a pack of dogs decided I looked like something worth chasing. Fortunately, their enthusiasm was short-lived.

It was about three in the afternoon when I pulled into Raines Resort Cabins and met Huan, the super-friendly host from Vietnam. He welcomed me with a big smile and, for reasons unknown, decided to put me next to two guys sharing a side-by-side cabin.

These two, somewhere in their 50s, were on a full-blown boys' road trip—hibachi grill, weed, beer, vodka, music. The whole setup.

At first, I wasn't in the mood to engage. In fact, I considered asking Huan if there was another cabin available. But after a shower, I stepped out onto the shared deck and, within minutes, hit it off with them.

They offered me beer, weed, and vodka. I turned them down. I still wanted to see how long I could go without alcohol, and I knew if I smoked weed, well, we all know that is the gateway drug to vodka. I learned that during the Satanic Panic era. Six days of *sobriety* wasn't exactly an impressive milestone, but it was something.

One guy was rail-thin, with long hair and a Fu Manchu mustache. The other was bigger—about my size.

I assumed they were professors. They laughed at that.

The thin guy ran a house-painting business in Boulder, Colorado. The other was a professional sports announcer from Buffalo, New York. They had rented an Escalade and had just come from *Dead & Company* at The Gorge Amphitheater in Washington.

A month prior, some guy had opened fire at the *Beyond Wonderland Music Festival* at the same venue, killing two and injuring three. They told me about the intense security they had to deal with at the show.

I never got into the Grateful Dead. Even Pink Floyd didn't enter my world until my senior year of high school when I watched *The Wall* in some dude's basement while enjoying some of the devil's lettuce. I was a skater punk. My cassette collection included *JFA, Agent Orange, Dead Kennedys, The Cramps,* and *Oingo Boingo.*

The only Grateful Dead song I knew was *Casey Jones.* Apparently, it was based on a true story about an engineer named Casey Jones who was driving his train too fast.

"Driving that train, high on cocaine.

Casey Jones, you better watch your speed."

They grilled up oysters they'd bought from a guy selling them out of a van down the street.

Species:	*Crassostrea gigas (Pacific Oyster)*
Origin:	*Netarts Bay, OR*
Flavor Profile:	*Sweet brine with robust meat and a melon-rind finish*
Suggested Pairing:	*Chablis*

They smoked a *lot* of weed and drank a *lot* of vodka. The conversation got funnier as the night went on, bouncing from music to road trip stories to random trivia.

At one point, the painter asked, "What's your favorite comedy movie?"

I didn't have a specific one. It depended on my mood. "Um, maybe *Big Trouble in Little China*."

The sportscaster went with *Blazing Saddles*.

The painter? *One Flew Over the Cuckoo's Nest*.

I didn't even bother trying to figure that one out.

Vintery, mintery, cutery, corn,
Apple seed and apple thorn,
Wire, briar, limber lock
Three geese in a flock
One flew East
One flew West
And one flew over the cuckoo's nest

CORY: 4
VP: 2

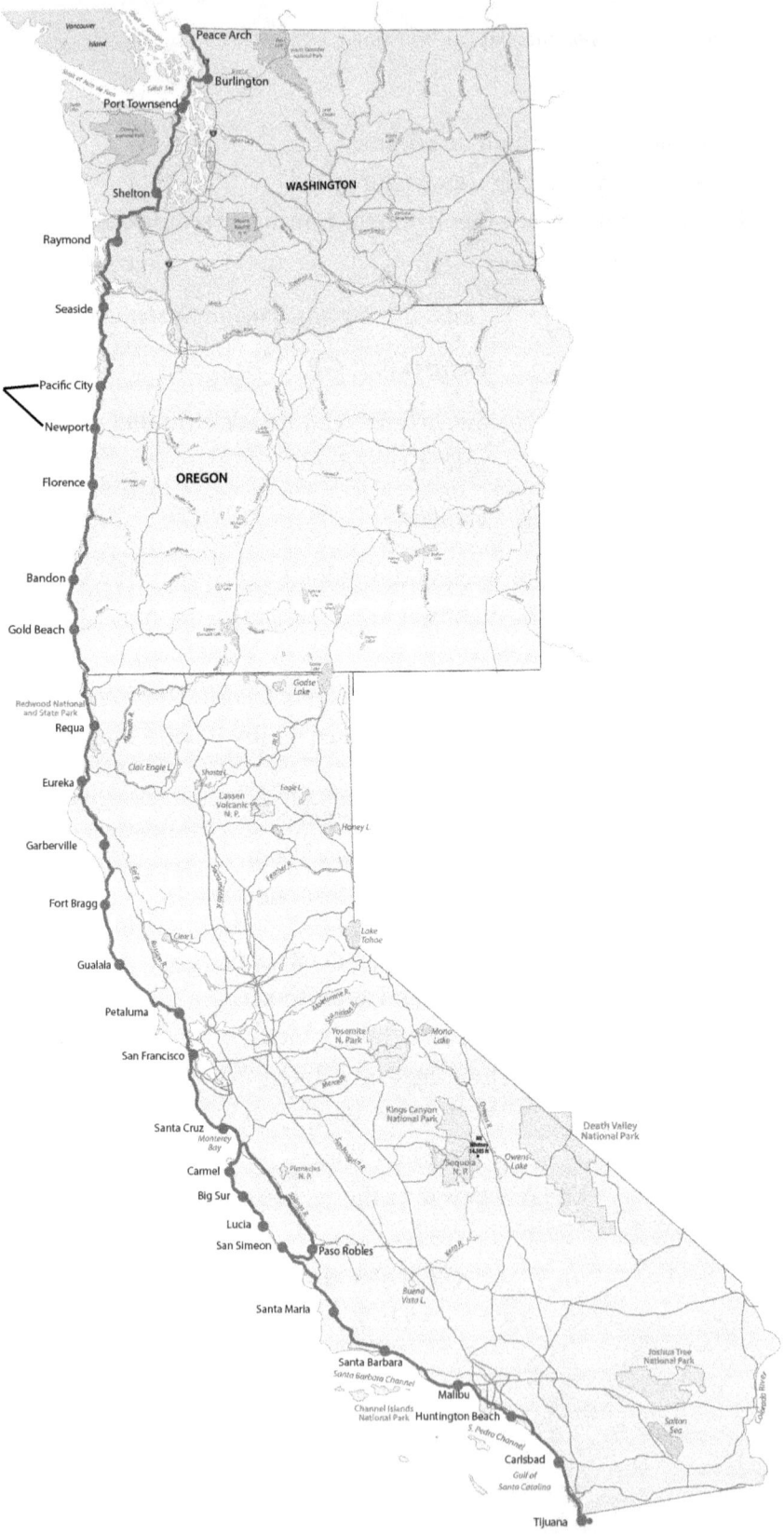

DAY 7

Peace Arch
Burlington
Port Townsend
Shelton
Raymond
Seaside
Pacific City
Newport
Florence
Bandon
Gold Beach
Requa
Eureka
Garberville
Fort Bragg
Gualala
Petaluma
San Francisco
Santa Cruz
Carmel
Big Sur
Lucia
San Simeon
Paso Robles
Santa Maria
Santa Barbara
Malibu
Huntington Beach
Carlsbad
Tijuana

WASHINGTON

OREGON

DAY 7 - JULY 12, 2023

Pacific City, Oregon to Newport, Oregon

49 MILES: 2,265' ELEVATION GAIN

"Good morning, D-Train. I hope you had a wonderful day yesterday riding your bike. And if you didn't, it doesn't matter because that was yesterday, and today is today. AND it looks like you're headed to Newport, Oregon. Your ride there should be sunny, high of 60°F. Not sure what check-in time is, but I'm assuming it's around three o'clock. It's a cloudy, rainy day here in Minneapolis, um, and I'm about to do battle with cars. Much, much different than riding a gravel bike. Hope you have a wonderful day, buddy. Talk to you soon."

Yesterday, I burned 3,000 calories and only ate Safeway pasta and two large oysters. Today, I woke up hungry.

As my neighbors, who were hungover, packed up their gear, they suggested I stop in town for breakfast at, wait for it… Grateful Bread Bakery.

I'd love to run into those guys again someday. Before they hit the road back to San Francisco, I gave them my info and told them my audiobooks were free if they wanted something to listen to on the drive.

The Grateful Bread Bakery was closed, so I settled for the Village Coffee Shoppe, where I enjoyed an unhealthy, greasy breakfast.

Next to me sat a group of four retirees, locked in a conversation I couldn't help but tune into.

"Government's trying to run our lives, not our country."

"It's not we the people anymore. It's they the lords and we the peasants."

"They just give my money away to people who could work."

"Now they want us to pay off other people's student loans. You know Bill Harper? They shut off his power because he owed fifty-five cents. How's he supposed to pay off someone else's damn student loan if he can't even pay fifty-five cents?"

On and on it went. Clearly not fans of the Biden administration.

I sipped my coffee, eavesdropped a little longer, and thought about the short day ahead—49 miles to Newport. I'd be there before lunch.

It was another near-perfect morning.

The road out of Pacific City curved around Nestucca Bay, and in three miles, I was back on Highway 101.

I turned into the unincorporated town of Neskowin, where a beautiful Haida salmon wood carving hung, welcoming residents and guests. The Haida people have lived in the region for over 12,500 years, considered masters of the sea and incredible artists.

A short walk up the beach led to Neskowin Ghost Forest, a stand of 2,000-year-old Sitka spruce stumps, remnants of a long-forgotten coastal forest. If ancient tree stumps aren't your thing, just north of the Ghost Forest is Proposal Rock, named in 1900 after Sea Captain Charley Gage proposed to Della Page there.

If neither of those things interests you, well… sometimes the best reason to stop in a place is simply because you're there.

A few yards along Highway 101, I passed a roadside cross for Sue Chavez (1962–2022). A dream catcher hung above it.

It was here that I hit the longest climb of the trip so far- 3.5 miles at 6%. Luckily, one of the two ascending lanes was coned off for maintenance, giving me a temporary bike lane of my own. About halfway up, I caught up with a utility truck slowly rolling ahead, dropping cones every few feet.

The guy on the back of the truck looked up and gave me a thumbs-up. "Nice work!"

The driver leaned out the window, grinning.

"Pop a wheelie!"

I laughed and threw him a shaka.

A *wheelie*? On a *climb*? Who did he think I was, Peter Sagan?

But just ahead, my *safe zone* disappeared. The coned-off lane ended, and I was back riding on the edge. Not two minutes later, a white pickup truck swerved directly at me. I yanked my handlebars to the right, hugging the shoulder as the truck overcorrected, plowing into the ditch.

Had I been twenty feet further up the climb, she would have hit me, and there would be a white cross erected for Cory Mortensen (1970–2023).

Shaken, I pulled off onto a lightly used double track—probably a utility road. I needed a moment to breathe and pee.

Wandering up the trail, I stumbled across a hidden campsite tucked deep in the forest. A fire pit sat in the center, surrounded by dense trees.

The west side opened to a cliffside view that was...absolutely breathtaking.

Under one of the trees, four bottles of Angry Orchard Cider had been left behind. Above them, two notes were nailed to the tree.

The first note was written on the back of a paper plate:

> Please leave it cleaner than you found it so
> we can all come back for years to come
> ☺
> Lewis Family
> July 2023 ♡

A second note was placed over the paper plate note:

> Lewis Family,
> Thank you for sharing your special, beautiful
> space. We picked up a lot of trash but are so sorry;
> someone dumped a fridge in this lovely Eden.
> We are grateful for you
> ♡
> J & J

With the white pickup erased from my memory, it was time to enjoy a 3-mile, 750-foot descent into Lincoln City. Twenty miles behind, twenty-nine to go.

I should have stopped in Lincoln City, grabbed a coffee, and sat on the beach, but I didn't. I was feeling strong, the fog off the ocean kept me cool, and visibility was poor, so I continued south. Just before Depoe Bay, a large sign read:

> # BI-PLANE RIDES
> # TODAY
> ### www.nwplanerides.com

You, dear reader, know where this is going. I pulled into the Siletz Bay State Airport-S45 and called the number. I had plenty of time, and I'd never been in a bi-plane.

No answer. I called again, still no answer, so I left a message and waited. I called one more time. Nothing. Well, it was not meant to be.

Five miles after the airport, I rolled into Depoe Bay. It was bustling with tourists and home to the "WORLD'S SMALLEST HARBOR," according to the sign on the bridge.

Another sign read:

> OREGON FILM TRAIL
>
> *ONE FLEW OVER THE CUCKOO'S NEST* - 1975
>
> The iconic fishing trip scene in the film adaptation of
> Ken Kesey's novel took place here in Depoe Bay.
> Jack Nicholson's character, Randle "Mac"
> McMurphy, staged an escape, led his fellow patients here,
> and commandeered a boat for a day of fishing.
>
> OREGON MADE

One Flew Over the Cuckoo's Nest, a comedy.

Next to the bridge was a Whale Watching Center filled with facts, displays, and science, and it provided binoculars for free. Gray, humpback, and blue whales are the most commonly sighted.

On his third trip around the world in 1778, Captain Cook wrote in his journal just a few miles south:

> "The land appeared to be of moderate height, diversified with hill and valley, and almost everywhere covered with wood. There was nothing remarkable about it except one hill... At the northern extreme, the land formed a point which I called Cape Foulweather from the very bad weather we soon after met with."

For most of today's ride, the road was flat—some rollers, nothing too taxing—except for one final half-mile, 500-foot climb before I could call it a day and chill in Newport.

Check-in at the Silver Sands Motel was at 4 p.m. *Sharp*. No exceptions. It wasn't exactly a great place. I had no desire to spend the rest of my day there; I just wanted to change out of my cycling clothes and do a little exploring.

Down along SW Bay Blvd, a stretch of bars and restaurants lined the waterfront along Yaquina Bay. I found Thai Port Restaurant—not as good as the last Thai spot, but it filled the void. Plus, the restaurant sat on a pier with a great view of the Newport Marina and the Yaquina Bay Bridge.

My phone rang; it was the bi-plane pilot.

"Hello, I saw you called. I was up flying. Couldn't answer—don't fly and text," he chuckled. Dry sense of humor—my kind of pilot.

"Oh, hey, yeah. I'm cycling the coast and passed your sign, ducked into the airport. Thought it would be fun to add a bi-plane flight into my day."

"When can you be here? I can get you up today."

"Yeah, well, I'm on a bicycle and am in Newport. So I'll chalk it up to a missed opportunity—not sure when I would be able to get there."

I checked Uber—$78 each way. Seemed steep.

Was I wimping out on an adventure? Maybe. I went back and forth but couldn't justify the expense. It wasn't just about the money; it felt selfish not to include Kate. She would *love* flying in an open cockpit over the ocean.

When we first started dating, I surprised her with a glider ride. She's a licensed skydiver and rode a Ducati Monster. No doubt, she'd give two thumbs up for an adventure like this.

Instead of soaring over the coastline, I spent the afternoon watching sea lions lounge at the Sea Lion Docks.

Sea lions are odd creatures. Whiskers. Fins instead of arms and legs. Fur instead of scales. Sharp teeth. Mammals that move faster in water than on land. Loud, stinky, seemingly lazy—yet somehow *apex predators*. Very odd. Very curious.

When I got back to the hotel, a new guy was at the front desk, hunched over the computer.

"You know, I could check you in early. Do you have any pets?"

"No, I'm on my bike."

"Okay, but just so you know—no pets in the room."

"Copy that."

I called Kate, texted some friends, did some journaling, and put on *Mission Impossible*. Tom Cruise. *He* would have gone back for the bi-plane ride. Hell, he would've flown the damn thing.

CORY: 5
VRP: 2

CALIFORNIA
1
PACIFIC COAST HIGHWAY

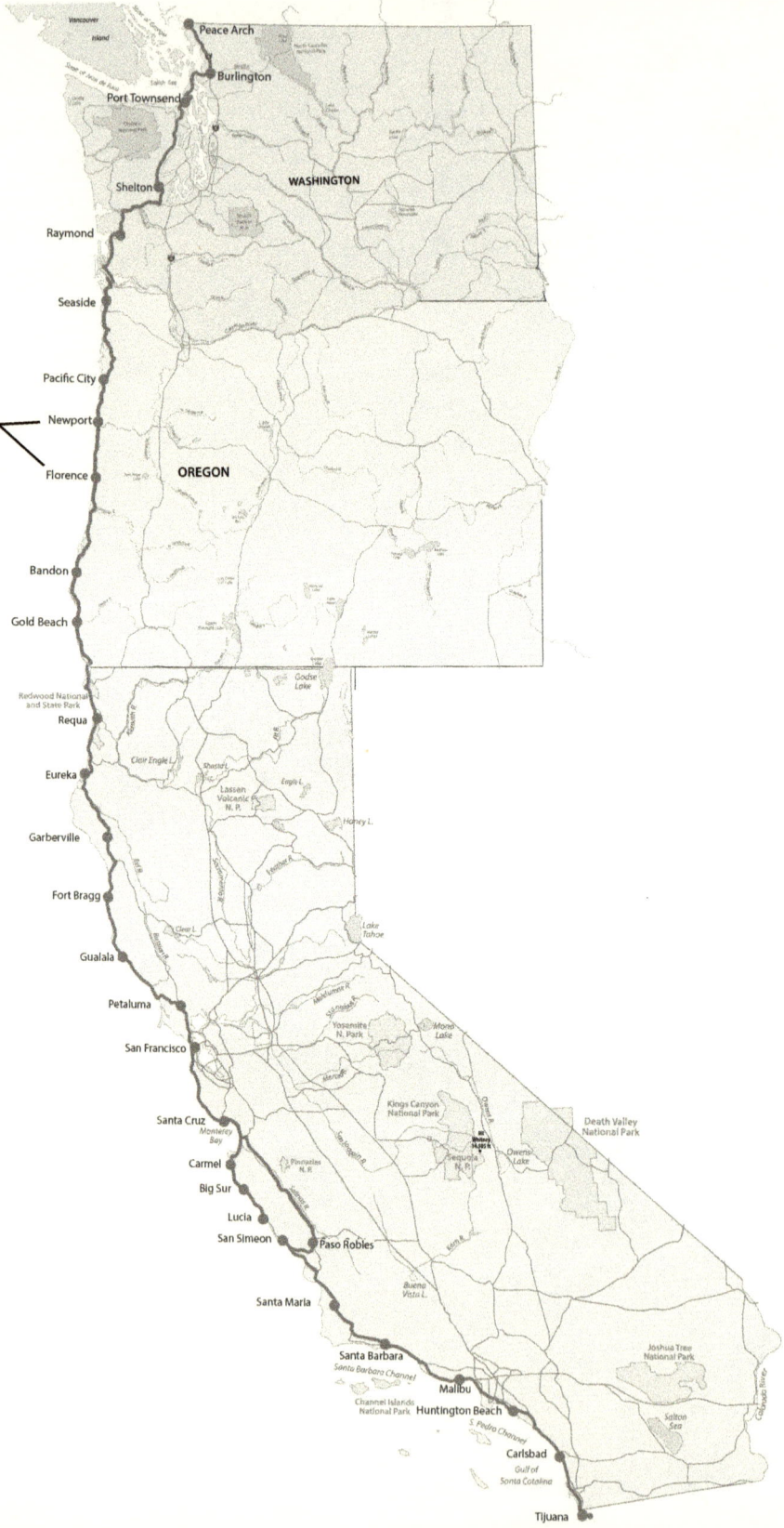

Peace Arch

Burlington

Port Townsend

WASHINGTON

Shelton

Raymond

Seaside

Pacific City

DAY 8 — Newport

Florence

OREGON

Bandon

Gold Beach

Redwood National
and State Park

Requa

Eureka

Garberville

Fort Bragg

Gualala

Petaluma

San Francisco

Santa Cruz

Carmel

Big Sur

Lucia

San Simeon — Paso Robles

Santa Maria

Santa Barbara

Malibu

Huntington Beach

Carlsbad

Tijuana

DAY 8 - JULY 13, 2023

Newport, Oregon to Florence, Oregon

50 MILES: 2,153' ELEVATION GAIN

"Good morning, D-Train! Welcome to another glorious day in your life. It's going to be about 67 degrees today and sunny. It's going to be a beautiful ride for you. I hope you enjoy the day, and just remember, like we said last night, 'the ride will come to you.' In a couple of days, you'll feel like a rockstar, and you'll be rad, and you'll think, 'there's no chain attached.' Anyway, have a glorious day today, buddy."

He attached a recommended podcast:

> ((🎙)) Podcast: THE END OF THE WORLD with Josh Clark
> Episode: Season 1, Episode 1
> *Fermi Paradox: Ever wondered where all the aliens are?*

After listening to Kevin's message, something wonderful happened. I was finally able to eke out a decent dump. Maybe I hadn't been eating enough, but for the past few days, very little had been produced in this matter. Today, July 13, 2023, things moved along nicely.

First stop: Chevron station. Time to check my lottery winnings. $4.00. Once again, I let it ride and bought two more tickets. You gotta pay to play.

Along the coastal road near Don & Ann Davis Park, overlanders had parked their Sprinter vans, turning the sidewalk into their front porch. Couples sat in camping chairs, sipping fresh-pressed coffee and watching the ocean crash against the shore.

Kate and I have talked about getting a Sprinter van—letting the road decide where home would be that night, that week, that month.

Rent out the house and let someone else pay the mortgage while we sip coffee and watch the tide roll in.

There was a time when society warned: *"If you don't get a job, you'll end up living in a van down by the river!"*

Now? That's the dream.

Just off the walkway were the skeletal remains of a whale. Next to them was a stone with the following words carved into it:

> Whales have been here
> forever. Their flesh has fed the
> people and been the occasion
> for celebration and feasting.
> Their bones have been made
> into tools and objects of status
> and ceremonial importance.
> The sighting of a whale still
> thrills all who see it. ·
> May it always be so!
>
> *—Robert Kentta*
> *Cultural Resources Director*
> *Confederated Tribes of Siletz Indians*

One of fourteen bridges designed by Conde McCullough along Highway 101, the Yaquina Bay Bridge is a masterpiece—both structurally and aesthetically.

McCullough believed bridges should be economical, efficient, and beautiful. He incorporated art deco obelisks, Romanesque arches, and Gothic spires into his designs, elevating them beyond mere infrastructure.

Sadly, many of his bridges have been demolished and replaced. But the Yaquina Bay Bridge? It remains easily my favorite along the 101.

Just past the bridge, a handmade sign caught my eye:

"OYSTERS—PICK YOUR OWN! $5"

Species: *Crassostrea gigas (Pacific Oyster)*

Origin: *Yaquina Bay, OR*

Flavor Profile: *Deep cups with creamy meats, sweet and mild with a melon finish.*

Suggested Pairing: *Pinot Noir*

Tempting.

Since we've got about 50 miles ahead of us, let me tell you the story behind this *D-Train* nickname that Kevin keeps referencing.

Obviously, it's yours truly. But here's how it all started.

It was 1999. I flew out to visit some friends in New York. After landing, I took a cab to their apartment in Brooklyn, dropped my bags, and within an hour, we were out on the town.

At some point in the night, I had one too many adult beverages. A very nice bartender politely suggested that, once I finished my drink, I should probably leave.

I took his advice.

Unfortunately, I left *alone*—without my friends, without a phone, and without any real clue where I was. I had spent maybe an hour in their apartment before heading out. No address. No map. No iThings to guide me.

But somehow, by some miracle, I made it back. When my friends arrived home later that night, they found me sitting on their stoop, waiting for them.

"How the hell did you find your way back?" they asked.

I shrugged. "I have no idea."

The next evening, we were out in Manhattan when I passed a guy in all leather, full beard, dreadlocks—the kind of guy you might instinctively avoid if you judged a book by its cover.

As I walked by, he grabbed my arm, grinned, and said:

"Dude! You were on the D-Train last night!"

"I really don't remember."

"Oh yeah, we were talking. You didn't know where your friend's apartment was, and I offered you my couch. Then, all of a sudden, you just got off at the next stop."

"That all sounds very plausible."

My friend, amused, chimed in:

"D-Train!"

The guy laughed. "Yeah, man, we were in the Bronx."

"Our apartment is in Brooklyn. How did you get from the Bronx to Brooklyn?" My buddy asked.

I just shrugged.

"Man, I'm just glad you made it back okay," the guy said. "Let me buy you a beer. Name's Mike—Mike Meselsohn. I'm the drummer for a band called Boiler Room."

He handed me a beer, gave me a copy of their album *Can't Breathe*, and invited us to a martini party in the Village. And just like that, *D-Train* stuck.

Who doesn't love New York.

D-Train isn't the only moniker I've picked up along the way.

The Doctor

When I was 22 or 23, I started dating this girl, and for our first four weekends together, we went to weddings for her various friends and family members.

For reasons unknown, I started signing the guest books as Dr. Cory Mortensen. It wasn't long before half her family thought I was an actual doctor.

To keep the story going, I bought a stethoscope and started showing up to her family events with it—acting like I had just pulled a 36-hour shift at the hospital.

Alfonzo

On one of my birthdays, my veterinarian friends got called away to deliver an alpaca. I asked if the owner would name it Cory in my honor. They had already chosen a name: Alfonzo.

Since the alpaca and I shared a birthday, the owners compromised—naming it Alfonzo-Cory.

El Presidente

When I owned my company, one of my first distributors was based in Mexico. When I flew down to meet them, they welcomed me with a gift basket—chocolates, a bottle of El Jimador Tequila, and a card that read: *"Bienvenido, **El Presidente** Cory Mortensen."*

Naturally, when I got back to my office, I had all my business cards, marketing materials, and email signature changed to read:

Cory Mortensen
El Presidente
EKHO Brand Americas, LLC
+001-612-702-80XX (Here's my number, call me maybe.)

El Presidente Deposed—After I sold my company.

Every morning, I expect an uneventful day. I treat it like a few-hour ride back home—get up, drink coffee, head out, and be done by lunch. Just another day on the bike, moving from Point A to Point B.

Cycling allows you to notice the forgotten and overlooked details of the landscape, certainly missed at 55 mph.

- A brief conversation with a construction worker holding a stop sign.

- An abandoned bridge, slowly being reclaimed by nature.

- A swimming pool shaped like a whale.

- A dinosaur, peering out from the trees.

- A metal sign, commemorating some event from centuries ago.

- A white cross, marking the place where someone's journey ended.

Everywhere has a story, some importance, some small detail waiting to be noticed.

I passed through small towns, places barely holding onto their names—just important enough to be a dot on a map:

- **Forfar** – Gaelic for Cold Point

- **Wakonda** – Great Creator of the Plains Indians

- **Tillicum** – Chinook for people, family, tribe

- **Yachats** – Dark water at the foot of the mountain

Places like *Devil's Churn* and *Thor's Well* demanded stops—if only out of curiosity about what godly forces would warrant such names. Both put on an impressive display of the ocean's power.

Today's ride featured rolling hills and dynamic coastal views—a wide shoulder, the sun offering just the right amount of warmth, and the wind at my back.

Further down the coast, Heceta Head Lighthouse stood watch— one of the most photographed lighthouses in the state. Not just a landmark, but also a bed and breakfast—a haunted one, at that. Its beam, the brightest in Oregon, reaches 21 miles out to sea—just 5.2 miles shy of a full marathon.

I arrived early in Florence. The Silver Sands Motel refused to budge on their check-in time, so I headed to the beach. Something epic happened here once.

In 1970, a 45-foot-long, eight-ton sperm whale washed up on the beach near Florence, Oregon.

The city, unable to decide what to do with the rotting, bloated carcass, left the problem in the hands of Highway Engineer George

Thornton. Taking a John Galt approach to the situation, George consulted Navy munitions experts and came up with a brilliant solution: Blow it up.

It's a known fact that dead whales can explode on their own due to the buildup of gases inside the carcass, but George wasn't about to wait around for nature to take its course.

With hundreds of onlookers, news cameras rolling, and enough dynamite to make Wile E. Coyote proud, George packed the whale with explosives and set the countdown.

At detonation, whale flesh rained down on the crowd, with some chunks flying as far as 800 feet. A massive slab of blubber crushed a car parked nearby.

The entire disaster was caught on film, and thanks to YouTube, it lives on as one of the most gloriously bad ideas in history.

What did we learn? We learned not to do it again.

My next stop was down on Bay Street, a lively mix of tourists and locals hanging out along the Siuslaw River.

As I took in the scene, my doctor's assistant called. She wanted to schedule my shoulder surgery—something I had finally agreed to and one of the many reasons I wanted to knock out this ride before being out of commission for a while.

My shoulder had been a mess for a while, but I ignored it. Years of wear and tear, and now time had finally caught up. It got to the point where I couldn't even push myself out of bed without sharp pain. Kate insisted I get an MRI. I did. Bam—surgery was in my future.

When I met with the surgeon, I asked a question that probably wasn't the best thing to ask a surgeon: "Isn't it possible that surgery could do more harm than good? Can't I just keep on keeping on?"

He leaned back and stared at me.

"You say you're in a lot of pain. You say you can't do the things you want to do, correct?"

"Yes."

"According to my computer program, you're healthy, so you'll probably live to be 83 years old. You're 53 now. Do you want to spend 30 years in the pain you're currently in, unable to do the things you love?"

"No."

"Call my office and schedule the procedure—or don't. Your call."

And with that, he walked out of the room.

I paid for the operating room and deductible, and in 32 days, I was going under the knife. They would:

- Reattach my bicep

- Repair a torn rotator cuff

- Shave down a bone spur

- Stitch up a torn coracoacromial ligament

Good times.

Across the street, a 308 GTS Ferrari straight out of *Magnum P.I.* sat parked along the curb.

A throwback to my youth. I imagined the owner—Hawaiian shirt, short shorts, mustache, the full Tom Selleck aesthetic. Then I saw him—balding, overweight, sucking in his gut to squeeze into the Italian sports car.

One day, Hollywood will ruin that series by turning it into a movie, and when they do, I'm sure Kate will drag me to it.

CORY: 5
VP: 3

CALIFORNIA
1
PACIFIC COAST HIGHWAY

DAY 9

Peace Arch
Burlington
Port Townsend
Shelton
Raymond
Seaside
Pacific City
Newport
Florence
Bandon
Gold Beach
Requa
Eureka
Garberville
Fort Bragg
Gualala
Petaluma
San Francisco
Santa Cruz
Carmel
Big Sur
Lucia
San Simeon
Paso Robles
Santa Maria
Santa Barbara
Malibu
Huntington Beach
Carlsbad
Tijuana

WASHINGTON

OREGON

DAY 9 - JULY 14, 2023

Florence, Oregon to Bandon, Oregon

75 MILES: 2,613' ELEVATION GAIN

"Good morning D-Train, welcome to another day in paradise. It is Bastille Day. If you don't know what that is… you can look it up. I'll give you some time to listen to some stuff while you ride. Um, anyway, um, looks like you got a day today, but you know what? It's not too bad. It's a 35-mile easy ride, have lunch. 35 miles after lunch, before you know it, your feet will be up drinking a cool beverage? I don't know, reading a newspaper, I wonder if they still have newspapers? Something like that. You're probably scrolling your phone while pooping. Anyway, hope you have a great day, um, it's supposed to be a beautiful day here in Minneapolis, and I'm just about ready to go, um, bring my child to daycare. So, anyway, hope you have a glorious day, my friend, and, um, enjoy!"

> **((🎙)) Podcast: REVOLUTIONS**
> **Episode: 12 3.11-The Fall of the Bastille**

Unfortunately, my headphones crapped out, which meant today's ride would be in silence.

Or, as Kevin put it, "Probably the proper way—nature be the soundtrack."

That's how he talks. He leaves out words and speaks as if he's narrating an old-world map. "Here be dragons," instead of "Here, one might find dragons."

Perhaps that's the result of a Wisconsin education.

Many will say it is dangerous to ride with headphones; I'm sure Bill Thorness would agree with that. I found a brand I will use until my last days. Shoks headphones sit on the outside of your ears, using bone conduction so you can still hear music, podcasts, audiobooks—whatever—while also hearing the traffic behind you.

The Silver Sands Motel had no air conditioning—a feature many places in the Pacific Northwest lack because the climate is usually mild— and the room was stuffy.

But this room felt thick with the scent of every traveler before me lingering in the walls. I could have upgraded. Should have upgraded.

I could have opened the window to let in some air, but that would have also made me an easy target for a break-in. Considering the riffraff loitering outside—the shouting matches, the drug deals, the occasional relationship blowout—I decided against it. Instead, I kept the window shut and wedged a chair in front of the door.

Not that it would actually stop anyone determined enough to break in and steal my Neosporin and toothpaste, but at least it would slow them down long enough for me to grab my knife and pretend to be fierce.

Instead, I stayed.

And, as a consolation, I found Ichiban Chinese & Japanese Restaurant, which sold me some of the spiciest beef lo mein I've ever had.

This, of course, led to early morning bathroom visits, but I do love me some spicy food—consequences be damned.

Before my headphones crapped out, I was listening to Neil Peart's book *Ghost Rider: Travels on the Healing Road*. I was surprised to hear about his motel choices as he rode his motorcycle around North and Central America. Some towns he ended up in offered limited options, but if given the opportunity, he seemed to prefer a motel built by a logging company in 1932 over the newer Marriott that offered all the unnecessary amenities we want but never use.

In 1997, Peart's only daughter died in a single-car crash at the age of 19. His wife Jacqueline, whom he had been married to for 23 years, died a year later from cancer. Neil attributed Jacqueline's death to a "broken heart," saying it was "a slow suicide by apathy. She just didn't care."

Seventy-five miles ahead of me. Yesterday, I was just thinking that all I had to do was ride my bike all day through this dramatic landscape, but this morning I was fixated on the hills I had seen on my Garmin's elevation profile. I was doing the one thing I told myself never to do:

"Never look at tomorrow's elevation when riding today's hills."

I wished that long days in the saddle produced more wisdom, more metaphors, more life-changing philosophical theories. Maybe they did—but by the time I had a chance to jot them down, they were gone.

I used my Notes app on my iThing with great frequency, but even with that modern convenience, I missed out on writing down what were undoubtedly profound thoughts which would have placed me on the same intellectual level as Nietzsche, Plato, and Bob Dylan.

When I first planned this route, I did so with the memory of my 31-year-old self. While I still approached life with that same reckless enthusiasm, the 53-year-old version of me often stepped in to remind me:

"Dude, you've already done this. Enjoy the ride. It's not a race. Nobody cares if you ride 50, 70, or 100 miles a day. Nobody cares how long it takes. Nobody cares if you even finish."

I made it all of 500 feet before ducking into The Little Brown Hen for breakfast. Armed with zero motivation and a long day ahead, I ordered a coffee and a bagel with lox.

The waiter poured my coffee.

"How far you going today?"

"Bandon. 75 miles."

"More like 80 miles. And big climbs."

That unsolicited response came from another customer—exactly what I didn't want to hear: more miles, big climbs.

Another guy chimed in: "That's a big push. Good luck."

Some days, the finish line feels unreachable. The whole day feels impossible. I've had these conversations with friends who do hundred-plus-mile rides in a day.

On paper, it looks easy. Just 70 miles, or 250 miles, depending on your tolerance for suffering.

Break it down: *Just take it ten miles at a time, bam—done.*

But once you're out there, the first climb comes. Then the second. Then the tenth. Then the wind, or the heat, or the cold, and suddenly, you're asking yourself:

"Why?"

It's a fair question.

Why challenge yourself when, honestly, no one really cares?

You run a marathon, tell your non-marathon friends, and their response? "Wow, that sounds hard. How far is a marathon again? Anyway, let's grab a beer."

At the end of the day, it's about you. Your willingness to do the thing—whatever that thing is.

It doesn't have to be physical. It could be financial, artistic, personal.

We get one chance at this life, and it feels wildly unfair that we spend our youth bursting with energy and lacking maturity, only to finally gain wisdom just as that energy begins to fade.

Was it Oscar Wilde who said: *"Youth is wasted on the young"*?

A year prior, Kate and I put our trust together. I wrote out a few extra things. One was a list of items I wanted my family to have.

While putting the trust together, I laid out my detailed funeral service, which Kate thought was arrogant of me. I rebutted, saying, if I died in a car accident tomorrow, do you want to figure out who will do the eulogy or what song to play? I included a case of *The Balvenie 12-Year Double Wood Aged Single Malt* to be provided to all those in attendance, to raise a glass to what I'd like to think was a life well lived. My nephews and nieces, who will essentially get everything, are tasked with a final assignment. I have put down six GPS coordinates around the world—some of my favorite places. They are required, as a family, to go to each of these places to spread my ashes, allowing me to share these special places with them. Their kids will never know who I am, and aside from perhaps a digital footprint—which I have requested to be deleted from all social media—and my books, no one will know I ever existed two generations from now.

I do not know who to attribute this quote or these words to, but as I get older, it hits home harder.

> In 100 years, we will all be buried with our relatives and friends. Strangers will live in our homes we fought so hard to build, and they will own everything we have today. All our possessions will be unknown and unborn, including the car we spent a fortune on, and will probably be scrap, preferably in the hands of an unknown collector.
>
> Our descendants will hardly know who we were, nor will they remember us. How many of us know our grandfather's father? After we die, we will be remembered for a few more years, then we are just a portrait on someone's bookshelf, and a few years later our history, photos, and deeds disappear in history's oblivion. We won't even be memories.

If we paused one day to analyze these thoughts, perhaps we would understand how ignorant and weak the dream to achieve it all really was.

If we could only think about this, surely our approaches, our thoughts would change, we would be different people.

Always having more, no time for what's really valuable in this life. I'd change all this to live and enjoy the walks I've never taken, these hugs I didn't give, these kisses for our children and our loved ones, these jokes we didn't have time for. Those would certainly be the most beautiful moments to remember, after all they would fill our lives with joy.

And we waste it day after day with greed and intolerance.

Kevin was right; I didn't miss the headphones. No voices in my head today aside from my own.

On all my cross-country rides, I never wore headphones. I debated whether or not to bring them on this trip but decided to in an effort to catch up on my audiobooks.

I passed two cyclists heading north, fully loaded, likely riding the Pacific Coast Highway from south to north. Most cyclists prefer the north-to-south route for two reasons:

1. Better views of the coast.

2. Prevailing winds are in your favor.

I gave them a nod, but they didn't return it.

I don't take things like that personally anymore. I used to, but after starting my company, I realized something: People either really like me, or they really don't, and I'm fine with both.

I'm blunt, unfiltered, and have a low level of empathy—but I'm honest, and no one ever has to wonder where I stand.

It also helps clear the clutter when it comes to friendships. I spend time with people who want to spend time with me and don't waste time trying to convince people who don't like me to like me.

"I'd rather be hated for who I am than loved for who I am not."
— Kurt Cobain

Did I just overthink a simple missed nod? Probably.

Fifteen miles in, I caught up with another cyclist, pushing his overloaded bike up one of the rolling hills. I assumed he had a mechanical issue because the climb was nothing to write home about.

Trying to make conversation, I quickly realized he was not happy. I greeted him, and he muttered something in German.

A quick look at his bike revealed no flat tyre and the chain was still intact.

Best I could figure? He just didn't have it in him to ride the hills. If this was his pace, it was going to take a long time to get to Mexico.

Just after Reedsport, I saw a young kid pushing his bike. If I had to guess, he was running away from home. I tried that once; it didn't pan out like I planned.

He had an old bike, a suitcase bungeed to the rear rack, and was wearing flip-flops.

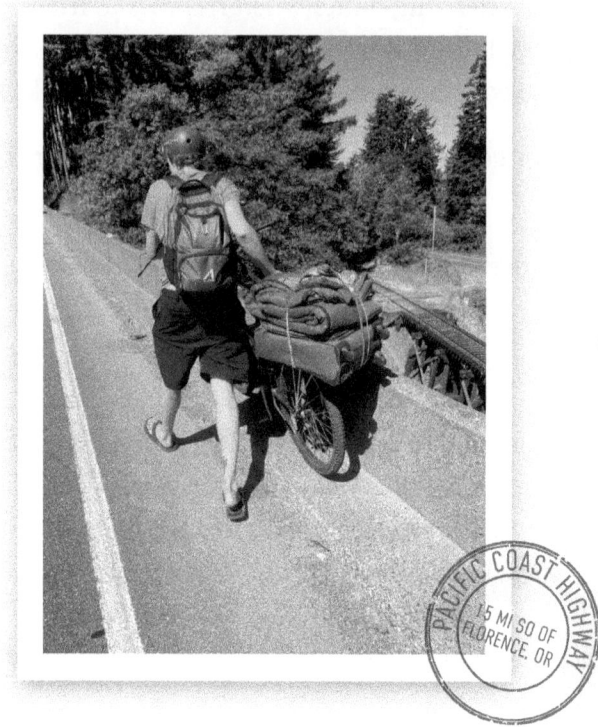

If he was trying to get away from where he was, he had a long way to go. And if he was trying to get somewhere else, he had an even longer way ahead of him.

I tried making conversation, but like the German cyclist, he wasn't interested.

I had seen more people on bikes today than any other day on this trip—none of them were in the mood to talk.

Passing along the sand dunes, I found myself racing a yellow and black butterfly. There was no winner—his flight was erratic and fast, and eventually, he disappeared.

Butterflies became more frequent. They were fun to watch, fun to ride with. And when one vanished, another would take its place.

At Coos Bay, I crossed the Conde B. McCullough Memorial Bridge—another stunning bridge designed by McCullough himself. Rising 280 feet above the water, it was a sight to behold.

Outside of the Starbucks, I saw a Kawasaki KLR650 with the words "Ticos on the Road" written across its tank bags.

In 1993, when I was in Costa Rica, I learned that Ticos (men) and Ticas (women) is what Costa Ricans call themselves as they have a habit of adding "-ico" to words.

Example: Instead of *chiquito* (small), they say *chiquitico*.

Inside, it wasn't hard to figure out who was riding the bike.

"*Hola, eres de Costa Rica?*"

"*Sí.*"

"*Ah… vi 'Tico' en tu motocicleta. Tico is Costa Rican, sí? Hablas inglés?*"

"Yes."

"*Bueno*, how far are you riding?"

"We started in Alaska. Heading to Ushuaia."

That journey—riding from Alaska to Ushuaia—is one of those things that sits on my list of things to do. The older I get, and the more I travel, the longer that list gets.

Between 2015 and 2017, Kate and I wandered around South America. In Peru, we met a guy who had driven his car from Los Angeles, and we ended up hitching a ride with him from Cusco, Peru, to Bariloche, Argentina.

He never made it to Ushuaia. Instead, he drove to Puerto Natales, Chile, then up to Buenos Aires, where he sold the car and flew home.

We met a few people on that trip who were riding or driving the Pan-American Highway—the longest road in the world.

I bought an Americano and a chocolate brownie and charged my phone.

Looking at the Ticos, I thought: "One day, I will make that ride happen. Car, motorcycle, bicycle—*it doesn't matter.*"

A mile south, I watched two hippie-esque nineteen-year-old girls strapping all their belongings to the top of a rusty 1970s sedan. They wore full-length dresses, the kind that looked like they had been stitched together from floral curtain fabric.

If there was ever a pair that should have been born 70 years ago, it was them. Their sedan should have been a VW Bus.

The smell of freshly cut timber filled the air, with piles of woodchips stacked between the road and the water, waiting to be loaded onto a cargo ship bound for somewhere far away.

A mural covered one of the buildings—Bigfoot hugging a robot, with the words "I LOVE YOU SO MUCH" scrawled above them.

I'm always ready for when the aliens return—the ancients who built all of this. One day I hope to meet Prometheus, the creator of humans from mud and clay.

Coos Bay felt like a place Jack Kerouac would have admired—a town where rivers, railways, and roads converged. A place where decisions were made—where to go next, or maybe, nowhere at all.

How would Kerouac have described Coos Bay?

Maybe something like:

"Whack, whack, whack—the axe sings its sharp tune through the hush-hush of the old green dream, trees sighing their last breath in the golden slant of the afternoon light, crashing down, breaking the hush, shaking the earth, and the leaves rise like startled birds. What did they whisper as they tumbled, as they lay upon the soft moss floor, waiting for the grinding hum of machines, the big hungry jaws of industry swallowing them whole?

And me, ah, old Billy's wine burning sweet in my throat, a fire in the belly, riding the rails, rattling along from Eugene, wind in the hair, dust in the teeth, chasing the ever-rolling road with a pocket full of change and a heart full of beat, beat, beat."

I am not a student of Kerouac, but I admire his prose. In a way, I would like to write like him, but I write how I write. Let Jack be Jack, and I'll let me be me. I tell my stories and thoughts in the way I know how. It's art, so there is no right or wrong. For the writer, there is only doing, sharing, writing—thoughts and opinions, smells and tastes. For the reader, there is imagination, absorbing, judging, contemplating, reviewing, and everything else art does so uniquely to each of us in its own way.

There is just one brain cell getting me through this day. I climbed the climbs, looking down at the road, not up at the challenge. To answer the question, "What do you do when you get to the top?" Answer: "Keep going."

The logging trucks are frequent here; there goes another one followed by an RV. A truck pulls a third wheel. All too close; I hope the drivers see me and give me a wide berth—they seldom do. I lived to ride another day, and that is a good thing. With each day, I celebrate the opportunity to ride, breathe, see, and smell another day because there are only so many.

As I rode into Bandon, I turned off Highway 101, lured in by the hustle and bustle of tourists.

Tony's Crab Shack, with its outdoor seating on the wharf and Crab Cooker Smokehouse, was perfectly positioned to tempt any seafood lover.

The sky was clear and the breeze gentle—it would have been a sin not to stop.

My ride was essentially done. The hotel was just a mile up the road, and I could only assume an early check-in wasn't in the cards.

Instead, I enjoyed a bowl of clam chowder and six raw oysters.

A totally random and interesting fact about oysters: apparently, they are protandrous hermaphrodites, which means they are all born male and, over time, become female—a transition that happens around year one.

Not sure which sex these tasty oysters were, but I ordered sex…er, six more.

By 3 p.m., I arrived at my home for the night—Sunset Oceanfront Lodging.

Not *technically* oceanfront, but close enough for government work.

The guy at the front desk was a retired long-haul trucker. He had been injured on the job, and now, in his 60s, he felt too old and too uneducated to get hired anywhere.

"One night, I checked into this very motel," he told me. "Got to talking to Bonnie, the owner. I asked if she had work. She asked if I could use a computer. I said, 'I don't even know how to turn one on.'"

"That was fifteen years ago. Now I manage the place. And I love every minute of my day. Let's get you checked in."

The hotel room was old and felt like a small cabin with a view of the ocean.

I took advantage of the washing machine near the parking lot—nine days in the same kit. It was about time my clothes got a proper wash.

A walk along the beach was the perfect way to end the day, watching as the sun set behind the profile of Princess Ewauna (*Face Rock*) and her cat and kittens (*Cat and Kittens Rocks*).

CORY: 6
VRP: 3

CALIFORNIA

1

PACIFIC COAST HIGHWAY

Peace Arch
Burlington
Port Townsend
WASHINGTON
Shelton
Raymond
Seaside
Pacific City
Newport
Florence
OREGON
DAY 10 — Bandon
Gold Beach
Redwood National
and State Park
Requa
Eureka
Garberville
Fort Bragg
Gualala
Petaluma
San Francisco
Santa Cruz
Carmel
Big Sur
Lucia
San Simeon — Paso Robles
Santa Maria
Santa Barbara
Malibu
Huntington Beach
Carlsbad
Tijuana

DAY 10 - JULY 15, 2023

Bandon, Oregon to Gold Beach, Oregon

55 MILES: 1,839' ELEVATION GAIN

"Alright. Good morning D-Train, welcome to Stage 10 of your glorious adventure. You had a good day yesterday; hope you got some sleep. Looks like it's going to be in the 60s but quite windy today. So, just keep your head down... and roll. Once again, it's probably just over 30 miles, then you have lunch, then you have another 30-mile ride, and you're all set. Enjoy the sights, uh, and you know, the idea of having Mother Nature as a soundtrack is probably not too bad. You know, not too bad at all. Anyway, good luck today; have fun. Huge mountain stage in the tour (Tour de France) today. I probably won't be able to watch because of this little person right here (referring to his 2-year-old daughter) but who knows, maybe I'll get lucky. You, my friend, will enjoy. Take care. Love ya, have a good one."

> 🎙️ **Podcast: HISTORY**
> **Episode: 205 *Napoleon Bonaparte Surrenders***

There was a dense fog this morning, visibility maybe one hundred feet; silhouettes of neighboring buildings were the most that could be made out. I sipped my coffee, staring west toward the sound of crashing waves.

The seagulls were there somewhere, calling out in the mist—navigating the dense fog with a confidence I envied.

I sat at the writing desk of this old motel, circa 1969, and typed a few notes onto my iPad.

After The Great Bandon Fire of 1936, the Brown family built a small duplex. Over time, it expanded to eight rooms. Then, in 1960, another fire burned down two-thirds of the building.

Between 1969 and 1971, the family rebuilt—bigger, better, stronger. And today, I sit here writing at a desk in a musty motel room in a building that refuses to give up.

A subtle reminder that, while the thought hadn't crossed my mind, I, too, must not give up.

Down in the lobby-slash-dining area, I grabbed a bagel and another cup of coffee from the basic breakfast spread.

The morning manager, preoccupied with her opening duties, made an off-hand comment about the monarch butterflies. Another woman, sipping hot tea, perked up with excitement.

"Yes! This is the middle of the Monarch migration. They travel from Canada to Mexico. I find them fascinating—the way they can move so effortlessly without the big ocean winds blowing them halfway across the state."

That was an interesting observation. How do these wafer-thin creatures stay so firm in their direction against winds that could hurl them off course? I inserted myself into the conversation.

"I've seen quite a few from Coos Bay to here. I didn't think much of it, but now that you mention it—yes, there have been an unusual number of butterflies."

I wondered—if a butterfly had a scent, what would it be? I imagine they'd smell like lemongrass.

One of the most fascinating things about monarch migration? It's a one-way trip. A monarch's lifespan is eight to nine months. After migrating 3,000 miles south, they lay larvae and die. Their descendants, with the same lifespan, then begin the journey back north.

But here's the mystery: How do billions of monarchs, who have never been to Mexico, instinctively find the Oyamel Fir forests of central Mexico at the exact same time each year? And how do their descendants, who have never been north, return to the exact places their ancestors came from?

I have a GPS, road signs, and a clearly marked highway, and I've already taken a few wrong turns.

Today was going to be a good day; I just knew it. My clothes were clean. My chain was freshly lubed. My headphones were still broken, leaving me alone with my thoughts—for better or worse.

The destination was just 55 miles south, and the forecast called for temps in the low 70s.

After dropping off my key, I jumped on the bike and started swerving between the yellow dashes in the center lane, proving (at 53 years old) that I still had world-class swerving skills. Once I hit Highway 101, I straightened up and settled in.

The road was flat, the shoulder wide.

In one hour, I had already covered fifteen miles. After an hour and a half, I was halfway done for the day.

I kept thinking about Coos Bay. That town had something. Not charm, exactly—something else. Something that mystified me. Maybe it was the way so many wanderers had passed through, searching for something even if they didn't know what.

From Bandon to Port Orford, the road kept its distance from the coast. I took advantage of the flat roads and tailwind.

My first stop of the day was Battle Rock Wayside Park, which looked out upon Port Orford, the small town for which it was named, the port littered with large rocks or perhaps tiny islands.

In 1850, the United States Congress passed the Oregon Donation Land Act, which allowed white settlers to lay claim to Indian land in western Oregon. Not sure if the native people had much say in the matter, and the way the act was written meant the tribes were not able to contest any settler's claim.

A year later, Captain William Tichenor dropped off nine poorly equipped men and a cannon to settle the area. "Here you go. Here are a couple of guns and a cannon. See ya in a fortnight."

The local Quatomahs, not pleased by the situation of having their land "settled" by white people, attacked the men with a force of over a hundred.

With one explosive eruption from the cannon, twenty-three Quatomahs were killed. The Quatomahs agreed the nine men could stay for fourteen days, then must go. The nine agreed.

Day fifteen came along, and three hundred Quatomahs attacked. Sadly, their chief was killed, and they retreated. That night, the nine fled north over a hundred miles, living off snails and berries, surviving to tell their tale that the Visitor's Center keeps alive.

This was just the beginning. The Rogue River Wars followed soon after, a brutal conflict between the U.S. Army and local tribes from 1855 to 1856.

I didn't start this ride thinking I would sprint it, but today I was making great time, averaging 15 MPH. Not fast by any means, but quick for this trip.

Port Orford returned me to the coast for a brief five-mile stretch before introducing a 250-foot climb that topped out at Humbug Mountain. Captain Tichenor named it after an exploration party he sent out that promptly got lost. He later claimed the name was chosen "to palliate their gross failure."

The road wrapped around the base of Humbug for four miles, adding another 200 feet of climbing for good measure. By the time

I reconnected with the coast, I was riding high above the ocean, the horizon stretching for miles.

The shoulder became considerably narrower, but drivers were respectful, occasionally reminded to watch out for us cyclists by bright yellow signs with a bicycle image that read "ON SHOULDER."

A few miles later, I passed a semi-truck on its side in the ditch. A quick glance at the tyre marks told a familiar story: maybe the driver got distracted, maybe a deer jumped out—either way, they swerved into oncoming traffic, overcorrected, and ended up sideways in the ditch. Two massive tow trucks were on the scene, with six guys standing around assessing the damage. A reminder of how quickly your day can go sideways—literally.

Thirty minutes later, I spotted a hiker. I was making good time and feeling conversational, so I slowed to chat.

"Hey, how's it going? You hiking the Pacific Coast?"

The guy had a scraggly beard, disheveled hair, a massive pack, and a billiard-style smoking pipe dangling from his lips. He took a long drag, exhaled, then responded with some indecipherable gibberish. The only words I caught were "every day" and "gotta keep in shape." Then he leaned forward, grinned like a lunatic, and let out a high-pitched hee-hee laugh.

I briefly considered asking him to repeat himself. Then I reconsidered. This guy probably knew exactly where to bury bodies so they'd never be found. I gave him a quick salute and moved on.

My hands were sunburned. My face also felt burned from the sun and wind. Having lived in Phoenix for the past five years and spent a tremendous amount of time outside, I go in every six months for skin cancer checks, which typically lead to having pre-cancer marks frozen off. That in itself should be enough to remind me to apply sunscreen, yet here I am riding the coast sans sunscreen.

The last twenty miles were a grind. I had assumed it would take about an hour and a half. That assumption was wrong. Any cyclist tackling this route gets a little surprise—first, a one-mile, 200-foot climb, followed by a short descent, and then a five-mile, 300-foot climb just to keep things interesting. The reward? Dropping down onto the Isaac Lee Patterson Bridge, another masterpiece from Conde McCullough.

In Gold Beach, at Jerry's Rogue River Museum, you'll find a rusted gun barrel hanging on the wall. It belonged to Hugo Mayer—better known as the "Hermit of the Craggies." He was described as an "elderly eccentric, wild-eyed, bearded, with shaggy hair." In 1934, Mayer ambushed and murdered his neighbor over grazing rights. He pleaded insanity. The jury wasn't buying it. He died in prison in 1961.

My hotel had a hot tub. Next door, a chowder house. Hot chowder, hot soak. Perfect end to the day. As I sat there, steam rising around me, I couldn't help but wonder—was that pipe-smoking backpacker some long-lost relative of Hugo Mayer?

Wouldn't surprise me.

CORY: 6
VP: 4

Peace Arch
Burlington
Port Townsend
Shelton
Raymond
WASHINGTON
Seaside
Pacific City
Newport
OREGON
Florence
Bandon
Gold Beach
DAY11
Redwood National
and State Park
Requa
Eureka
Garberville
Fort Bragg
Gualala
Petaluma
San Francisco
Santa Cruz
Carmel
Big Sur
Lucia
San Simeon
Paso Robles
Santa Maria
Santa Barbara
Malibu
Huntington Beach
Carlsbad
Tijuana

DAY 11 - JULY 16, 2023
Gold Beach, Oregon to Requa, California
73 MILES: 3,600' ELEVATION GAIN

"Good morning D-Train, hope you had a wonderful night's sleep. You get to go to California today; that's kinda fun. Popping your head into California, checking it out, then the next day popping it out of California, know what I mean? Know the best part about going to the... UK? Flying to Amsterdam. Anyway, um, hope you have a wonderful day today. It's a bit of a long one; once again, break it up, you know. Stuff before lunch, stuff after lunch. No big deal. Monster day today in the Tour de France. Should be a banger, so to speak. Hope the weather is good out there. I think it's going to be. Um, keep trucking; your body is starting to adjust to all of this. Now you just need to work on getting ahead of it. But it's going to be beautiful. You have a good one, man. Ride fun... ride run... ride fun... have fun riding... ride well... ride fun... I think ride fun. Anyway, take care, buddy."

> ((🎙)) Podcast: **HISTORY**
> Episode: **206 Saturday Matinee: Fiasco: The AIDS Crisis**

I woke to the sound of a foghorn moaning in the distance. Short, methodical bursts—haunting, like something pulled from an old black-and-white horror film. The kind where lighthouse keepers go mad from isolation, haunted by the ghosts of doomed sailors.

The fog hung thick over the coastline, shrouding the massive rocks that jutted from the sea. Eerie. Mysterious. For a moment, I half-expected to see the vengeful spirits of leprous mariners, victims of the Elizabeth Dane shipwreck a hundred years ago. Maybe this was Antonio Bay, Oregon—the cursed town from *The Fog*.

Then, reality. The only specters emerging from the mist were cars, trucks, and a motorcycle blaring Billy Joel's *We Didn't Start the Fire* so loud I could hear it clearly over the rumbling exhaust pipes.

This was my last day in Oregon, and I had savored every mile of it. The state offered everything—dense pine forests, rolling sand dunes, grueling climbs, exhilarating descents, and a coastline that seemed pulled from a postcard. Cozy little towns, gypsies and overlanders, lumber trucks, RVs and motorcyclists, clear-cuts and reforestation. Sea lions barking on the rocks, cypress trees twisting in the wind. Oh!—and the seafood.

Today, I would enter California.

"The Golden State."

"El Dorado."

"The Golden West."

"The Land of Milk and Honey."

"The Land of Sunshine and Opportunity."

I had crossed two states, yet I still wasn't even halfway. It's a bit mind-bending when you consider just how long the California coast is. For perspective, from the Oregon border to the Mexican border is roughly the same distance as:

- Amsterdam to Florence, Italy

- Tegucigalpa to the Panama Canal

- Hanoi to Saigon

- Brisbane to Melbourne

- New Delhi to Goa

To add another reference to the sheer size of California—you can fit Moldova, Portugal, North Macedonia, Belgium, Kosovo, the Netherlands, Switzerland, Luxembourg, and Slovenia all inside its borders without overlapping. And to top it off, California is the fourth largest economy in the world, trailing only China, Germany, and Japan.

The day started with a long, three-mile climb. A cold, miserable, not-what-I-signed-up-for kind of climb. I wasn't in the mood for it. I pulled out my phone and fired off a text to Kate and Kevin:

"I'm done!"

Of course, I wasn't done. I had 73 miles ahead of me. I knew that. But complaining felt necessary.

Kate and Kevin weren't the comforting type. I didn't expect them to respond with, "Oh no, poor you!" No, their responses were predictable. Either they'd ignore me, or they'd say:

"Shut up and keep going. You're riding your bike along the Pacific Coast. Enjoy the ride."

Neither of them responded. Which, in its own way, was their way of saying:

"Shut up and keep going. You're riding your bike along the Pacific Coast. Enjoy the ride."

Fair enough.

At the top of the next climb, I spotted a historical marker. Reason enough to stop.

Oregon History
Cape San Sebastián
Spanish explorers were the first to explore the North American Pacific Coast, beginning fifty years after Columbus discovered the western continents. Sebastián Vizcaíno saw the cape in 1603 and named it after the patron saint of the day of his discovery. Other navigators—Spanish, British, and American— followed a century and a half later.

Now there was a whole lot that could be said about this horribly distorted bit of history. Clearly, Spanish explorers were not the first to explore the North American Pacific Coast since there was a large American Indian population here. Then there was the whole

Columbus discovering western continents, but I just don't have the energy to go down that rabbit hole of misinformation. But good on Cape San Sebastián and the Spanish explorers for naming the place.

The reward for those two climbs? A screaming descent into Pistol River Beach. Along the way, I passed Pistol River Loop, N Bank Pistol River Road, Pistol River State Scenic Viewpoint, and finally crossed over the Pistol River itself.

The Tolowa people called the river *chvt-ler'sh-chvn-dvn taa-ghii~-li~*. Then, in 1853, a settler named James Mace dropped his pistol in the river during a Rogue River War skirmish. And just like that, Pistol River was born.

The road hugged the coastline for a while before veering back into the woods. More climbs—short ones. No Bigfoot, just rolling hills.

At "Arch Rock Point," there was a turnout that hung 200 feet above the ocean, offering views of Leaning Rock, Black Rock, Yellow Rock, and Arch Rock, which science says was created over eons of erosion from wind and waves grinding down the rocks and forming these magnificent geographic features.

However, it wasn't eons of erosion that made these rocks. No, my friends—it was Coyote.

Long ago, Coyote played a cruel trick on the other animals and the Tolowa people. As punishment, they stranded him on Arch Rock, leaving him to starve. But Coyote, always clever, gathered mussels and tossed them into the water. One by one, the mussels magically grew into small islands, creating a path for him to escape back to shore.

So, was it millions of years of erosion?

Or magic mussels?

I'll let you decide.

The Pacific Coast attracts its fair share of free spirits. With plenty of dirt pullouts along the highway, there's no shortage of spots for overnight parking. It may not be technically legal, but if you're going to sleep in your car, you'd be hard-pressed to find a more spectacular backdrop.

At one pullout, I passed a guy stretched out on a cot beside his station wagon. Next to him: a cooler, a hibachi grill, and a full weight-lifting set. It looked like he planned on settling in for a while.

I stopped for a moment, watching as he slept, wondering what had led him here.

Did his wife kick him out?

Did he lose it all in Vegas?

Or did he just wake up one day and decide the vagabond life was the life for him?

Hell, I've been coddiwompling my entire life.

Not a fan of heights, the Thomas Creek Bridge—Oregon's highest—was a bit of a mental humdinger. A simple truss bridge with low rails, I cursed Ivan Merchant for not making them taller. I had no choice but to ride straight down the middle—cars be damned.

If there was a view, and I know there was, I couldn't tell you about it. My eyes were locked on the centerline, my only goal: getting back onto *tierra firma* as fast as possible.

Some heights don't bother me. Not sure why this one got to me. The Astoria-Megler Bridge was longer, high enough, but it didn't faze me. None of the other bridges along the way had, either. But this old hunk of metal and asphalt? It sent me straight into survival mode.

Damn you, L'appel du vide.[9]

---

9 In English, the Call of the Void, the urge to want to jump knowing the outcome would be death. Something I struggle with.

At Whaleshead Viewpoint, a thin cloud drifted off the coast. A couple stood nearby, holding hands.

Maybe a proposal was about to happen.

Maybe he had brought her here to say he was sorry, promising to be a better man.

Or maybe *she* was the one who soured the relationship.

I had hoped the name Whaleshead was tied to some legend, like a forbidden love story between a young Rogue River Indian couple.

Nope.

Just a rock that looks like a whale's head.

For the next couple dozen miles, the road flattened out. No more long climbs, no more rollers. I settled into a nice, steady rhythm.

Brookings. Home to Oregon's largest Monterey Cypress tree, planted by Harrison Blake in 1850. Also, the site of something far more interesting—an event you probably never heard of because when it happened, Uncle Sam covered it up.

On September 9, 1942, Nobuo Fujita launched his floatplane from a Japanese submarine aircraft carrier. Yep. Turns out, the Japanese had *submarine aircraft carriers*.

His mission? Drop incendiary bombs on the forests outside Brookings, ignite a massive wildfire, and bring destruction to the American mainland.

Lucky for Brookings, the forest was too wet. The fire never caught.

While it's true that between 1944 and 1945, Japan sent over 10,000 balloon bombs toward the U.S.—and about 300 made it, and tragically, one killed Elyse Mitchell and her five children during a church outing, Nobuo Fujita remains the only Japanese pilot to have ever bombed the U.S. mainland during WWII.

Twenty years later, Brookings invited him back and made him an honorary citizen.

Nobuo arrived carrying his family's 400-year-old samurai sword as a peace offering, fully prepared to commit hara-kiri if the town rejected him.

They didn't.

When he died, his family spread his ashes at the bombing site. His family sword now hangs in the Brookings library.

I stopped at a Starbucks tucked away in a Fred Meyer. Chilled to the bone, I ordered a coffee, charged my phone, and contemplated the next 40 miles, knowing there was a 1,200-foot climb before the day was over.

Turns out, this Fred Meyer had an electronics section—something I'd never seen in a Fred Meyer before. I picked up a pair of off-brand headphones, a knockoff of the Shokz I'd come to love.

I sent a text to Kate and Kevin.

"Forty miles and a 1,200-foot climb to go."

Kate responded first. "You can do it!!!!!!!"

Kevin took a different approach. He sent a voice recording with his nine-year-old daughter, Aida.

Kevin: "Action."

Aida: "You got this!"

Kevin: "You got what?"

Aida: "You got to climb the mountain."

Kevin: "He can do it, can't he?"

Aida: "You can do it."

Kevin: "You know Cory can do it, right?"

Aida: "Yes, you got this, Cory. You can climb the mountain. But I'm sorry for saying 'I-assa.'"

Kevin: "Why are you sorry for saying that?"

Aida: "Because it's funny."

Kevin: "What's funny?"

Aida: "I-assa."

Kevin: "What's 'I-assa'?"

Aida: "I-assa boudie butt."

Kevin: "Boudie butt? Is he on first base?"

Aida (laughing): "Yesssss."

Kevin: "Boudie butt can't be on first and second."

Aida ended with a wordless tune, humming into the mic.

Six miles later, I reached the border.

Another cyclist had his bike leaned up against the "Welcome to California" sign.

"Hey, let me take your picture for you."

"Thank you. I'm Mike."

"Cory."

Mike had started in Seaside, Oregon, eight days ago. No set destination, no schedule. This was his first time riding cross-country, his first time really riding a bike outside of commuting around town in New Jersey.

"I had a blood clot. I was overweight. Drank too much. Decided I needed to do something about it."

He had been eating three whole pizzas a week. And don't get him started on the beer.

"I've lost 20 pounds just by commuting to work. And now I'm out here, realizing I packed way too much. I keep giving stuff away when I find someone who needs it. I gave my camp stove to a guy living in his car. Now I just stop at restaurants. You look like you're traveling light."

"Yeah, I've done a few long-distance rides. The more I do, the less I take. No need to carry food on the coast—there are towns everywhere. I planned ahead, booked hotels and motels along the way. I ride all day, so I just have some mechanical gear, tubes, tools, flip-flops, an extra t-shirt, and shorts. That's about it."

We talked a little more, but I was eager to keep moving.

"Nice to meet you, Mike. See you down the road."

"I doubt it—you're pretty fast."

Two miles later, I came across a hiker.

Full backpack. Old-school aluminum external frame. Looked like something I had in Boy Scouts.

His name was Jake. Twenty-four years old, hiking the Pacific Coast. And by the looks of it, loving every second.

"Walking, huh? How far do you go in a day?"

"Twenty-six miles. I don't like hiking at night."

"What's the final destination?"

"San Diego. Hoping to find a job when I get there. If I don't, I'll just keep going…someplace."

I'll keep going…someplace.

Fucking *yeah*, kid. That's how you do it. Once you reach the top of the mountain—*keep going*.

I was thirty-one when I finally decided to sell everything and go. I was gone for two years. After that? I started a company and went from living out of a backpack to being El Presidente of my own business.

Jake figured it out at 24.

One day, he'll be a CEO.

NASA hired George Land in the 1960s to study creative genius. What he found was… depressing.

- 98% of 3–5-year-olds were considered creative geniuses.

- 30% of 10–14-year-olds were considered creative geniuses.

- 12% of 15–18-year-olds were considered creative geniuses.

- 2% of adults were considered creative geniuses.

- Land identified two forms of thinking:

- **Divergent Thinking** → Imagination, new ideas, creativity.

- **Convergent Thinking** → Judgment, evaluation, analysis.

He concluded that traditional education kills creativity.

I graduated in the bottom 5% of my high school class. Ironically, I still gave the graduation speech alongside the valedictorian.

My dad was 100% against me going to college. He thought the military was a better option. Looking back, I kind of regret not enlisting. But at the time, being told what to do? *Not my thing.*

So, I went to university instead. I quickly learned that the game was simple: regurgitate whatever the professor tells you.

It hit me hard in three classes my freshman year:

- **Philosophy** → Overthought my papers. Got D's.

- **Advanced English Literature** → My interpretations didn't match the professor's.

- **Creative Writing** → Got a C for being *too* creative.

The 'A' students work for the 'C' students. The 'B' students work in government, and the 'D', 'F', and dropouts own the company.

The sun finally peeked out, and for the first time all morning, I was warm.

I thought about Jake. If he kept up his 26-mile-a-day pace—assuming he didn't take any rest days—he'd hit San Diego by November.

At Crescent City, I grabbed some water and a sandwich at a Starbucks, which is a great place to charge your phone. Nobody seems to care how long you hang out.

As I rolled out of town, I passed Tsunami Lanes Bowling Alley.

In 2001, my cousins Amy and Becky, and Becky's then-boyfriend (now unmentioned ex) and I spent a few days biking the Oregon coast, finishing in Crescent City. To celebrate, we played a few rounds of psychedelic bowling at this very spot.

I snapped a picture of the bowling alley and sent it to Amy and Becky.

"22 years ago, cousins. Let's do another ride."

A mile past Crescent City, the last big climb of the day began. I was entering the Redwood Forest. Massive trees surrounded me as the road climbed for over five miles at a 6% grade.

A few times, I had to surrender and walk. The breaks were short—I'd push for a bit, then get back on the bike. The road twisted and climbed, winding through the towering Redwoods.

At the summit, my reward: a seven-mile descent. Max speed? 46 mph, tucked behind a delivery truck, drafting. The entire Pacific Ocean stretched out before me, exposed in all its grandeur.

Trees of Mystery was a delightfully tacky wayside attraction that I normally would have ridden by, but there was a giant statue of Paul Bunyan and Babe the Blue Ox that required a photo.

Not too far down the road, a sign read:

THE YUROK TRIBE
WELCOMES YOU
Aiy-yu-kwee

The Yurok have fished here for over 10,000 years. This is also where my 25th great-grandfather, Sir Francis Drake, encountered them in 1579.

My day was done.

I rolled up to The Historic Requa Inn, where I was greeted by Cass, the innkeeper.

"Your name is Cass?"

"Cass, like Mama Cass."

She set down a large plate of fresh chocolate chip cookies. I grabbed three.

Did I look old enough that she just assumed I'd know who Mama Cass was? That I grew up listening to The Mamas and the Papas (which, to be fair, I did—on vinyl)?

Or maybe Cass just figured everyone shared her taste in flower-power music. I doubted the young couple checking in behind me had any clue who Mama Cass was—or had ever used a rotary phone.

"Looks like your room is ready. You can park in the lot behind the building."

I sat there, still sweating in my cycling gear, helmet on, eating a cookie.

"Oh… are you biking?"

"Yep. I'll just bring my bike to my room."

Her eyes widened. It was as if I'd just told her I planned to bring a goat inside.

"Um… you see the…"

"I typically just bring it to my room."

"Um, I don't think… in your room? No, no… um, where is your bike now?"

I pointed.

It was sitting in the main sitting room.

"Oh, wow, I see. Hmmm… you brought your bike inside. Huh. Well… there's a storage shed in the back. Would that work for you?"

"Sure, no problem."

Cass was from Tucson, Arizona. She and her husband ran a self-defense company. She had a lot of guns, which surprised me because she wore a large crystal around her neck and dressed like… well, *Mama Cass.*

She was in the middle of a divorce.

"Best thing to happen to me," she said before I could even get out the obligatory sorry to hear that.

"I have a friend up here who told me to stay with her. This place was looking for an innkeeper, so I took the job. Been here six months. Happiest I've been in decades."

I stored my bike, grabbed what I needed—clothes, charging cables, iPad—and went to my room. Then, straight to the outdoor hot tub.

I texted a picture of my current situation to Kate, then opened an audio message from Kevin. It was a short essay written and spoken by Brother David Steindl-Rast.

"A Good Day

You think this is just another day in your life. It's not just another day; it's the one day that is given to you today. It's given to you. It's a gift. It's the only gift that you have right now, and the only appropriate response is gratefulness. If you do nothing else but cultivate that response to the great gift that this unique day is, if you learn to respond as if it were the first day of your life, and the very last day, then you will have spent this day very well.

Begin by opening your eyes and be surprised that you have eyes you can open, that incredible array of colors that is constantly offered to us for pure enjoyment. Look at the sky. We so rarely look at the sky. We so rarely note how different it is from moment to moment with clouds coming and going. We just think of the weather, and even of the weather we don't think of all the many nuances of weather. We just think of good weather and bad weather. This day right now has unique weather, maybe a kind that will never exactly in that form come again. The formation of clouds in the sky will never be the same as it is right now.

Open your eyes. Look at that.

Look at the faces of people that you meet. Each one has an incredible story behind their face, a story that you could never fully fathom, not only their own story, but the story of their ancestors. We all go back so far. And in this present moment on this day, all the people you meet, all that life from generations and from so many places all over the world, flows together and meets you here like a life-giving water, if you only open your heart and drink.

Open your heart to the incredible gifts that civilization gives to us. You flip a switch and there is electric light. You turn a faucet and there is warm water and cold water—and drinkable water. It's a gift that millions and millions in the world will never experience.

So these are just a few of an enormous number of gifts to which you can open your heart. And so I wish for you that you would open your heart to all these blessings and let them flow through you, that everyone whom you will meet on this day will be blessed by you; just by your eyes, by your smile, by your touch— just by your presence. Let the gratefulness overflow into blessing all around you, and then it will really be a good day."

I sat there, letting the words sink in, taking in where I was.

A historic inn along the Klamath River, deep in the Klamath Valley. Soaking in a hot tub, digitally connected to the world.

For a brief moment today, I was complaining because I was cold and had to climb hills. Then I realized today I also got to ride along the Pacific Ocean and through the Redwood Forest. It had really been a good day.

CORY: 6
VP: 5

Peace Arch

Burlington

Port Townsend

WASHINGTON

Shelton

Raymond

Seaside

Pacific City

Newport

Florence

OREGON

Bandon

Gold Beach

Redwood National
and State Park

Requa

DAY 12

Eureka

Garberville

Fort Bragg

Gualala

Petaluma

San Francisco

Santa Cruz

Monterey
Bay

Carmel

Big Sur

Lucia

San Simeon

Paso Robles

Santa Maria

Lassen
Volcanic
N. P.

Honey L.

Lake
Tahoe

Yosemite
N. Park

Mono
Lake

Kings Canyon
National Park

Death Valley
National Park

Mt.
Whitney
14,505 ft

Sequoia
N. P.

Owens
Lake

Buena
Vista L.

Santa Barbara

Santa Barbara Channel

Malibu

Channel Islands
National Park

Huntington Beach

S. Pedro Channel

Joshua Tree
National Park

Salton
Sea

Carlsbad

Gulf of
Santa Catalina

Tijuana

DAY 12 - JULY 17, 2023
Requa, California to Eureka, California
66 MILES : 2,404' ELEVATION GAIN

"Good morning, D-Train. I hope you slept well! You're rolling into Eureka today, which will be kind of fun. Um, yeah. I think you've got this, man. Once again, you're not racing; you're just a dude riding a bike. That's all you're doing. It's all good; everything's fine. Take a breath, look around, and enjoy the day. It's quite the honor to get to do this. Alright, so that's a lot of positive things to think about. In any case, it's a rest day on the Tour [de France], so nothing going on there. And, um, at least in the Flanders front, I woke up to a baby who puked all over herself, so there's that. Anyway, have a good ride, man. You're going to kill it today, one way or another. Take care, man."

(((🎙))) Podcast: HISTORY
Episode: 513 The Russian Royal Family is Executed

Typically, my bike is in the room with me, making it easy to pack up. This morning, I had to make a few trips—down the hall, down the stairs, out to the shed, and back. Not a big deal, just slowed things down a bit.

With only sixty-six miles ahead of me, I wasn't in a rush. I sat in the sitting room, sipping coffee and watching the fog drift over the Klamath River.

I wished Kate were here. She'd want to spend a week exploring the trails, walking the coast, soaking in the hot tub, drinking wine, and reading a book.

I filled my water bottles, locked my door, and made my way back to the lobby for another cup of coffee. I charged my phone and decided I'd finally finish Neil Peart's *Ghost Rider* now that I had a new pair of headphones.

The clouds were low. No sun, no wind. Just damp air hanging at 55 degrees. Another day for gloves and a jacket.

I made the mistake of checking the elevation profile. Immediate regret. A profile I wholeheartedly disapproved of. There was a lot of climbing ahead. And so, with a single pedal stroke, the day began.

My Garmin (HAL 9000) had a mind of its own today, constantly beeping at me, trying to reroute me down roads I had no interest in. I ignored it, sticking to Highway 101 until I hit the turnoff for the Newton B. Drury Scenic Parkway, a road that cut through Redwood National Park.

Who was Newton B. Drury?

I realized I should probably start keeping track of all these names—these roads, bridges, and parks dedicated to people I knew nothing about. As for Newton B. Drury? He was the Director of the National Park Service and Executive Director of the Save the Redwoods League.

Seems fitting.

An eerie mist wove through the towering trees, soft and ghostly, curling around the trunks of impossibly enormous Redwoods. I imagined the forest creatures watching me with curiosity as I swerved down the middle of the road, weaving from one side to the other, climbing higher and higher.

- Some of these trees were over 2,000 years old.

- Their seeds germinating while St. Paul sat in prison in 58 AD.

- They were saplings when Pompeii was destroyed.

- By the time the Chinese invented paper, they were just getting started.

- When Rome fell, they were a respectable 352 years old.

- By the First Crusade, they had fully matured.

- When the Pilgrims landed at Plymouth Rock, these Redwoods were celebrating their 1,562nd birthday.

The oldest recorded tree was Prometheus until it was killed in 1964 by a geographer named Donald Rusk Currey. He was using a coring tool to determine its age when the tool got stuck. So, in a moment of absolute genius, he decided to cut the tree down. Turns out, it was nearly 5,000 years old.

Today, the oldest known tree is Methuselah, estimated at 4,856 years old.

Some of the Redwoods disappeared into the low clouds, like Jack's beanstalk. The sun fought to break through, but the clouds won the battle.

I snapped the obligatory pictures, one with my bike against a tree for scale.

Halfway through the park, the road rewarded me with a long, twisting descent.

At the south entrance/exit, a couple of PCH bike riders pulled out in front of me, leaving the Elk Prairie Campground. Turning south onto 101, I spotted a giant bull elk statue.

Then another. Then one of their heads moved. Not statues.

A huge bull elk stood right there on the roadside, a cow nearby. As I made a few photos, the two cyclists rolled up beside me. I pointed. "You see that?"

One of them nodded. "Yeah, we had dozens of them in our campsite last night."

Crossing Lost Man Creek, I wondered how it got its name. The obvious answer: at some point, a man got lost here.

Around the bend, a huge herd of female elk, cows, grazed in a field. One looked up and ran alongside me for a short while. Abruptly, she stopped, flicked her ears, and went back to grazing.

A few miles later a road crew had traffic backed up just before Orick. I rode past the stopped cars along the shoulder, pulling up alongside two other cyclists—a father and daughter.

"Is your name Wesley?" the man asked, pointing at my cycling jacket.

It had the name Wesley printed in a logo, a design a friend had made for me back when I started a bicycle brand a long time ago in honor of my dad.

"No, it's my dad's name. I named my company after him."

"My name is Wes," he said, motioning to his daughter. "This is Lisa. Where are you headed today?"

I had to think about it. I couldn't remember.

"Eureka. Heading to Eureka. Started at the Canadian border 11 days ago."

He nodded at my gear. "Traveling kind of light. You doing a credit card ride?"

"Yeah, I've done the tent thing. Gave myself about 25 days to knock this out. You guys?"

"Started in Vancouver. She'll be a freshman at Cal Poly, so we're riding to get her there for orientation. Then I'm continuing on to Santa Barbara, where we live."

"Wow, that's really cool. Showing up to college orientation after biking down the coast with your dad from Canada? No other students will be worthy of your awesomeness."

She smiled.

The flagman flipped the sign to green, and we rolled south.

I stopped to watch the waves at Redwood Creek Beach, catching up with the pair again at a general store a few miles up the road. That was the last I saw of them.

My Garmin insisted I turn onto McDonald Creek Road, a route showing a 1,200+ foot climb. I ignored it and stuck to 101. Turns out, my choice skipped the climb I'd been dreading all day.

Not only was there no climb, but the road somehow kept descending—almost impossibly, like an M.C. Escher drawing in perpetual motion.

In McKinleyville, I took an exit and nearly got hit by a bus. Entirely my fault. I had pulled out in front of him, assuming he'd slow down. He did not. Lesson learned.

The Hammond Trail was a welcome reprieve—peaceful, winding, and eventually spitting me out onto rough farm roads.

The final stretch into Eureka took me over the Richard F. Denbo Memorial Bridge, spanning Arcata Bay and Tuluwat Island, previously known as Indian Island.

On February 26, 1860, European immigrants searching for gold massacred over 200 women and children of the Wiyot Tribe using axes, knives, and guns.

Arcata's local newspaper, *The Northern California*, described the scene:

> "Blood stood in pools on all sides; the walls of the huts were stained, and the grass colored red. Lying around were dead bodies of both sexes and all ages, from the old man to the infant at the breast. Some had their heads split in twain by axes, others beaten into jelly with clubs, others pierced or cut to pieces with Bowie knives. Some struck down as they mired; others had almost reached the water when overtaken and butchered."

That same day, 58 more Wiyot were killed a few miles up the coast. Days later, another 40. No one was ever charged with the murders.

Bret Harte wrote an editorial in *The Northern California*:

> "A more shocking and revolting spectacle was never exhibited to the eyes of a Christian and civilized people. Old women, wrinkled and decrepit, lay weltering in blood, their brains dashed out and dabbled with their long gray hair. Infants scarce a span long, with their faces cloven with hatchets and their bodies ghastly with wounds."

In 2014, the Eureka City Council voted not to apologize to the Wiyot tribe but instead wrote this:

> "As mayor of Eureka, on behalf of the city council and the people of Eureka, we offer our support to the Wiyot Tribe and reaffirm our commitment toward healing the Wiyot people's wounds and continuing to work toward establishing better relationships rooted in reconciliation. The continuation of the Wiyot Renewal Ceremony is a step toward the healing of the wounds that have been a scar on our community."

I'll just leave that there for you to chew on.

The second bridge, the A.M. Bistrin Memorial Bridge, dropped me into Eureka.

It was 1:30 p.m. My day of cycling was over.

I was happy with my early arrival, but checking into my motel? That would have to wait—another hour and a half.

So, who are Richard F. Denbo and A.M. Bistrin?

- Richard F. Denbo was the manager of the Eureka Chamber of Commerce for 20 years and was responsible for getting the bridge named after him built.

- A.M. Bistrin was a successful businessman who saved Eureka from having a freeway plowed through it.

Eureka's Old Town is listed on the United States National Register of Historic Places, home to over 145 Victorian buildings. Turns out, it's also considered one of the best art towns in the country.

Geographically speaking, it's the westernmost city in the lower forty-eight with a population over 25,000. I guess Eureka had more going for it than I initially gave it credit for.

Trivia Break:

- Westernmost point in the lower 48: Cape Alava, WA.

- Westernmost town in the lower 48: Neah Bay, WA.

After a few zig-zagging laps through Old Town, I settled on a large, empty Mexican restaurant. I wheeled my bike into the bar, pulled out my phone and charging cables, and waited.

And waited.

And waited.

I waited so long, I probably could have poured myself a few drinks, and no one would've been the wiser.

Finally, an extremely overweight bartender emerged from the back room, dripping with sweat. Upon seeing me, he ducked into the kitchen, then returned with a bowl of chips and two flavors of salsa.

Kate was in Chicago for work. She texted to say she was having a great time with her colleagues and was excited to meet up in a few days. The plan: She'd fly to San Francisco, rent a car, and drive the coast, meeting me at each destination while still working remotely.

For now, it was me and a burrito.

CORY: 7
VP: 5

Peace Arch

Burlington

Port Townsend

WASHINGTON

Shelton

Raymond

Seaside

Pacific City

Newport

OREGON

Florence

Bandon

Gold Beach

Requa

Eureka

DAY 13

Garberville

Fort Bragg

Gualala

Petaluma

San Francisco

Santa Cruz

Carmel

Big Sur

Lucia

San Simeon

Paso Robles

Santa Maria

Santa Barbara

Malibu

Huntington Beach

Carlsbad

Tijuana

DAY 13 - JULY 18, 2023
Eureka, California to Garberville, California

65 MILES : 3,335' ELEVATION GAIN

"Good morning D-Train, hope you had a wonderful evening. Great ride yesterday, got in early. Great work, nice job, awesome effort. Happy ride; it sounds like. In any case, you're in California. You like California. Because it's California. In any case, exotic California. Um, alright. You have 67 miles today, once again not too tough; it should be pretty fun. I imagine that highway is getting beautiful, transitioning from the Pacific Northwest's pine tree rainy stuff, and soon you'll have big vistas to see. Um, big day today in the tour, individual time trial with a nasty climb at the end or in the middle, I don't really know. I'll find out when I get to work, um let's go Pogacar; in any case, you're killing it, dude. I hope you're having a great time, and um, we'll talk soon. Have a great ride, my friend."

((🎙)) **Podcast: HISTORY DAILY**
Episode: 514 The Great Fire of Rome

The Travelodge was…acceptable.

Situated just off Highway 101, its parking lot and surrounding area were home to Eureka's homeless, men and women wandering in circles, shouting unintelligible things at all hours of the night.

It's an unfortunate situation, really. One that seems impossible to solve.

In 1729, Jonathan Swift wrote *A Modest Proposal*—a satirical essay that mocked the British ruling class by offering a solution to Ireland's poverty and overpopulation problem that the ruling class was ignoring.

His suggestion? The poor should sell their children to the wealthy for food—going so far as to offer a range of recipes for preparing them.

It was meant to wake up the leaders to the issue. Jean-Jacques Rousseau took the opposite stance when he famously said: "When the people shall have nothing more to eat, they will eat the rich."

Fast forward to university. That year, my professor assigned us to write a convincing argument and present it to the class. Most of my classmates delivered Public Service Announcements:

- "Why You Should Wear a Condom."

- "Why You Shouldn't Drink and Drive."

I took the Jonathan Swift approach. I wrote a satirical persuasive essay arguing that we should exterminate the homeless. I asked the audience to reframe their thinking. Not as killing people. But as simply removing mold from the cheese. Knowing full well this wasn't a real solution, I concluded:

"The catch is—what someone else considers mold, you may consider cheese. Meaning: judge not, lest ye be judged." I like that word 'ye'; it solves the pronoun issues. "Gather ye rosebuds, while ye may."

I suppose it was not that unique of an argument, after all—Soylent Green is people!

Now, allow me to redeem myself and assure you I am not a bad guy. In 2019, I was competing in a sprint triathlon in Phoenix. I had just started the run portion, turning onto a bridge along the course when I saw him.

A homeless man, standing on the edge, ready to jump. Thirty-five feet below him—the Salt River riverbed. How no one else on the course saw him still baffles me. I ran over, grabbed him. We struggled. I tried to pull him off the railing. Another runner ran up and helped. Together, we gained control of him.

I talked to him and told him he was important. I watched as his face went from anger to confusion, then he started crying. Eventually, the police arrived and took him away.

Later, I called the police department to check on him. They wouldn't share any details. I'm sure they held him for a while and then released him. But then what?

- What happened to his tent?

- All of his belongings?

- What happens to him now?

What happens to all of them? The ones who kept me up all night outside the Travelodge in Eureka. The forgotten who lurk in the shadows of society—the ones we try to ignore as they approach our cars at red lights, holding a cardboard sign that reads: "Homeless. Please help."

I made coffee and turned on the TV for background noise. The lead story: the Crimea Bridge, smoldering after an explosion.

I packed up, checked tyre pressure, lubed the chain, and stuffed my street clothes into my handlebar bag. Then, a text from Eddie.

I've tried to convince my nieces that Eddie is Santa Claus, but they're not buying it. Sometimes, the nieces are clever. Other times… not so much.

One winter, the girls stayed with Kate and me for five weeks. At the time, we were landscaping our front yard. One day, boulders were dropped off. The girls went wild, climbing all over them, jumping off into the dirt.

The oldest asked where boulders come from.

My dad would have said, "The stork brings them."

But since they had already watched the truck dump them, I took a different approach.

"You grow them. Want to grow a boulder?"

"YES!"

I told them to find a rock and pick a spot in the front yard. They dug a little hole, placing their rock so part of it stayed exposed—because it needed sunlight to grow.

"Now, you have to water it. Twice a day."

And they did. Every morning. Every evening.

The landscaping crew caught on. Every couple of days, before the girls woke up, they swapped out the rock for a slightly larger one. The girls were thrilled, watching their boulder grow.

A year later, they asked how big the boulder had gotten.

"It died. Nobody was there to water it."

They don't believe Eddie is Santa Claus, but they do believe rocks can grow into boulders.

Eddie's text was a picture: a plate of biscuits and gravy.

"Post Crusher breakfast. Cory's favorite! Don't eat it often, but figured I earned it."

He was at Buck's Restaurant in Ishpeming, Michigan, which is the Upper Peninsula—a.k.a. the Yooper, a.k.a. the U.P.

Ishpeming has grown on me over the summers I've spent up there mountain biking.

If I ever had to go into the witness protection program, I'd want to be sent to the Yooper. No one would think to look for me there.

The Crusher that Eddie was referring to is a gravel bike event with various distances put on by a fella named Todd Poquette, who started 906 Adventure Team. The 906AT not only helps kids develop resilience with its Adventure Teams; it is also there "to create a more resilient community by empowering people to discover the best version of themselves through outdoor adventure."

That mission statement makes Todd sound like a stand-up guy, but it's his penance for being the creator and race director for the following epic, soul-crushing races all up in the peninsula:

- **The Polar Roll** – 15, 30, 150 miles. Dead of winter. Fat bike, studded tyres required; or you can snowshoe it.

- **The Crusher** – Advertised distances: 40, 100, 200 miles. Actual distances? 54, 130, 225 miles.

- **The Marji Gesick** – 80% failure rate. You can ride or run it. Options: 50, 100, or, if you hate yourself, 200 miles. (Actual distances? 61, 109, 218 miles.) Pro-cyclist Jeremiah Bishop called it the "hardest single-day mountain bike event in America."

I have attempted the Marji 100 three times—on a rigid single-speed twice, then on a full-suspension mountain bike.

Did Not Finish (DNF). Every. Single. Time.

Then I tried the Marji 50. DNF.

My first Polar Roll attempt? Start line temp: -9°F. DNF. I came back a month later and finished it.

The Crusher 40 (54 miles)? Did that one with Kevin and Eddie. Later, Kevin and I tackled the 100 (119 miles). We rode for 18 hours. We missed the last three-mile section of singletrack in the darkness of night. We did the miles. Still need to go back and finish the course.

Eddie? He just finished the 200-mile Crusher. 17 hours. On a single-speed.

I first met Eddie at a mountain bike race at Afton Alps, Minnesota.

A name that exaggerated the place, its longest run is 3,000 feet with a 350-foot vertical drop. Not exactly the Alps.

That's not to say it's an easy mountain bike course. I was actually a decent rider back then, and I still hated racing there. I was only there to get points toward an overall season ranking.

Somewhere on the course, I reached for a water hand-up. Eddie came up behind me, rubbed my tyre—BAM. I went down. He ran me over, said "Sorry!" and kept going.

Now, that might sound like a dick move, but it happens in racing. I knew it wasn't intentional, but I was still pissed. I got up and kept riding.

In the singletrack, Eddie—who had somehow figured out my name—shouted: "Great job, Cory!" I muttered something like, "Yeah, whatever."

At the finish line, Eddie was there—smiling, holding a beer. I took the beer and walked away. That's how our friendship started.

In his younger days, Eddie was a Ski Jumper; he was on the US World Junior Team, 1983-84. The kind that goes down those massive jumps, sails for hundreds of yards, lands like it's nothing. Until one day it wasn't nothing.

He stuck on the takeoff, bounced on the knoll of the landing and shattered both ankles. Shattered both ankles. Shattered everything between his knees and feet.

First verdict from the doctors? Amputation. That didn't happen. But they told him he'd never walk normal again. Now, 40+ years later...he's one of the fastest, strongest cyclists out there. And one of the nicest guys you'll ever have the pleasure to know.

Heading south on Highway 101, I passed Fort Humboldt State Historic Park.

After his time fighting in the Mexican-American War, Ulysses S. Grant was tasked with leading a few hundred people from New York to San Francisco by ship.

No Panama Canal yet; it wouldn't be completed until 1917. They traveled down to Panama, crossed the country by land, then continued by ship up the Pacific Coast.

Once in San Francisco, Grant was sent to Oregon, where he developed sympathy for Native Americans, witnessing white business owners cheat them out of supplies. In 1854, Captain Ulysses S. Grant was stationed at Fort Humboldt for a few months. His job? Protecting settlers from the local tribes.

Keep in mind, this was six years before the good people of Eureka slaughtered 200+ Wiyot women and children. So, who really needed to be protected?

While at Fort Humboldt, Grant became a heavy drinker. Given the choice to resign or reform, he resigned. However, his resignation was never submitted. Instead, he went on to become General Grant, won the Civil War, became the eighteenth President of the United States, and now adorns the $50 bill.

What if his resignation had been accepted? What would history look like without Ulysses S. Grant?

I was riding along the Roger M. Rodoni Memorial Interchange, which turned into the Dave Ghilarducci Memorial Freeway, crossing over the R. Fleisher Memorial Bridge, where the road changed names again to the Sam Helwer Memorial Highway.

A piece of cloth hung from the guardrail. It read:

"DEATH TO ~~FRANCE~~ Liberty – Independence.
Benjamin Colwill. Friends…?

I had no clue what that note on the guardrail meant. Maybe Benjamin Colwill will read this and let me know.

These are the small details you notice when crossing the country on a bike at 12 mph.

- Roger M. Rodoni – Killed in a car accident on Highway 101, just south of the interchange he had been advocating for. That, Alanis Morissette, is irony.

- Dave Ghilarducci – Fire chief of Rio Dell, California.

- Richard Fleisher – Declared a casualty of the Korean War on September 3, 1950.

- Sam Helwer – Worked for the California Division of Highways as a District Engineer.

Twenty miles south of Eureka was a turnoff to the Avenue of the Giants. The avenue added a few more miles to my day, but it was worth it. I was teleported into a magical wonderland of Redwoods towering to the clouds, like their brothers and sisters I passed through yesterday.

All alone on the road, I pulled out my phone and made a video, assigning Woody Guthrie's *This Land is My Land* as the soundtrack:

"This land is your land, this land is my land, from California to the New York island. From the Redwood Forest to the Gulf Stream waters…"

I enjoyed the whole day and pulled back on the throttle, just pedaling like I would on the way to the grocery store. I was on pace to make it to my night's stay by 1:00, and check-in, I'm sure, wasn't until 4:00.

The Immortal Tree, a 1,000-year-old, 258' tall Redwood, 14' in diameter; it survived:

- The flood of 1964.
- Forest fires.
- Lightning strikes.
- Lumberjacks.

Next to it, a gift shop. I bought postcards for Kevin's daughter, Aida, and my nieces.

Nearby, The Eternal Tree House—a gutted Redwood stump turned "tree house," surrounded by a collection of mythical, psychedelic wood carvings and sculptures.

Worth stopping if only for its oddity. At Myers Flat, they let you drive through a Redwood tree for $10. Not quite as thrilling as it sounds. If I were single, I could update my Match.com profile: *"I like poetry, long walks on the beach, and cycling through Redwood trees."*

With 15 miles to go, I stopped at Redwoods Market & Deli. I grabbed a sandwich and water and sat on a bench, watching the residents of the 95554 zip code go about their loitering.

Dean Creek Resort was a former motel, now dressed up with tacky lawn ornaments, RV camping in the back, a pool and creek for cooling off, and a small store with limited, overpriced options.

The owner was a 70-ish-year-old hippie, barely 4'10". She swore like a sailor and had zero patience for bullshit. As long as you followed her rules, life was good. Deviate, and God help you. I really liked her.

I bought a non-alcoholic Lagunitas IPA and jumped into the pool.

Taking advantage of the hot, dry air, I washed my clothes in the shower, hung them outside on a clothesline, then fell asleep for an hour.

Before the office closed, I ducked in to grab some nibbles. The old hippie was drinking a big glass of whiskey and offered me a glass.

"I drink hops and whiskey. Sometimes water and whiskey. I like my whiskey, so most of the time I just drink whiskey."

Instead, I grabbed another N/A Lagunitas, some hot pockets, and ice cream. None of which satisfied me, but my options were limited, and I didn't know what I wanted; I just knew I wanted something.

She asked what I did for a living.

"I'm an author. And you're going to be in my book about this ride."

She grinned and pulled out a book. Her son's book, *Going for a Bike Ride: West–East by Daniel Locascio and Samson Hatae*. A multi-hundred-page coffee table book—a photographic journey of their bike ride across the U.S.

"Here, take this to your room. I think you'll enjoy it. It's my only copy, so don't spill anything on it."

She knocked on my door before leaving, "Hey, I just bought your books on Amazon, now remember to write only good things about my place."

Dean Creek Resort. Five stars!

CORY: 8
VP: 5

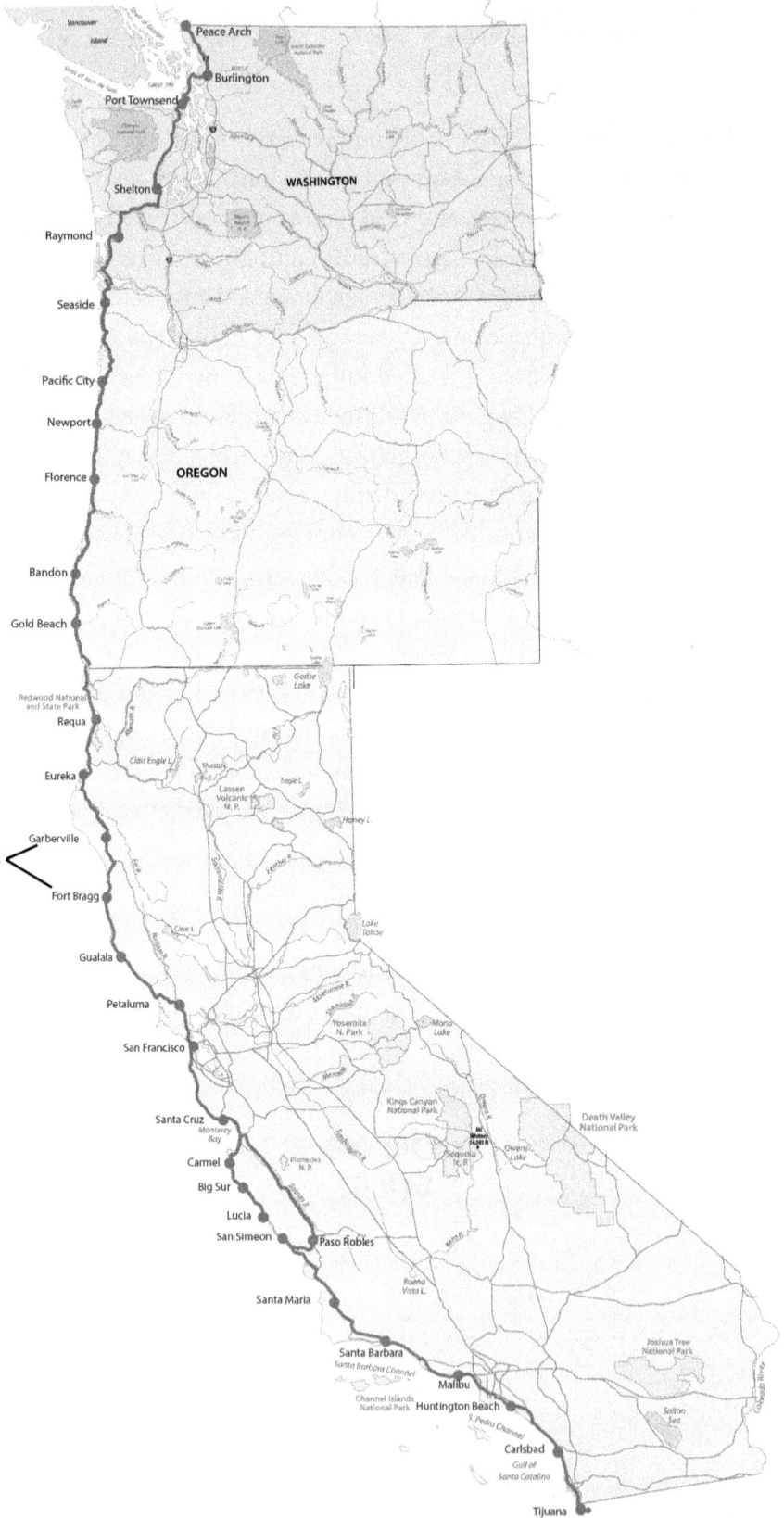

Peace Arch
Burlington
Port Townsend
Shelton

WASHINGTON

Raymond

Seaside

Pacific City
Newport

OREGON

Florence

Bandon
Gold Beach

Redwood National
and State Park
Requa

Eureka

Garberville
DAY 14
Fort Bragg

Gualala

Petaluma

San Francisco

Santa Cruz
Carmel
Big Sur
Lucia
San Simeon   Paso Robles

Santa Maria

Santa Barbara
Malibu
Huntington Beach

Carlsbad

Tijuana

DAY 14 - JULY 19, 2023

Garberville, California to Fort Bragg, California

72 MILES : 5,946' ELEVATION GAIN

"Good morning, D-Train, another beautiful day in California. Off to Fort Bragg today. Fort Bragg, probably some special forces there or something. Fort Bragg sounds very familiar. Anyway, enjoy the day, enjoy the fun, enjoy the route. A monster day in the tour again; I think it's that way all the way till the end. Anyway, congrats. Tour de Cory, tour de California, tour de you. I hope you have fun, enjoy yourself. Rooting for ya. Um, I hope that Lagunitas… Lag-u-ni-tas was very good last night. Um, anyway, take care, buddy, have fun."

> **Podcast: HISTORY DAILY**
> **Episode: 515 -** *Maurice Garin Wins the First Tour de France*

Opening the door to bring in the fresh cool air, I made some coffee and wrote some witty notes on the postcards to my nieces and Kevin's daughter.

With the door open, some dude, wearing a drug rug, worn-out jeans, and work boots, popped his head into my room.

"Is anyone in the office?" he asked.

"I don't know, just ring the doorbell."

"I'm starving!"

"So am I. There are no restaurants or markets I know about outside the office store."

He looked at a map outside on the wall.

"Do you know how far…"

"Probably not, just biking through," I interrupted.

"Me too. I started in Seattle, trying to get to Monterey. You know how far that is?"

"Well," I thought for a moment, "I plan on passing through Monterey on Monday."

"Wow." He stroked his beard. "What day is it today?"

I had to think about that. "Wednesday."

He started to walk away, then popped his head back in my room. "Got any weed?"

"What?"

"Weed, got any weed?"

"No, I'm doing this trip sober; I've been drinking non-alcoholic beers and avoiding dispensaries."

He smiled, "Good for you."

I assumed he was homeless. Then again, under the circumstances, so was I. My guess? He did just enough to get by—cutting wood, clearing brush, burning trash. It didn't matter. As long as he made enough to eat, score some weed, and kept a roof over his head.

Maybe he'd just been dealt a bad hand and never figured out how to escape it. Or maybe he was like Robert "Bobby" Eroica Dupea—born into a wealthy family, a Harvard-educated pianist, but disillusioned by the bourgeoisie, choosing instead to live a simple, unencumbered life.

With 815 miles behind me, and a projected distance of 1,850 miles, I'd be—at 912 miles—*theoretically* halfway done.

Un día más cerca de México.

With 72 miles ahead, one big climb, and plenty of heat until I hit the coast, my plan was to be out the door by 7 a.m. By 7:30, I dropped the key off and tried to have a conversation with a cat that happened to be watching me.

Cory: "Well hello kitty, what's your name?"

Cat: Blank stare

Cory: "Are you hungry? So am I, but I have no food."

Cat: Continued blank stare. Licks its leg.

Cory: "Well, I'm off. Have a nice day, kitty."

Cat: Continues to lick its leg.

Not long after, the glorious scent of bacon filled the air. Then weed, then bacon again, then weed. I wanted to find the source and partake in both.

At Benbow, I had a choice:

- Stay on the 101

- Take Benbow Drive, a quieter route that added a few extra miles.

I saw no reason to change course and stuck with the 101. Smart choice? No idea. Unfortunately, the shoulder soon narrowed, traffic picked up, there was no shade from the sun, and the climbs kept coming.

At the Eel River Bridge, the 101 became a single lane and seemed to suddenly fill up with logging trucks. Past the bridge, I stopped at "Legend of Bigfoot"—a roadside attraction to escape the trucks and because I was curious. The shop sold everything from metal Bigfoot lunchboxes to Bigfoot t-shirts to wooden chip and dip trays in the shape of Bigfoot's foot.

Out back was a psychedelic landscape of colorful metal marshmallows and tree trolls. The only thing missing was a hookah-smoking caterpillar.

Across the way was a diner that offered breakfast, weed, and various touristy items. Next to that was a gas station where I bought a latte and six Powerball tickets, and fell into a conversation with two twenty-something tattooed lesbians whose dog sat next to me on the bench and demanded all of my attention.

Tourism seemed to keep this little part of California going. There was the "One Log House," which, if you haven't figured it out, was a house made out of a hollowed-out redwood log. Next to that was the Grandfather Tree, which is older than the Mayan civilization. Down the road was Confusion Hill, which offered a gravity house, the largest sculpture carved from a redwood, a miniature train that took you into the redwoods, and if one had a keen eye, they might see the elusive Chipalope—a distant evolutionary cousin to the Jackalope found in the Dakotas.

I stopped at the Peg House, a very welcoming place where live music was played in the outside courtyard. "The Swamp Stump" was playing live this Saturday with special guests "Barnfire, Lost Bayou Ramblers, and Accordion Soul Music." Additionally, there would be a crawfish boil, dancing, games, and local beer available.

The Peg House history was literally bolted to the side of the building:

Built on the original site of Gill's Airport, the Peg House was built by Hans Hauer around 1961. The building is a traditional Danish structure, built without nails from hand-hewn beams. "Never Don't Stop."

In Leggett, a sign read:

"Drive-Thru Tree. Turn Left. ½ Mile."

Sure. Why not? Another day, another drive-thru tree. What else do I have to do today?

Passing a post office, I ducked in to mail the postcards. The postal worker took them and glanced at me. "$1.75."

She started stamping the postcards.

"$1.75? That's truly amazing. Slap $1.75 worth of stamps on me and mail me home."

I laughed. The postal worker didn't laugh. Didn't even smirk, so instead of standing there sweating in my bike outfit, I looked at the wanted posters until she asked me to pay.

I wasn't entirely joking. Between 1913 and 1915, it was actually possible to mail children via the U.S. Postal Service. The last one sent was six-year-old Edna Neff, mailed from Pensacola, Florida, to her dad in Christiansburg, Virginia, for fifteen cents.

The first time I really thought about postage was when I spent two years traveling the world and would send my sister a postcard from each country I visited. One day, sitting in a bar in Venezuela, I bought a stamp for under a dollar and thought about how crazy it was that I could send a card halfway around the world for under a dollar.

The whole system baffled me. How did it even make money? Turns out, it all has to do with the Universal Postal Union in Berne, Switzerland, and the reason you can buy something from China on Amazon and pay no shipping while USPS still has to deliver it without getting paid. Something I heard on NPR, so it has to be true.

It was hot, I hadn't eaten, I still had 44 miles left, and I was about to start a 4.2-mile, 1,200-foot climb. West on US 1, the road dropped—a tease—then the real climb began.

The occasional views toward Huckleberry Pass were breathtaking, and every part of me wanted to stop, rest, and take them in, but I knew if I stopped, I'd lose momentum, and momentum was everything. This was, hands down, the hardest climb since I had left the Canadian border; the descent was one of the most thrilling. Back along the coast, which I hadn't seen in two days, the temperature dropped about 20 degrees.

Five years earlier on this stretch of road, Jennifer and Sarah Hart loaded up their GMC Yukon with their six adopted children, whom they had been physically and mentally abusing. Jennifer, behind the wheel, opted to drive the family off a one-hundred-foot cliff—familicide. The prettiest landscapes hold the saddest tales.

The aged Westport Community Store, offering gas and groceries, seemed like a mandatory stop, if for no other reason than curiosity. Built around the time the town was originally established in 1879 and originally named Beall's Landing, the store had a great deli and housed hundreds of rubber ducks in every color and size imaginable.

Which, of course, led to the obvious question: "So… what's up with all the rubber ducks?"

Every year the town holds The Great Rubber Ducky Race. Things to consider before entering:

- **Size counts.** Within the allowed size limits, the smaller your duck is, the faster it will be.

- **Caution! Strong headwinds.** Breeze off the ocean can push your duck back if it is high and wide.

- **Don't run aground.** There are shallows and rapids that can catch your duck if it floats too deep in the water.

- **Don't get upset**. Many manufactured toy ducks have trouble staying upright and may even run the whole race upside down. Prevent this by attaching a weight to the duck's bottom; a quarter held on with masking tape works well.

Why did Westport change its name from Beall's Landing? James Rodgers came from the East, opened a lumber mill, and, with his influence, renamed the town as a contrast to his hometown Eastport, Maine.

Rolling into Fort Bragg, I had my heart set on a steak; instead, I enjoyed Raffaele Esposito's creation and ended up with a pizza from Mountain Mike's Pizza. Wah wah wah.

The guy in the room next to me was on a motorcycle tour with some buddies. I ran into him while hanging my clothes out to dry on our shared railing.

"I used to ride my motorcycle cross-country in my 20s. Now I ride my bicycle," I told him.

He laughed.

"I used to ride my bicycle. Now I ride a motorcycle. Do it while you're young—because when you hit 70, you start feeling 70."

CORY: 9
VP: 5

Peace Arch
Burlington
Port Townsend
Shelton
WASHINGTON
Raymond
Seaside
Pacific City
Newport
Florence
OREGON
Bandon
Gold Beach
Redwood National
and State Park
Requa
Eureka
Garberville
Fort Bragg
DAY 15
Gualala
Petaluma
San Francisco
Santa Cruz
Monterey
Bay
Carmel
Big Sur
Lucia
San Simeon
Paso Robles
Santa Maria
Santa Barbara
Santa Barbara Channel
Malibu
Channel Islands
National Park
Huntington Beach
Carlsbad
Gulf of
Santa Catalina
Tijuana

Vancouver
Island
Strait of Juan de Fuca

Goose
Lake
Clair Engle L.
Eagle L.
Lassen
Volcanic
N. P.
Honey L.
Clear L.
Lake
Tahoe
Yosemite
N. Park
Mono
Lake
Pinnacles
N.P.
Kings Canyon
National Park
Mt.
Whitney
14,505 ft
Sequoia
N.P.
Owens
Lake
Death Valley
National Park
Buena
Vista L.
Joshua Tree
National Park
Salton
Sea
S. Pedro Channel
Colorado River

DAY 15 - JULY 20, 2023

Fort Bragg, California to Gualala, California

58 MILES: 2,517' ELEVATION GAIN

"Good morning, D-Train. How are you doing today, buddy? Hope you had a good day in the saddle. I saw your video—I'm a bit envious. Very beautiful, very fun. In any case, you've got a fun ride today: thirty up, thirty down. Boom. Done. No problem. You're probably feeling pretty good by now. Maybe your taint isn't feeling so good, but it will all come together. Looks like the tour has been decided, eh? At least you're not going to miss the greatest tour of all time. So that's good. Or maybe you've been watching anyway. I don't know. Anyway, hope you're digging the gravel bike. Enjoy California. I can't pronounce where you're going because I only glanced at it while I was driving. Anyway, ride on, brother. Have a good one. Love ya, take care."

> (((🎙️))) Podcast: **HISTORY DAILY**
> Episode: **516** *The German Military Tries to Assassinate Hitler*

"Hey, let's see if we won anything." I handed my lottery tickets to the clerk at the gas station.

He ran them through the machine. "Wow, look at that—you won $5."

He reached for the cash drawer.

"Whoa, whoa, whoa. Let's let that ride. Get me six more tickets."

From behind me, a voice chimed in.

"Congratulations."

I turned to see a younger guy with a cheek piercing and a small tattoo under his left eye.

"Thanks, man."

"Where are you biking to?"

"Today? Gualala."

"Wow, that's far. I used to live there. Do you think you can make it?"

I tried not to sound cocky.

"Oh, yeah. Just fifty-eight miles. Looking forward to grabbing a steak when I get there."

"Well, there's a great seafood place—Gualala Seafood Shack. Can't miss it. I used to live there; that's how I know."

We both walked outside.

He nodded toward his bike.

"This is my ride, man. Pretty sweet."

He hopped on a foldable electric bike, lit a cigarette, and in the most *Napoleon Dynamite* exit possible, rode off.

The ride to Gualala was pure bliss—ocean to the right, woods to the left. Little inns and B&Bs dotted the roadside.

Ten miles in, beneath me ran the 800-mile-long, 30-million-year-old San Andreas Fault.

The Little River Market looked like a good place to stop.

A sign on the door read:

"No public bathroom. Bathroom 200 feet north."

Below it was a hand-drawn map of the building, with an arrow pointing north and a bold "200 FEET" scrawled above it.

I grabbed the breakfast of champions—a ham and cheese croissant and a Diet Coke. At the register, the woman ringing me up asked:

"How far are you going?"

"Gualala."

"Well, it's about an hour by car, if that helps you."

"Thanks. Short day today—60 miles."

She glanced out the window.

"Gonna be hot today."

I checked my phone—72°F.

"I was just up in Leggett. It was 85°F. It's nice and cool here along the coast."

She nodded.

"Well, if you're going to Gualala, you're gonna come across a bridge. When you do, go right. Don't go left."

"I was just gonna follow Highway 1."

"If you go left, you'll end up in Cloverdale. You don't want to do that. Go right at the bridge."

"Got it. Right at the bridge. If I see a sign for Cloverdale, I won't go that way."

"That's right. Don't go to Cloverdale. A lot of people miss that turn."

"Don't go to Cloverdale."

It sounded like a Monkees song. As I walked out the door, I started humming *Last Train to Clarksville…*

> *Take the last train to Cloverdale*
> *And I'll meet you at the station*
> *Don't take 128*
> *Or I'll miss my reservation.*
> *Don't be slow.*
> *Oh, no, no, no.*

I wasn't as hungry as I thought. A couple of bites from the sandwich, a gulp of Coke, and then the rest went into the bin outside the Little River Market.

Reaching the intersection to Cloverdale, I realized the lady at the Little River Market had over-exaggerated the possibility of missing the turn. There were two signs:

```
┌─────────────────────────┐
│     ← Cloverdale        │
└─────────────────────────┘

┌─────────────────────────┐
│     → Gualala           │
└─────────────────────────┘
```

Not exactly a *Choose Your Own Adventure* moment.

One brutal climb stood between me and Gualala—short, but with three switchbacks that had me dropping into my granny gear. Halfway up, a group of motorcyclists passed me. One tooted his horn. I recognized the jacket—my neighbor from last night's motel in Fort Bragg.

For thousands of years, this land was home to the Pomo Indians—living peacefully among the dense forests and grasslands perched above the Pacific. Then the Spanish missionaries arrived, befriended the Pomo, converted the Pomo. And then they enslaved the Pomo.

As if things couldn't get any worse for the Pomo, along came Andrew Kelsey and Charles Stone—two land-grabbing settlers who took whatever the Spanish weren't using and forced any remaining Pomo to work the land they stole while taking liberties with the Pomo women.

The Pomo had enough, and Kelsey and Stone were killed. A justifiable ending, but not the end of the story.

The U.S. Army got wind of the murders, sent in troops, and proceeded to slaughter 100 Pomo women and children and forced the survivors onto reservations. Then came disease. The Pomo population plummeted from 3,000 to 400.

Today, the Pomo population has rebounded to over 10,000, and for any metalheads reading this, Chuck Billy, lead singer of Testament, is one of them.

Today, Gualala is a quaint little town of about 2,000 people. None of them are Pomo.

I found the seafood place the guy on the electric bike told me about earlier.

As I rolled up, there he was—the guy from Fort Bragg, standing with his motorcycle buddies.

"I can't believe how fast you got here on your bicycle."

He shook my hand and introduced me to a few of the guys.

All of them were 70+, and one guy? 80.

"This guy got pulled over today for speeding," he said, nodding toward the octogenarian.

"The cop looked at his license, saw his age, couldn't believe he was still riding a motorcycle—and gave him a warning."

The eighty-year-old grinned. "It's all about staying active; you start feeling eighty when you hit eighty."

CORY: 10
VP: 5

Peace Arch
Burlington
Port Townsend

WASHINGTON

Shelton

Raymond

Seaside

Pacific City

Newport

Florence

OREGON

Bandon

Gold Beach

Redwood National
and State Park

Requa

Clair Engle L.

Shasta L.

Eagle L.

Lassen
Volcanic
N. P.

Honey L.

Eureka

Garberville

Fort Bragg

Clear L.

Lake
Tahoe

Gualala

DAY 16

Petaluma

San Francisco

Yosemite
N. Park

Mono
Lake

Santa Cruz
Monterey
Bay

Carmel

Big Sur

Lucia

San Simeon

Paso Robles

Pinnacles
N. P.

Kings Canyon
National Park

Mt.
Whitney
14,505 ft.

Sequoia
N. P.

Owens
Lake

Death Valley
National Park

Santa Maria

Buena
Vista L.

Joshua Tree
National Park

Santa Barbara
Santa Barbara Channel

Malibu

Channel Islands
National Park

Huntington Beach

S. Pedro Channel

Salton
Sea

Carlsbad

Gulf of
Santa Catalina

Tijuana

DAY 16 - JULY 21, 2023
Gualala, California to Petaluma, California

78 MILES: 2,731' ELEVATION GAIN

"A good morning, D-Train. Take two of this message. The message went through some random Bluetooth device, which stinks because it was a gooood message. It was a very fun message. Anyway, in California, enjoying the ride—another day in paradise for you. Hope everything... hope you're enjoying everything. Ummmm. Just a day away from San Francisco, where you will meet up with your lovely wife. One more day of bachelorhood, so to speak. Hope you're digging the flat pedals, although you're probably a flat pedal master by now. Though I do not recognize that as being true. There are no such things as fla... anyway, I don't care. It doesn't matter what color... what color. Well, it doesn't matter what color your pedals are. But it doesn't matter what kind of pedals you have—at least, it shouldn't matter. I guess, I don't know, maybe if you had triangle pedals, that would be kinda odd. Um, maybe those are Look pedals. You know what! It doesn't matter; pedals don't matter. I'm not getting in the middle of that. Anyway, enjoy your ride—49 miles. Why don't you ride around in a circle for a mile and make that 50? 25 for lunch, 25 for bed. Whatever. So close to San Francisco. It's going to be great, man. Enjoy the ride; love you, man. Take care."

> (((🎙️))) **Podcast: HISTORY DAILY**
> **Episode: 517 *The Scopes Monkey Trial***

Originally, I had mapped out a leisurely 48-mile ride to Bodega Bay, envisioning an early arrival at a cozy resort. The plan was to indulge in seafood, perhaps take a dip in the ocean, and unwind. The following day, a 78-mile journey to San Francisco would reunite me with Kate.

However, the thought of tackling 78 miles and arriving exhausted prompted a revision. Instead, I decided to push on to Petaluma today, leaving a shorter ride into San Francisco tomorrow for my rendezvous with Kate.

Some friends questioned why I didn't continue south from Bodega Bay passing through Point Reyes into Sausalito. Honestly, I hadn't given it much thought.

The morning greeted me with biting cold; the sun was concealed behind thick clouds. The road stretched out, flat and fast, leading me to the 155-year-old Stewarts Point Store. It seemed everyone within a 20-mile radius had the same idea.

Renowned for its bakery and coffee, the aroma of fresh doughnuts was intoxicating. The store also showcased the Richardson family heirlooms: an 1888 baby buggy, a 160-year-old wheelbarrow, and turn-of-the-century fishing traps.

With thirteen miles behind me, just before eight, I entered the store, eager for a sweet treat and a latte. However, a long line of patrons with ample time on their hands made me reconsider. I decided to press on to Bodega Bay, just thirty-five miles south. Given today's pace, I'd be there by 10 a.m.

The fog thickened, transforming the woods into a misty, almost mystical landscape. Hawthorne's *Young Goodman Brown* popped into my head; this is the scene where Young Goodman came across the devil—I was sure of it.

Fort Ross was a major Russian settlement established by Ivan Kuskov in 1812. This multicultural community welcomed various groups, including the Pomo, Aleuts, Ukrainians, Poles, Belarusians, Finns, Germans, Estonians, Lithuanians, and Latvians. Together, they cultivated the land and built a thriving settlement.

Unfortunately, smallpox began to wipe out the Indians. As luck would have it, the Russian vessel *Kutuzov* arrived from Peru in 1817.

With it came the smallpox vaccine, which was given to fifty-four residents of Fort Ross. To prevent further spread, only vaccinated individuals were permitted entry into the fort.

The question we are asking ourselves is why did a Russian vessel from Peru have the smallpox vaccination?

After the Spanish spread smallpox throughout South America, King Charles IV of Spain, who had lost his daughter to smallpox, also realized his workforce was diminishing in South America. In 1803, armed with Dr. Edward Jenner's newly developed smallpox vaccine, he sent the Balmis-Salvany expedition to South America with three directives:

1. Vaccinate the masses free of charge with the vaccine Dr. Jenner developed.

2. Teach the domains how to prepare the smallpox vaccine.

3. Organize municipal vaccination boards to record the vaccinations performed and have serum ready for future vaccinations.

It took over three years to complete vaccinating millions. Dr. Jenner later said of the expedition, "I don't imagine the annals of history furnish an example of philanthropy so noble, so extensive as this."

Today's work began just after Fort Ross—a 5.75-mile climb that didn't let up. At the top, a massive road construction project blocked the way. No way around it. I queued up with the cars and waited 20 minutes before a construction worker finally gave the go-ahead. Unfortunately for everyone stuck behind me, the next stretch of road was narrow, lined with concrete barricades, and barely wide enough for one car. This meant they had no choice but to follow me at 12 mph for over a mile.

The descent led me into Jenner, a tiny port town completely swallowed by fog. Gas was $5.99 a gallon, which was still cheaper than the 16 oz Americano at Café Aquatica—$4.95. A gallon of Americano would cost $39.60. Perspective.

A friend had recommended I grab a craft beer from the gas station here, claiming it was pretty damn good.

Instead, I just took a photo of my bike in front of the station. I had made it this far without alcohol, and it was still morning.

Bodega Bay had gone to the birds. Literally. This was where Alfred Hitchcock filmed *The Birds*.

I stopped at The Birds Café, where they had:

✓ A bird on the street sign.
✓ A bird on the side of the building.
✓ A bird on the menu.

It reminded me of that Portlandia skit: "Put a bird on it."

I ordered a couple of fish tacos, enjoyed the amazing weather, washed it down with an Americano, and then hit the road for Petaluma, 31 miles away.

The temperature jumped 20 degrees as I moved away from the coast. Rolling into Valley Ford Market, I grabbed some water and took advantage of the porta-potty out back. Normally, I'd just pee on the side of the road, but the timing worked out.

The door read "Vacant." I opened it. A woman screamed. I caught her midstream.

When she walked out, she smiled. "I should have locked the door."

Back on the road, a roadie passed me at a ridiculous pace. I kept pedaling and soon hit my last road construction zone of the day. The flag woman smiled and said:

"Petaluma's just fifteen miles down the road. Ready? Set? GO!"

She flipped the stop sign to SLOW, and I took off... slowly.

Later, I passed a sign that read: "SLOW FOR FLOWERS." Which made me smile.

My stay for the night was a Marriott property. Thanks to my Marriott loyalty status, they let me check in early. Fifteen minutes after checking in, I was sitting in the hot tub, looking up things to do in San Francisco after picking up Kate.

CORY: 11
VP: 5

Peace Arch

Burlington

Port Townsend

WASHINGTON

Shelton

Raymond

Seaside

Pacific City

Newport

Florence

OREGON

Bandon

Gold Beach

Redwood National
and State Park

Requa

Eureka

Garberville

Fort Bragg

Gualala

Petaluma

DAY 17

San Francisco

Santa Cruz

Carmel

Big Sur

Lucia

San Simeon

Paso Robles

Santa Maria

Santa Barbara

Malibu

Huntington Beach

Carlsbad

Tijuana

DAY 17 - JULY 22, 2023

Petaluma, California to San Francisco, California

48 MILES: 1,894' ELEVATION GAIN

"Good morning, D-Train. Another day, another wonderful experience. All of you are headed to San Francisco. Dock of the bay, baby. Dock of the bay. You get to meet up with your lovely wife, Lady Kate. And up, yeah. A little bit of civilization. Well, I guess you've been staying at fancy hotels, so it's all good. Anyway, I have a little special guest announcer this morning. Can you say something please? (talking to his daughter) In a mousy voice: 'Good job, Cory.' What do you want? Well, that's pretty good; he's been riding his bike for a couple of weeks now. How crazy is that? 'You can ride it; you can do it, Cory.' I think that about sums it up, my friend. Love you, buddy. Have a good ride. Take care."

((🎙)) Podcast: HISTORY DAILY

Episode: 518 Saturday Matinee: The History of Egypt

and

((🎙)) Podcast: HISTORY DAILY

Episode: 211 The End of the Warsaw Ghetto

Big day today. Not the ride—the ride would be easy, mostly downhill and flat, with a couple of punchy climbs thrown in for good measure. Today was big because Kate was flying in. I planned to leave at 6 a.m.; her flight was scheduled to arrive at 12:12 p.m. If I could maintain an average speed of 15 mph, I'd have enough time to reach the hotel, shower, take an Uber to the rental car lot, pick up the car, and then pick her up. Bam, crackerjack.

Instead, I left at 7 a.m. As I arrived in Novato, Kate sent me a text: "Delayed. Maintenance issue. I don't land until 1:39 p.m."

Excellent, I thought. I have time. I was just twenty-five miles from the hotel and maintaining a respectable speed of 18 mph.

Soon, I was in San Rafael and jumped on an amazing bike trail filled with runners, walkers, individual cyclists, and cycling groups. I latched onto the wheel of a roadie, locked in at 23 mph, with no intention of taking the lead. When we hit a big climb, he dropped me like a bag of rocks.

In Sausalito, I received another text from Kate: "Looks like 1:45 arrival. Just about to board."

That allowed me to stop, find a coffee shop, and charge my phone. One medium Americano, please. I sat on the sidewalk overlooking a very hazy San Francisco skyline, temperatures in the mid-70s. Countless road cyclists were heading to and from San Francisco. I decided I wanted to live here.

After the coffee, with just under eight miles left, it was time to cross the famous Golden Gate Bridge. I had driven over it several times; biking across it was an entirely different and thrilling experience. Its impressive scale, the view, the wind, the size of the massive steel cables and bolts. Suspended 200 feet above the water at the bridge's crown, it posed a bit of a mental struggle for those of us with "L'appel du vide." A short railing and a massive safety net protect you from potential doom. I stopped halfway across and watched the sailboats navigate around Point Diablo, fishing trawlers heading back from sea, and container ships heading west. I looked down at the massive $224 million suicide deterrent net. Since its completion, the number of suicides has significantly decreased, dropping from an average of thirty per year to eight.

Just below the south side of the bridge near Fort Point National Historic Site are a pair of painted yellow hands on a black sign on a chain-link fence at the end of the road: "Hopper's Hands." Below them are a pair of yellow dog paws.

Ken Hopper, a steelworker on the bridge, noticed that runners would run down to the chain-link fence at the end of Marine Drive, touch the fence, and then turn around to continue their run. So he had the signs made as a sort of "High Ten."

The hands have another meaning. The Golden Gate Bridge has been the most used suicide site in the world. Ken, along with many of the steelworkers on the bridge, are trained in suicide rescue; Hopper has prevented thirty people from jumping but unfortunately lost two. The yellow hands also seem to say, "This is a turning point," not a "dead end," to all those thinking about jumping.

I noticed a sign in the back of a pickup truck that read, "San Francisco Marathon."

"Is that tomorrow?" I asked the driver.

He nodded affirmatively.

I texted my nephews, Micah and Elijah, with whom I'd recently run a half marathon. Elijah completed the full marathon. "OK lads, get on a plane. San Fran marathon is tomorrow," I wrote. Elijah responded enthusiastically, "I'm down. My body has had time to recover, so it's time to hop back in action." Micah, true to form, didn't reply; he's like his dad in that way.

My hotel was a couple of miles south of the wharf. After checking in and showering, I caught an Uber to the car rental lot. When I picked up Kate, I had Taylor Swift playing on the radio. She had mentioned wanting to see Swift live in Europe in 2024.

"So, we're Swifties now, eh?" she said with a smile as she got into the car. I asked her thoughts about seeing *Les Misérables*.

"Oh babe, I've been traveling all day. Can we just grab a glass of wine and relax somewhere?"

Between Kate's ten-day trip to Sweden and Norway, our brief reunion before my departure, and her work trip to Chicago, it was already July 22nd. The summer was half over, and we'd only spent about two weeks together.

CORY: 12
VP: 5

Vancouver
Island
Peace Arch
Burlington
Port Townsend

WASHINGTON

Shelton

Raymond

Seaside

Pacific City

Newport

Florence

OREGON

Bandon

Gold Beach

Redwood National
and State Park

Requa

Eureka

Garberville

Fort Bragg

Gualala

Petaluma

San Francisco

DAY 18

Santa Cruz
Monterey
Bay

Carmel

Big Sur

Lucia

San Simeon
Paso Robles

Santa Maria

Santa Barbara
Santa Barbara Channel
Malibu
Channel Islands
National Park
Huntington Beach

Carlsbad

Tijuana

Death Valley
National Park

Kings Canyon
National Park

Yosemite
N. Park

Mono
Lake

Lake
Tahoe

Honey L.

Lassen
Volcanic
N. P.

Joshua Tree
National Park

Salton
Sea

DAY 18 - JULY 23, 2023

San Francisco, California to Santa Cruz, California

78 MILES: 2,935' ELEVATION GAIN

"Goooood morning, D-Train. Alright, now you're going to Santa Cruz. Santa Cruz, great brand of skateboards. That's good. Hope you had a good time in San Francisco with your lovely lady. Um, you got a long day ahead of you today. Just remember: 40 miles, eat lunch, 40 miles—no big deal. You're in California. You're in the cool part of California, lots of things to see. Good, probably well-paved roads. Alright, man, have a great ride; it's going to be a glorious Sunday, dude. Take care, man. Love ya. Bye."

> ((🎙)) **Podcast: HISTORY DAILY**
> **Episode: 212** *Saturday Matinee: Wild West Extravaganza*

Waking up next to Kate was awesome! Between her trip to Norway and a week-long work trip in Chicago, she was exhausted and mentioned she might be getting sick.

About twenty years prior, I had ridden this section to Carmel, where my cousin Becky was living. When I arrived, she asked how long I was staying and if I had a place to stay. I was on the tail end of a two-month leave of absence. Pointing to my tent, I told her I had about two weeks left before I had to get back to work. She had a friend with a house in Carmel Highlands who was looking for someone to house-sit. Giddy up.

While at the house, I started writing my first book. Three days before I was to return to work, I made a decision that would change my life. I called my employer, told them I wasn't coming back, left my bike at Becky's, walked out onto Highway 1, and hitchhiked south—destination unknown. I was gone for two years.[10]

I was eager to hit the road, revisiting the route that had once liberated me and unveiled the person I was meant to be. I told Kate where the rental car was parked, kissed her on the forehead, and texted her the address of the hotel in Santa Cruz. "Sleep in as long as you want and indulge in room service," I suggested.

Heading toward the coast, I encountered runners participating in the San Francisco Marathon and cheered them on. Having run sixteen marathons myself, part of me yearned to join them; another part was relieved to be on my bike instead.

My first marathon was on a whim. A friend I hadn't seen in ages invited me to lunch. When I saw her, I exclaimed, "Maria, you look radiant!" She revealed she'd just completed her first marathon and encouraged me to try it. I joined a running group and, despite struggling through half a mile initially, completed my first marathon three months later.

Soon, I found myself at Ocean Beach. I paused to take a photo and sent it to Kate. "You're going to have a great drive today, babe. Take your time; I've got a lot of miles ahead of me."

About an hour later, a cyclist approached me and matched my pace.

"You ride for the Crossniacs?" he asked, noting my cycling jacket emblazoned with their logo.

"You know the Crossniacs?"

"Yeah, my buddy Bill from Minnesota is a member. We've tried recruiting him to our team, but he insists on wearing his Crossniacs kit."

"I used to sponsor them back in the day. I had a bicycle company called Wesley, named after my dad who passed away. I put it on the back burner after selling my heart rate monitor company. I raced with them as an amateur, Cat 4/5. The rest of the guys were beasts. One even took second at nationals about a decade ago. Time flies."

---

10 Shameless plug, my books *Unlost* and *Embracing Bewilderment* are about the two-year adventure.

As we approached a climb, he was far stronger than me, and I urged him to go ahead. It's remarkable how small the world can be sometimes. I've had a lot of small world situations, but hands down my favorite was in 2002. I was on a ship with about ninety runners from all over the world heading down to run the Antarctica Marathon. During small talk, one of the ninety runners *from all over the world* started talking with me. Long story short, it turned out she not only knew my uncle Steve, but my aunt Mary, Uncle Richard, and Grandma Heckenlaible.

At Pacifica, a strong tailwind pushed me south. In Miramar, I stopped to grab some water and check if my Powerball tickets won. All losers—I'm done with the Powerball, at least for now.

In Half Moon Bay, I was drawn to the surfers carving up the waves while skateboarders were at a nearby park, "thrash'n." The scene echoed Spicoli's mantra: "All I need are some tasty waves, a cool buzz, and I'm fine."

A guy was selling Bonsai plants out of his van by the roadside, and model remote control planes were doing acrobatics at the RC airfield.

Beachgoers at Gregorio worshipped at the altar of Poseidon, basking in the sun and surf. An incredibly fast couple on road bikes overtook me while I was doing 20 mph. With the tailwind, I got cocky and invited myself to draft behind them; my speedometer jumped to twenty-four, then twenty-six. When he looked back, saw I was drafting, and accelerated, I conceded after a couple of miles—spent, with no way to keep that pace.

Later, the winds at Waddell Beach offered a spectacle of kiteboarders dancing across the water.

One thing I asked Kate to bring was a new pair of headphones; the off-brand ones were useless. I delved into the backlog of podcasts Kevin had sent and started listening to Jack Kerouac's *The Dharma Bums*. Truman Capote once quipped about Kerouac's style, "That's not writing; it's typing."

Some have compared my writing to Steinbeck's, specifically *Travels with Charley*—a comparison that leaves me ambivalent, given my dislike for Steinbeck's prose.

As I pedaled southward along the Pacific Coast Highway, I heard two honks from a car horn. It was Kate, smiling and waving as she pulled into a scenic overlook to wait for me and take in the ocean view. After a brief conversation, we agreed to meet for lunch at the Whale City Bakery in Davenport.

Life with Kate has always been an adventure. When we married, I had just sold my business, and two months later, we both sold our houses and relocated to Dallas—a significant move, especially for Kate, who had spent her entire adult life in Minneapolis. The transition wasn't easy for her, but we knew my contract would end in two years. We had already decided to sell everything and travel the world indefinitely. Given this plan, we didn't invest heavily in making new friends in Dallas, which was hard to do since we both traveled 50% of the time for work. When together in Texas, we explored the state: visiting bluebonnets in Hill Country, spending weekends at dude ranches, deep-sea fishing in the Gulf, and visiting Luckenbach. As we left Texas for an unknown destination, we hiked Guadalupe Peak—the state's highest point at 8,751 feet. Big Bend remains on our list.

After leaving Dallas, we found ourselves living in a tent or crashing on friends' couches until we sold the car, grabbed our backpacks, and headed for South America. There, we spent two years trekking, exploring, and volunteering.

Upon returning to the United States, a friend shipped our road bikes to Dallas, and we rode from there to Minneapolis. The plan was to stay for the summer and then head to Southeast Asia for a few years. However, unexpected opportunities arose: I landed a consulting gig, and Kate received an offer she couldn't refuse—a Chief Legal Officer position. We still haven't made it to Southeast Asia together, but it will happen someday. In the meantime, we embark on smaller adventures, like cycling the Pacific Coast Highway.

At Whale City Bakery in Davenport, we enjoyed a simple lunch. Known for its fresh, daily-baked goods, the bakery offers a variety of pastries and desserts that often leave patrons craving more. The welcoming atmosphere, complemented by the ocean breeze, made it a perfect spot for our midday break.

Inside the bakery, a collection of notes from previous visitors adorned the walls. One particularly heartwarming message caught my eye:

"I come from China. I'm seven years old. I like this restaurant. The food is delicious. Enjoy the summer holiday. – Ena M."

The cozy ambiance, coupled with its delightful breakfast offerings and outdoor seating, made it an inviting spot. Adjacent to the bakery stood the Davenport Jail Museum—a modest two-cell jail constructed in 1913, which saw limited use before its decommissioning in 1934.

I had no appetite. After my latte, I left Kate to bask in the sunshine, enjoying her book and avocado toast breakfast. With just nine miles remaining, I felt a surge of energy, although I hadn't eaten anything substantial in the last 50 miles. The caffeine coursed through me, making me jittery and eager to tackle the final stretch.

Aided by a favorable tailwind, I reached Santa Cruz in twenty minutes. Spotting a fruit vendor by the roadside, I purchased a large bag of grapes, gobbling them down as I waited for Kate.

"Gobbled"—that's a weird word. Gobble. Gobbling. To gobble. Gobble gobble. From the Middle English word "Gobben": to drink or swallow greedily.

At the hotel, I showered with my cycling clothes on, old school like Kate and I did when we were in South America. I grabbed the wet clothes and hung them out to dry in the courtyard, where I met a lady, accompanied by her dog, who felt the need to tell me about how her whole family was dead, how her uncle yelled at her dog, and now the dog has all these issues. She was waiting for her girlfriend. The conversation veered into such bizarre territories that I nearly considered ordering a shot of tequila.

I eavesdropped on another conversation. A woman, likely in her 50s, confided to her friend about her dissatisfaction with her marriage: "The kids are grown, he's complacent, and I want to create a new life without him."

Marrying later in life, I understood the desire for reinvention. Reflecting on my journey, I've embodied many personas, pursued various dreams, faced numerous failures, taken right turns when I should've gone left, moved on when staying might've been wiser, and lingered when I should've moved forward. Yet, all those decisions—good, bad, or indifferent—led me here. I appreciate the person I've become, cherish the woman I married, and value our home and shared adventures. The challenging times have shaped who I am today, and for reasons beyond my comprehension, Kate loves that person. So, here's to the good times, the bad times, and the present moments that define us.

Kate asked me to pick up some zinc, Vitamin C, ginger ale, and a COVID-19 test kit. She tested positive and called our clinic for instructions on what to do. Their response was to get rest.

We live in a house divided when it comes to a few things. The last shot I got was a tetanus vaccine after falling on some sharp rocks while hiking in the mountains at night. I slipped, and the cut went deep, almost severing the tendons in my hand. Before that, it was yellow fever when I was in Central America.

When COVID-19 emerged, I chose not to get vaccinated—not out of an anti-vaccine stance, but due to skepticism about the rapid development, testing, and approval of the vaccine. Learning that manufacturers were granted immunity from potential lawsuits further fueled my doubts.

It reminded me of past government experiments like:

- **Tuskegee Experiment** - A secret study where Black men who were infected with syphilis were left untreated to study the disease's progression.

- **Operation Sea-Spray** - The U.S. Navy sprayed bacteria over San Francisco to test biological warfare dispersion in the civilian population.
- **Operation Top Hat** - The U.S. Army tested chemical and biological decontamination methods on unwitting soldiers without proper consent framed as field exercises.
- **Operation LAC** - The U.S. dispersed biological agents from planes over large areas to study how they spread.
- **Project SHAD** - Military tested chemical and biological weapons on U.S. sailors, often without consent.
- **MKUltra** - The CIA ran illegal mind control experiments using drugs like LSD on unknowing subjects.

Such historical experiments have left me wary of governmental intentions.

On the flip side, Kate was vaccinated. During the middle of the pandemic, I was sick. Kate was convinced I had COVID, so we went in for an antigen test. Results: Kate tested positive; I was negative. We then took the PCR test later that day. Results: both of us negative.

That was one of the problems I had regarding the pandemic. Don't get me wrong; I do not deny it took a toll, but here was a perfect example of my skepticism. Her positive test will show up in the data as another positive. However, the fact that she tested negative later that day will not erase that positive record, so were the numbers inflated?

When Kate told me the response from the doctor was, "Get rest," I couldn't help but reflect on how, two years prior, such a diagnosis might've led to the hotel being shut down or even city-wide quarantines. Now, the guidance is simply to rest.

CORY: 13
VP: 5

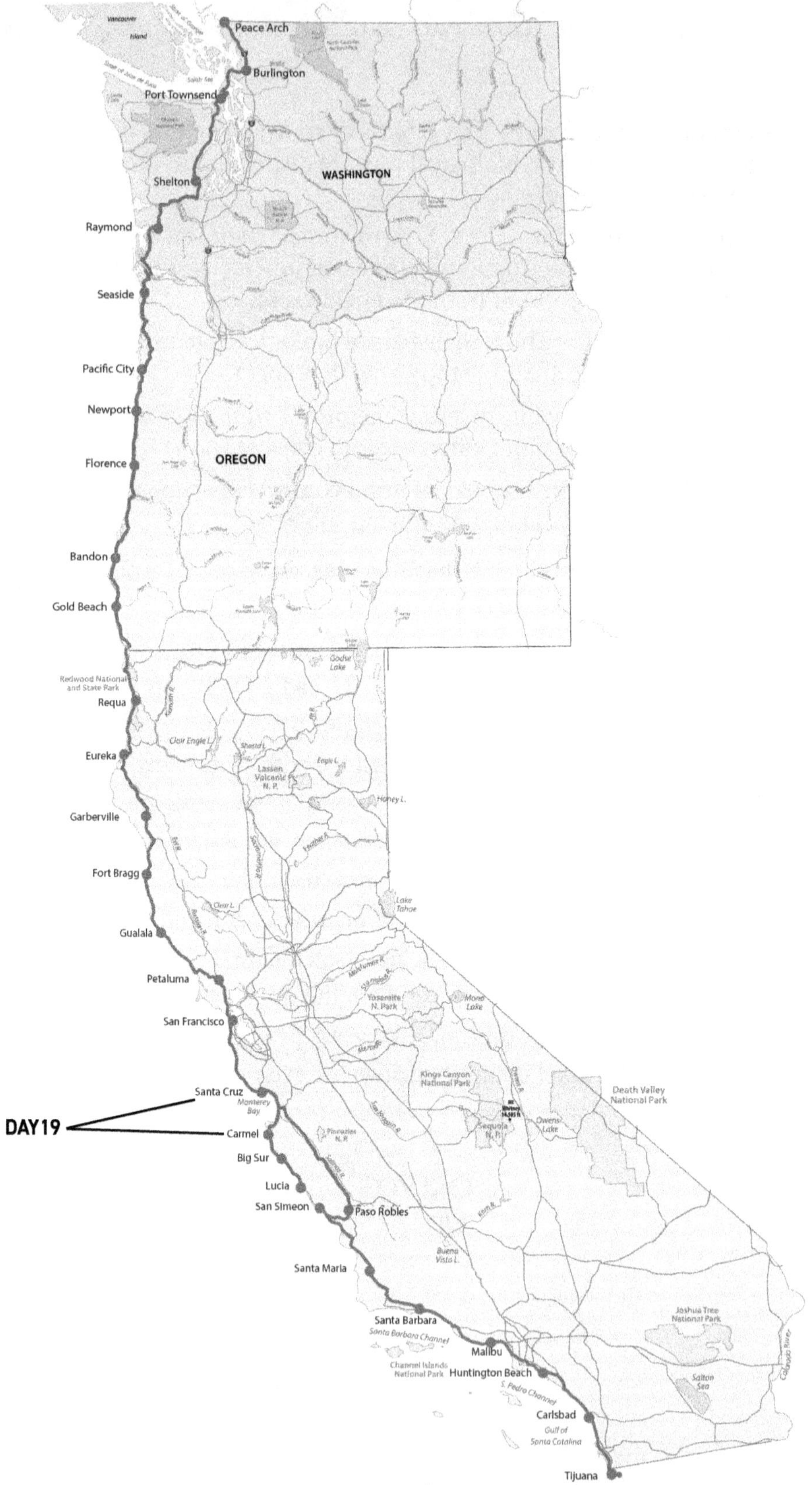
Peace Arch
Burlington
Port Townsend
Shelton
WASHINGTON
Raymond
Seaside
Pacific City
Newport
Florence
OREGON
Bandon
Gold Beach
Redwood National and State Park
Requa
Goose Lake
Clair Engle L.
Lassen Volcanic N. P.
Eagle L.
Honey L.
Eureka
Garberville
Fort Bragg
Clear L.
Lake Tahoe
Gualala
Petaluma
Mono Lake
Yosemite N. Park
San Francisco
Kings Canyon National Park
Death Valley National Park
Santa Cruz
Monterey Bay
DAY19
Carmel
Pinnacles N. P.
Sequoia N. P.
Owens Lake
Big Sur
Lucia
San Simeon
Paso Robles
Buena Vista L.
Santa Maria
Santa Barbara
Santa Barbara Channel
Joshua Tree National Park
Malibu
Channel Islands National Park
Huntington Beach
S. Pedro Channel
Salton Sea
Carlsbad
Gulf of Santa Catalina
Tijuana
Colorado River

DAY 19 - JULY 24, 2023

Santa Cruz, California to Carmel, California

63 MILES : 1,746' ELEVATION GAIN

"Good morning, D-Train. Alright, man, I think you've got about ten days left on this journey of yours. You are in Carmel today—don't think they would like it to be called Carmel, but it could be called that. Anyway, hope you have a glorious day! The Tour de France is over; Pogacar did not win, but Jonas Vinegaard did. Peter Sagan is now retired. Cavendish is retired, too. I don't know. Anyway, hope you have a glorious ride today, man. You've come pretty far. Enjoy the day, my friend. Be one with the bike, be one with the ride, let it come to you, sir. Have a good one, man; take care."

> **(((🎙))) Podcast: HISTORY DAILY**
> **Episode: 519** *The Rediscovery of Machu Picchu*

It was nice having the car; the bagel shop was about a mile away, and if I were just on the bike, I might have skipped breakfast, as I've done pretty much this whole trip—finding something along the way or just riding all day and grabbing dinner at the end. I wanted to get Kate some food, and her request was a whole wheat bagel with peanut butter and an almond milk latte. She was feeling really bad but wasn't going to let a Chinese-manufactured disease slow her down.

According to *TV Guide*, the top ten biggest news moments are as follows:

1. John F. Kennedy Assassination

2. Moon Landing (did we or didn't we?)

3. September 11 attacks

4. President Nixon's resignation

5. Gulf War

6. O.J. Simpson trial

7. *Challenger* explosion

8. Rescue of Baby Jessica

9. Election-night debacle (Gore vs. Bush)

10. Death of Osama bin Laden

But those all happened before the breaking news that was coming out of Santa Cruz, California.

A rogue sea otter known only as 841, has been eluding authorities for weeks in the Santa Cruz area, harassing seals and stealing surfboards from surfers.

Helicopters, divers, and even a 200-yard-long net have been deployed, but 841 has managed to maintain her freedom. Viva 841, you elusive surfboard-stealing, seal-harassing sea otter.

Soaring down into downtown Santa Cruz, I jumped onto Highway 1—this stretch is technically off-limits to cyclists and pedestrians. But with just four miles, light morning traffic, and a generous shoulder, I figured I'd chance it. If a cop pulled me over, I'd feign ignorance with a terrible accent: "Vhat, you mean I no can ride bicycle on road? Vhy? In Europe, we ride all roads all times!" More likely, I'd just pay the ticket, acknowledging my inability to do accents. That said, for reasons unknown to me, I have been asked on random occasions what country I was from because of my accent.

Pedaling through Santa Cruz felt like a trip back in time. The maze of turns led past aging houses—once affordable havens for surfers in the '70s, now million-dollar properties awaiting demolition to make way for luxury oceanfront homes and condos. Every time I ride through Santa Cruz heading south, I get turned around or miss a turn;

it's like the place has some sort of energy that messes with my inner sense of direction.

The Santa Cruz Beach Boardwalk is the oldest amusement park in California and home to the fifth oldest roller coaster in the United States—the Giant Dipper. There is also Charles I.D. Looff's hand-carved carousel, complete with a Wurlitzer, which was installed in 1911.

I felt bad for Kate. I was so excited for her to be here—enjoying the ocean, the surf, the small cafés, and relaxing while she worked—and there she was, with the 'Vid.' Well, at least that's what the $26 COVID test box from Walgreens said. I sent her a text to let her know I'd arranged for a late checkout, so she could sleep in as long as she wanted.

Southwest of Watsonville sits the Redman Hirahara Farmstead, a place with a history that speaks to both hardship and resilience. Originally owned by a Japanese-American family, the Hiraharas, their lives were upended in 1942 when they, like thousands of other Japanese-Americans, were forcibly sent to internment camps. Most families in similar situations lost everything—homes, land, businesses.

Thanks to the kindness of locals, their farmstead was preserved. When the Hiraharas returned after the war, they didn't just reclaim their home; they opened its doors to other displaced Japanese-Americans, offering shelter and jobs working on the farm to those trying to rebuild their lives. It stands as a monument to community and perseverance, now listed on the National Register of Historic Places.

Further down the road, Elkhorn Slough is a sprawling salt marsh that serves as one of California's richest estuaries. Home to sea otters, harbor seals, and red-legged frogs hidden among the reeds, the slough is home to nearly 700 species of plants and animals. Birds of all kinds—pelicans, egrets, curlews—fill the sky and shallows, creating an amazing place for wildlife watchers.

It's easy to get caught up in the forward motion of a ride, always thinking about the next mile, the next stop. Just like the person behind the name of a bridge, an old farmhouse, and a random marsh, these elements make bike trips so rewarding.

After La Selva Beach, San Andreas Road led me away from the ocean into a unique landscape of farming and agriculture. You'd think this coastline would have been swallowed up by developers and multimillion-dollar homes. Instead, there were miles of fields with hundreds of migrant workers hunched over, harvesting produce and loading it into cardboard crates. These crates would then be transported to distribution centers, eventually reaching grocery stores far from the fields where they originated. And then, as I shopped in my grocery store in the desert, where no one should live, I pondered whether or not I should pay $12 for three containers of pre-sliced watermelon.

Instead of my audiobook, my playlist for the day was a mix of Soul Coughing, Cake, Old 97s, White Stripes, and the Beastie Boys. Had I had a radio, I would have tuned on K-PIG radio, which I first heard in 2001 and fell in love with, but it required a subscription. The station features folk, blues, rock, and Americana music that fits right in here in the eclectic Monterey Bay area.

For the first time on this trip, I faced a headwind—a relentless force that felt like it was coming at me at a hundred miles an hour, even if it was only ten. I stopped in Marina to grab a drink and checked the "Find My Friends" app to see where Kate was. She was just four blocks away, parked at Marina State Beach. Deciding to surprise her, I biked over. She was feeling a lot better; perhaps it was a false positive on the COVID test.

From here, I had 15 miles to go and two hours before check-in. My Garmin warned me of a 3.3-mile climb ahead. Doing some quick math, I figured it would take me about two hours to knock out the remaining miles and took off.

The ride was fantastic—a smooth trail carved through sand dunes, leading me straight into Monterey. In 2018, over 1,000 octopuses (*aliens?*) were discovered near Davidson Seamount, an underwater mountain two miles below the surface off the coast of Monterey.

Scientists dubbed the area "Octopus Garden"—a deep-sea nursery where the creatures cluster together to lay eggs and raise their young.

Of course, there was no mention of UFO wreckage at the site. But had there been, we all know how that would have been covered up—chalked up to a "rogue weather balloon" or an "untethered buoy."

Speaking of cover-ups, close to my home in Phoenix, there's a place called Dreamy Draw, a name stemming from the effects of mercury mining in the area. Miners, affected by mercury exposure, reportedly experienced hallucinations, appearing "*dreamy*" as they descended the draw.

But Dreamy Draw isn't just miles of hiking trails; it also has something that makes absolutely zero sense: a dam in the desert, where there is no water.

According to local legend, a UFO crashed there in 1947. The story goes that instead of removing the wreckage, the government simply built a dam over it. Shortly after, Highway 51 was constructed nearby. (*Area 51*)

Leaving Monterey felt like the *bitter end*—because soon after, the 3.3-mile climb began.

Glancing at my Garmin, I saw the grade at 6%—manageable.

Then 8%—okay, legs are feeling it now.

I turned a corner—10%.

Another turn—12%.

Then, just when I thought I'd reached the worst of it, the road kicked up to 16%.

That's the kind of incline where walking feels like a workout, and cycling feels like a bad decision. My speed dropped to 3.5 mph, and my daily average plummeted from 15 mph to 12.3. I wanted to get off the bike and push, but instead, I muscled through it, cursing at my Garmin, my life choices, and the entire concept of gravity.

I could have opted for a detour—the 17-Mile Drive through Pebble Beach—a beautiful route along the Monterey Peninsula, past world-famous golf courses, windswept cypress trees, and coastal cliffs. I had ridden it before, and for anyone looking for what to see and what to do on this ride, I highly recommend adding it.

But today? No chance. Adding seventeen more miles to my ride in exchange for avoiding this climb was not on the menu.

I followed my Garmin religiously, and in return, I was served 16% grades and existential despair. But ahead lay Carmel, my promised land, filled not with milk and honey but with hot tea, succulents and overpriced meals.

At times like this, I am baffled that chains don't just snap or bottom brackets crack. The amount of power being generated is incredible, and I'm one step below an amateur. I can't comprehend the torque on the frames of those professional sprinters kicking out 1,200+ watts each day at the Tour de France.

In the world of road bike racing, there are the following categories:

Category 4/5:	Everyone starts at Cat 5. 24-27 mph average, 32-33 mph max.
Category 3:	26-30 mph average, 35-40 mph max.
Category 2/1:	28-32 mph average, 42-47 mph max.
Pro:	Elite riders racing with national teams.
Category 6:	Made up category for the rest of us.

Back at the hotel, I showered, grabbed some of the free chocolate from the lobby, and flopped onto the bed.

I really wanted a drink. Not wine, I'm not a fan. Not beer, I don't really like that either. What I wanted was a single malt.

"I think I want a drink," I said, more to myself than to Kate.

"Well, have one."

"Yeah, but I kind of want to wait until the end of the trip."

"Well, quit complaining about it, then, and just wait."

She went back to work. I grabbed a bottle of water and headed out to the deck, overlooking the garden of our hotel, catching up on emails and some writing.

My buddy Brian, who lives out in Carmel Valley, had been following my Strava and sent me a message. We agreed to meet up in the morning and ride to Big Sur together. I hadn't seen him in a few years and was looking forward to catching up.

Later, I walked into town and grabbed a pizza at Il Fornaio Carmel. Kate, still not feeling 100%, opted to stay back at the hotel.

While waiting at the bar for the pizza, I broke down and ordered a large glass of Macallan 12. It was… fine. Not as satisfying as I'd hoped, but that didn't stop me from ordering another.

The bartender was one of those guys who poured based on how much he liked you. Based on the four-finger pour sitting in front of me, he must have really enjoyed our conversation. By the time the second glass was gone, I had a solid buzz going as my pizza finally arrived.

It's funny, after a few weeks or months off drinking, I always forget how much I don't actually care for alcohol. It's not really the taste I miss—it's the ritual. Sitting in a certain chair, at a certain time, with a certain glass. It's the process more than the product.

Next to me, a couple from Green Bay, Wisconsin, struck up a conversation. They had sold everything after their eight kids moved out and were now living in an RV full-time.

"Carmel is our favorite place," she said, swirling her wine. "And his company just happens to have a conference here. So as I see it—" she grinned, raising her glass—"It's a paid vacation."

Her husband laughed and ordered another beer.

Many coastal towns have a daily ritual. Just before sunset, people make their way down to the beach. Some walk along the water, others play with their dogs, some spread out a blanket, pop a bottle of wine, and settle in.

When that special moment comes—when the last golden sliver of sun sinks below the horizon—everyone stops what they're doing, turns west, and watches. And then, as if on cue, there's a quiet round of applause.

Tonight, sans Kate, I watched another day disappear into the Pacific.

CORY: 13
VP: 6

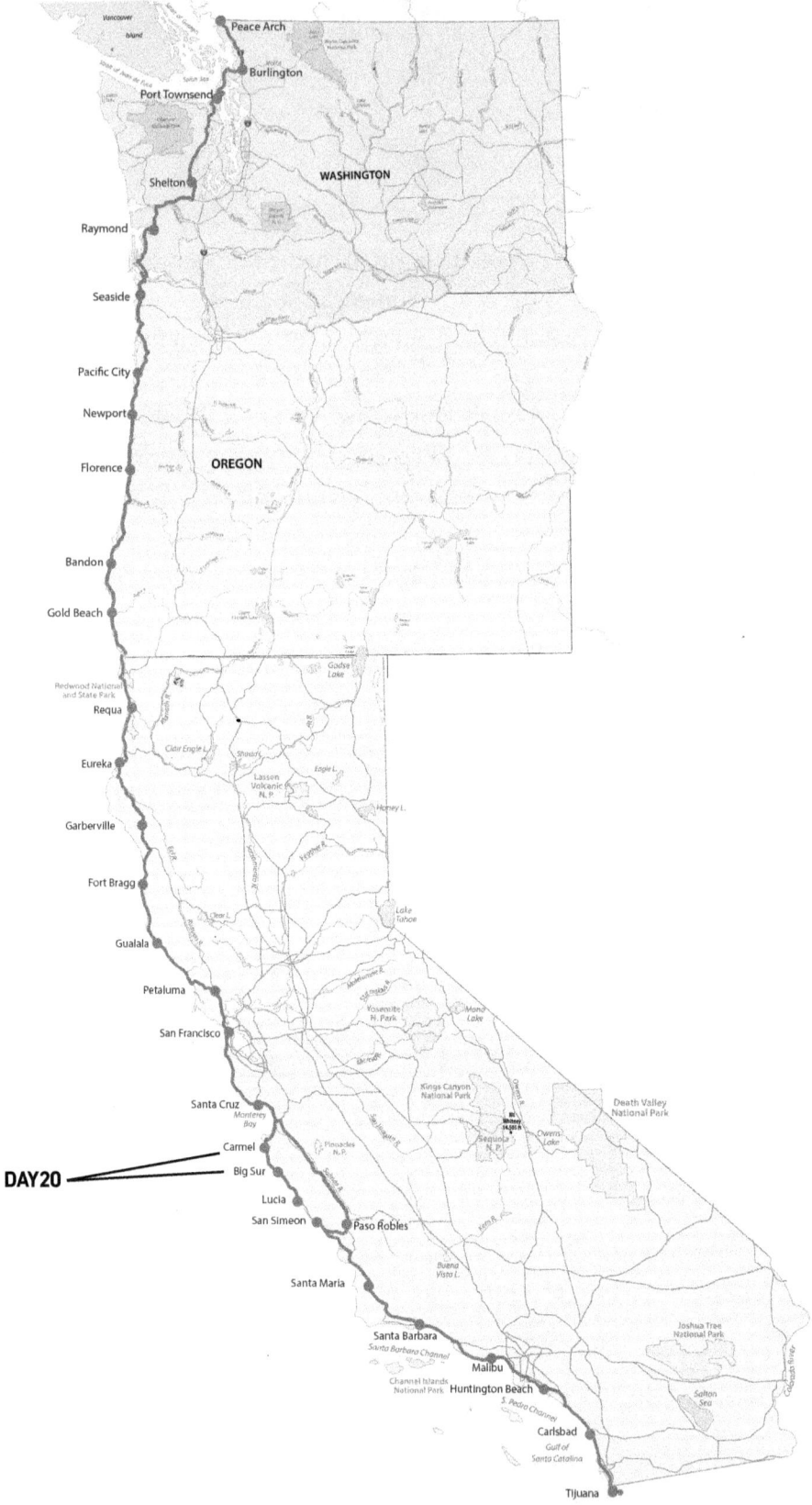

Peace Arch
Burlington
Port Townsend
Shelton
Raymond
Seaside
Pacific City
Newport
Florence
Bandon
Gold Beach
Requa
Eureka
Garberville
Fort Bragg
Gualala
Petaluma
San Francisco
Santa Cruz
Carmel
Big Sur
Lucia
San Simeon
Santa Maria
Santa Barbara
Malibu
Huntington Beach
Carlsbad
Tijuana
Paso Robles

WASHINGTON

OREGON

DAY20

DAY 20 - JULY 25, 2023

Carmel, California to Big Sur, California

25 MILES: 2,190' ELEVATION GAIN

"Good morning, D-Train man. Welcome back to another day in the life of an adventurer. There you go. Alright man, short day. 25 miles; you might go longer. If you don't, you've earned it. Have a good one man: BIG SUR! I've never been there. I hear it's pretty cool. Hope you have an enjoyable day. Thinking about you every day. Have a good one. Take care. Love ya, have a good ride."

> **((🎙)) Podcast: HISTORY DAILY**
> **Episode: 520 *Bob Dylan Goes Electric***

I was awake by 5 a.m., checked the pre-market stock news, and then opened my email. One was titled "Thank you."

"Hello Cory,

I certainly could wax poetic about my appreciation and enjoyment of your book, *The Buddha and the Bee*, but instead will just say thank you. I recently finished my doctorate in music education and have begun reading "for fun" again - this book reminded me not only of how much I love to read but how much I love and miss bikepacking.

Thank you for sharing your adventure so beautifully. It brought me great joy.

—Jamie"

Well, that was a wonderful way to wake up.

The next bit of great news was Kate had broken her fever and was feeling much better.

Taking the car, I drove to Safeway to grab the all-important coffee, and that's when I ran into Ken. His bike had everything but the kitchen sink: quilts, bags piled high on the back, a guitar strapped to the front, and his front handlebar bag adorned with all sorts of mementos: feathers, religious medals, keychains, and a tiny stuffed animal.

"Been living on my bike for seven years," he said with a smile.

I told him where I started and where I was headed.

He sort of gazed at the tops of the trees, as if scanning a map in the sky or looking for UFOs.

"Yeah, yep. I've ridden pretty much all that, heading south now. Maybe Modesto. Not sure. Should be there in a week. How you plan on getting through the slide?"

He was referring to a major mile-long landslide on the Pacific Coast Highway that had shut the road down for all traffic until November, maybe December.

"I heard a lot of people wait until the road crews leave, then pass through. But I might have worked out an alternative plan."

I didn't go into detail, but if I couldn't get through, Kate would meet me on the north side, and we'd drive back up to the south side of the slide. I'd miss a mile of the PCH, but with all the missed turns, detours, and side trips, I had more than made up for that.

"Yeah," Ken nodded. "A couple of people got stuck in there, not sure how. One guy tried to go through at night but got lost—didn't have a headlamp." He laughed. "Some people think they can do what they can't do."

He took a sip from a stainless steel cup, watching me over the rim.

"I hope to see you at Pfeiffer Park. There are some tables in the back by the parking lot. I like to sit there for a few days and read."

Back at the hotel, I texted my cousin Freddy, who lived in Topanga Canyon. His driveway was essentially the starting line for Tuna Canyon Road, a one-way descent into Malibu where kids with fast cars liked to race down—with an average of one death per year.

Weeks ago, I told him I'd be there tomorrow, but now it was looking more like the 30th.

He replied, letting me know that he and his wife would be in Scotland but still offered Kate and me his house for the night.

Freddy's generosity didn't surprise me. In 2014, I spent a month in Los Angeles for work—trade shows, conferences, trainings. Kate and I had just gotten married, and instead of spending a month apart, she arranged a few weeks of meetings in LA so we could be there together.

One night, we visited my Uncle Charlie and Aunt Diane in Palm Springs.

"You know your Aunt Mary and cousins Becky and Freddy are at the Fancy Food Conference in Anaheim, right?"

I didn't.

It turned out Becky and Mary had already gone home, but Freddy was still in town, staying at his girlfriend's place in Topanga.

Later that night, Kate and I were back in LA, just in time to see Air Force One take off. I posted a photo on Facebook, which caught the attention of my Uncle Johnny.

"You guys are in LA? Aimee, Addie, and I are at the W Hotel in Hollywood—you should stop by."

The W was ten minutes from where we were staying.

Soon we were on the roof of the W, drinking cocktails with family we hadn't seen in ages.

"Freddy's in Topanga. Let's call him."

Freddy gave us an address and told us to pick up pizzas on the way.

We jumped in the car, grabbed pizzas at Endless Color, and spent the rest of the night in Topanga, with family, food, and laughter.

And that's just how my family works.

I was meeting my old friend Brian today.

We met in 2003, both of us just starting our businesses—he was a college student running a web design company, and I was a 33-year-old who had just spent two years traveling the world with no job prospects and no college degree. So I did the most logical thing: with no business experience what-so-ever, I started a heart rate monitor business.

We were opposites yet kindred. He was straight as an arrow, while I had a bong sitting on my desk when we first met—or so he tells me.

I was using Microsoft FrontPage, a program that allowed anyone who could turn on a computer to build a crude website in a matter of days. As my company grew, I realized I needed a more professional online presence, so I hired Brian to build my website. That's how we became friends.

Over the years, Brian would drag me away from the office for bike rides, a much-needed escape. I was a workaholic and had no money, so the only thing I could afford to do was ride my bike.

Late at night, driving past my office, Brian would text me: "Cory, go to bed. There's nothing you can accomplish at 11 p.m. that can't be accomplished at 6 a.m."

For two years after starting my company, I slept in the office—not because I wanted to, but because I was too broke to afford rent. I had a hammock strung up in the back and showered at my uncle's house. The bakery next door, Great Harvest Bread Company (shout out), took a liking to me and gave me a warm sample of bread and a cup of coffee every morning. One morning, when they found out I was dumpster diving for boxes to ship my products in, they started setting boxes aside for me.

There I was, shipping fitness equipment in doughnut boxes, some still hardened with frosting.

How I managed to start that company, not knowing anything about business, grow it, and eventually sell it still baffles me. It just goes to show what happens when you mix hard work, perseverance, and stubbornness together.

Sprinkle in a little luck and a dash of "fuck you, don't tell me I can't do something," and you too can be successful.

In 2005, Brian, my sister Sara, and Erik (a young guy who worked for me for a short while) entered the Minnesota Border to Border, a four-day endurance event.

Our team name was HTBTC—Hope to Beat the Cutoff.

- **Day 1:** 200-mile bike ride.

- **Day 2:** 200-mile bike ride.

- **Day 3:** 50-mile run.

- **Day 4:** 50-mile canoe.

We finished in fourth place by six seconds. Had we been just six seconds faster at any stage, we would have made the podium. If we ever did the race again, our team name was either going to be:

1. "Six Bloody Seconds"

2. "Team Upchuck"—since every single one of us puked on Day One from pushing too hard.

Brian eventually sold his company, stayed in Minneapolis for a bit, and then moved to Monterey, California, with his growing family. Now he lives in Carmel Valley, ten years younger and 130 pounds lighter than me.

We had coffee, and he shared how much he loved being a dad. He encouraged me to move out here, especially after I told him how much Kate and I love spending time in Carmel and had been looking at houses. The only thing stopping us is California's insane taxes.

Then we got on the bikes. It was 25 miles to Big Sur. We had all day—well, I did anyway. For Brian, this would be a roundtrip...trip; he still needed to get home.

Somewhere along the way, Brian shared some news about his health. A gut punch. But he was optimistic. He knew there was no cure, but he wasn't going to let it take control of his life. If anything, he was going to fill it up even more.

I hoped he'd take it easy on this old dude. He didn't. He took off, leaving me in the dust. Laughing, I thought to myself: *So, it's going to be like that.*

Most of my friends are competitive, and while I know I'm not the fastest, I like that they push me. I raced mountain bikes for a while, and one year Kevin and I bought On-One single-speed mountain bikes from the UK—$250 for the bike, $250 to ship it.

I am a weak climber, and I figured a single-speed would force me to get better, pushing through the pain. That year, I trained hard, and by the end of the season, I finished third in the state for my age group. As a reward, a buddy who owned a bike shop had a custom titanium Eriksen single-speed built for me.

I caught up with Brian, and he pulled back on the throttle. When I finally got beside him, he smirked. "Still not much of a climber, are you?"

"*Nope.*"

He did most of the talking, and I did most of the suffering, trying to keep up with his pace. Thanks to the landslide, there was almost no traffic, allowing us to ride side by side on the shoulderless highway.

He pointed to some kelp-filled coves.

"I like spearfishing in those."

"You go alone?"

"Yeah."

"Are you free-diving or using a tank?"

"I free-dive."

I stared at the thick forest of kelp swaying in the current.

"Dude, that's a lot of kelp. You have a good knife? Do you carry a Spare Air[11]?"

"No."

"I'm buying you one. I'm buying you ten. You have a family—I don't want to find out you got caught up in some kelp and drowned."

Brian shrugged it off, more concerned about something else in the water.

"Yeah, there's a great white that's been lurking around."

"You ever see it?"

"Nope. But I'm sure it's seen me."

He changed the subject.

"You know, when the road is open, over 4.5 million people drive down it every year, and there isn't a single bathroom between Big Sur and Gorda."

He wasn't wrong.

"I think they do that to keep traffic moving. I also think they should require a pass, like the national parks, for nonresidents, to maintain it."

I've driven this road countless times, and I'd happily pay a toll for the privilege. But no amount of money is going to stop the landslides that shut it down.

- In 2017, a massive slide at Mud Creek buried the highway. It took over a year to clear.

- Then there's the lack of toilets, which means more people shitting on the side of the road.

- Travelers assume they can camp anywhere for free. Sometimes, that doesn't end well.

11 A small scuba tank that provides about ten minutes of emergency air.

Take the Soberanes Fire, for example. A careless camper from Florida started a fire that got out of control, burning down 132,000 acres and fifty-seven homes, and killing one person.

Up ahead was Bixby Bridge, one of the most iconic landmarks along the Pacific Coast Highway. Built in 1932, it required 300,000 board feet of Douglas fir. A single 8-foot 2x4 is 5.34 board feet, meaning 56,180 two-by-fours were used, and 825 trucks delivered 178,200 cubic feet of concrete and 600,000 pounds of reinforcing steel—all constructed five years before the highway would even be built to connect to it.

Labor used to build the highway consisted of prisoners from San Quentin, paid $0.35 a day and promised a reduced sentence in exchange for their labor. It's said that John Steinbeck worked on the construction of the highway which is about as Steinbeck as you can get.

I made the obligatory photo stop, then enjoyed the 2.5-mile descent into Big Sur.

For the runners of the Big Sur Marathon, this is a 2.5-mile climb. At the top, they're greeted by "Grand Piano Man," a guy in a tuxedo who plays a grand piano at a viewpoint next to the bridge. For 17 years, the piano man was Jonathan Lee. Before he passed away in 2004, he found Michael Martinez, who has carried on the tradition.

Passing Point Sur Light Station, I looked down at an old research station. At least, that's what they called it.

In reality, it was one of thirty top-secret Navy underwater listening stations used to track Soviet submarines, only to be shut down in 1984 after Navy Warrant Officer John Walker, a Soviet spy, told the Russians we were listening. Walker died in prison in 2014.

My dad was in the Navy during the Cold War, a navigator on a Constellation. They flew from Midway Island to the Aleutians and back, keeping an eye on the Russkies. After he passed, his friend Tom invited me to a few Navy reunions. During one, he shared something I had never known. *"Congress never authorized a Cold War service medal. They don't consider it a war, just a conflict. That means the Veterans of Foreign Wars don't accept Cold War vets."*

"Poor is the nation that has no heroes, but poorer still is the nation that, having heroes, fails to remember and honor them."
—Cicero

The entire ride today was a hit. As we wrapped up the final miles into Big Sur, it heated up as we pulled away from the coast and entered Andrew Molera State Park. I offered Brian a ride back, to which he chuckled, "Cory, it's just 25 miles. Got plenty of time, and it's a great ride. Call me when you come back to town, and we can all have dinner." With that, he headed north. Getting older, while my friends are distant in terms of miles, I feel blessed for those I call friends and even more blessed for those that answer the phone.

Big Sur has a sort of magic to it; many famous artists have found it to be their muse. In today's world, with its multi-million-dollar homes carefully hidden in the landscape, there is one charming yet slightly annoying feature Big Sur offers—or doesn't offer. It is easier to find a black cat in a coal cellar than to find cell service and Wi-Fi.

Clearly, I should have shared that with her before I left, but assumptions were made. I assumed Big Sur would have cell service, something I should have known it didn't. In 2022 Kate had completed the Big Sur Marathon, and in 2021 we came out to look at property with our real estate agent, who told us there was, in fact, no cell service and very limited Wi-Fi.

I ducked into the Restaurant at Big Sur River Inn and ordered a local IPA because I was thirsty after biking many miles. That, and I was no longer not drinking until I got to Mexico. A lady sat down next to me at the bar, ordered a glass of wine, and said to the bartender, "Oh, I love your style," commenting on his wardrobe. Uninterested, or perhaps just indifferent, he responded, "Thanks. I guess. It's the only clean clothes I have," then disappeared for ten minutes.

While the service was poor, the restaurant had, much to my surprise, Wi-Fi. I told Kate to meet me at the bar; we'd have lunch and enjoy what Big Sur had to offer.

CORY: 14
VP: 6

CALIFORNIA
1
PACIFIC COAST HIGHWAY

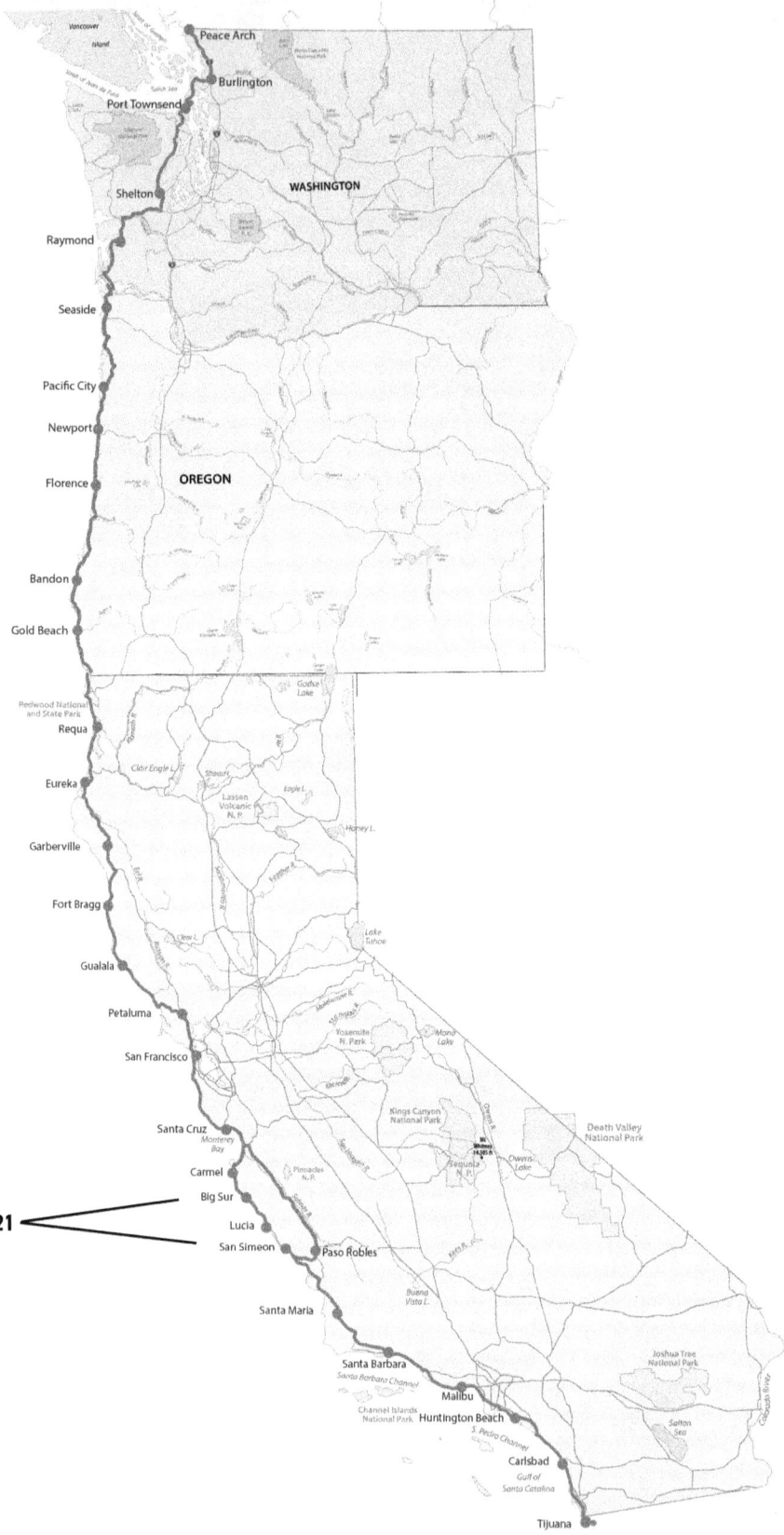

Peace Arch

Burlington

Port Townsend

WASHINGTON

Shelton

Raymond

Seaside

Pacific City

Newport

OREGON

Florence

Bandon

Gold Beach

Requa

Eureka

Garberville

Fort Bragg

Gualala

Petaluma

San Francisco

Santa Cruz

Carmel

Big Sur

DAY 21

Lucia

San Simeon

Paso Robles

Santa Maria

Santa Barbara

Malibu

Huntington Beach

Carlsbad

Tijuana

DAY 21 - JULY 26, 2023

Big Sur, California to Paul's Landslide a.k.a. Lucia, California

`20 MILES: 2,720' ELEVATION GAIN`

Paso Robles, California to San Simeon, California

`30 MILES: 1,931' ELEVATION GAIN`

"And a bright and wonderful morning to you, D-Train. Welcome to the day. Hope it goes well. Hope yesterday was a nice, relaxing zig-zagging back across the median road day, and today you've got a fun one. Thirty up, eat, thirty down—boom, end of story. Good ride. It's going to be good. California. Not sure where you're ending up in California as far as pronunciation goes. I just glanced at it, and I…I need glasses; I can't read it because it's on my phone…yes. Anyway, enjoy the ride. Enjoy the day. You're doing a great job. You only have like a week left, which should be sad or great. Not sure where you're at in the headspace, but it's awesome, man. It's awesome; it's a hell of a trip. Nice work, enjoy the day. Take care, buddy, love ya."

> (((🎙️))) **Podcast: HISTORY DAILY**
> **Episode: 521**
> ***The Signing of the Americans with Disabilities Act***

It was well known that a landslide had shut down the Pacific Coast Highway 25 miles south of Big Sur. The PCH Facebook page I was following had all sorts of discussions about it. Some said the troopers were keeping an eye out for cyclists and turning them back, while others suggested that if you waited until the road crew left, you could sneak through.

The silver lining in all of this was there was almost no traffic. My plan was to ride to the north part of the slide, then Kate would pick me up, and we would drive to the south part of the slide, allowing me to miss out on only about a mile.

Over the years, more than fifty-five landslides have shut down the highway. Before me was Paul's slide, which had been blocking the highway since January 2023. My PCH Facebook group was all speculating on its reopening around November—it finally opened in June 2024.

Unfortunately after Paul's slide was cleared, part of the road fell into the ocean at Rocky Creek Bridge, and a few miles from that, the Regents Slide occurred in March 2024, shutting down an even larger section of the PCH than Paul's slide did. In April 2024, the Dolan Point Slide was added to the list.

In August 2024, one cyclist attempted to navigate the Regents Slide. Unfortunately for me, his name was Cody Mortensen, which led to people asking if it was I who decided to cross the slide, fall over 100 feet, and had to be airlifted out with a concussion. It was not me.

PCH Tip – If the construction crew says, "If you attempt to cross it (the slide), you will probably die," it might be a good idea to rethink your plans of crossing the slide.

A sign read: "1,500 feet: road ends."

I pedaled up to the where the road was blocked off, the rubble of the landslide just beyond, making the desire to try to pass through enticing.

To my right, was Lucia Lodge, recently made famous after the prequel to *One Flew Over the Cuckoo's Nest*, where Nurse Ratched lived in Ryan Murphy's series *Ratched*. Observation: I never would have thought there would be three references to that movie in this book.

Another car pulled up, and a lady got out.

"Sir, do you know why the road is closed?"

She had either ignored all the signs or thought they didn't apply to her.

"Big landslide."

"When will it open? We're heading to San Diego."

"November or December, from what I've read."

Her face dropped.

"So… do I have to go all the way back to Monterey?! ¡Ay Dios mío!"

"Enjoy the drive."

Kate arrived and I loaded my bike into the car and headed back north.

Kate worked while I drove the two hours. We stopped at an abandoned wayside that Tesla had cleverly converted into a charging station, shaded by a canopy built of solar panels.

After ten years of marriage, Kate isn't shy about letting me know how much she hates my driving—a universal marriage problem. Personally, I think she's just jealous of how incredibly skilled I am behind the wheel. I'll concede that I have a slight tendency to be a little heavy on the pedal.

As Jack Burton said in *Big Trouble in Little China*: "I never drive faster than I can see."

If we had gone back to the south side of Paul's Slide, the ride to San Simeon would have been 39 miles. Instead, Kate dropped me off in Paso Robles, which was 44 miles away from San Simeon. In hindsight, I should have stayed on Highway 46, also known as Green Valley Road. But for no explainable reason, I took a right onto Santa Rosa Creek Road.

These mountains were for real; it was incredibly hot, and one of many bumpy descents claimed one of my water bottles. Santa Rosa Creek Road threw endless climbing at me, with cracked pavement, bumps, no shoulder, and heavy patches. The sections lined with trees provided a nice break from the relentless sun. Unfortunately, those shaded areas were home to swarms of mosquitoes and deer flies, and on the climbs, I was an easy, slow-moving target.

With five miles to go before dropping into Cambria, I was out of water. I passed a table set out along the side of the road with baskets of fruit available for purchase through an honor system. I would have paid $10 for Gatorade, $20 if it was ice cold. Instead, all that was left was a lime, lemon, and avocado.

Cambria provided me with fluids and a cool ocean breeze. Kate texted, "You okay?" I replied, "Mountains were a suffer fest; took a lot longer than I thought." She responded with a thumbs up and the hotel room number. I still had seven miles to go, all straight into a headwind.

The San Simeon Lodge was more of a motel than a lodge, but it was clean and quiet, with a bar/restaurant attached offering typical bar/restaurant food.

That night, my temperature started to rise; my throat was sore. I was getting sick.

CORY: 14
VRP: 7

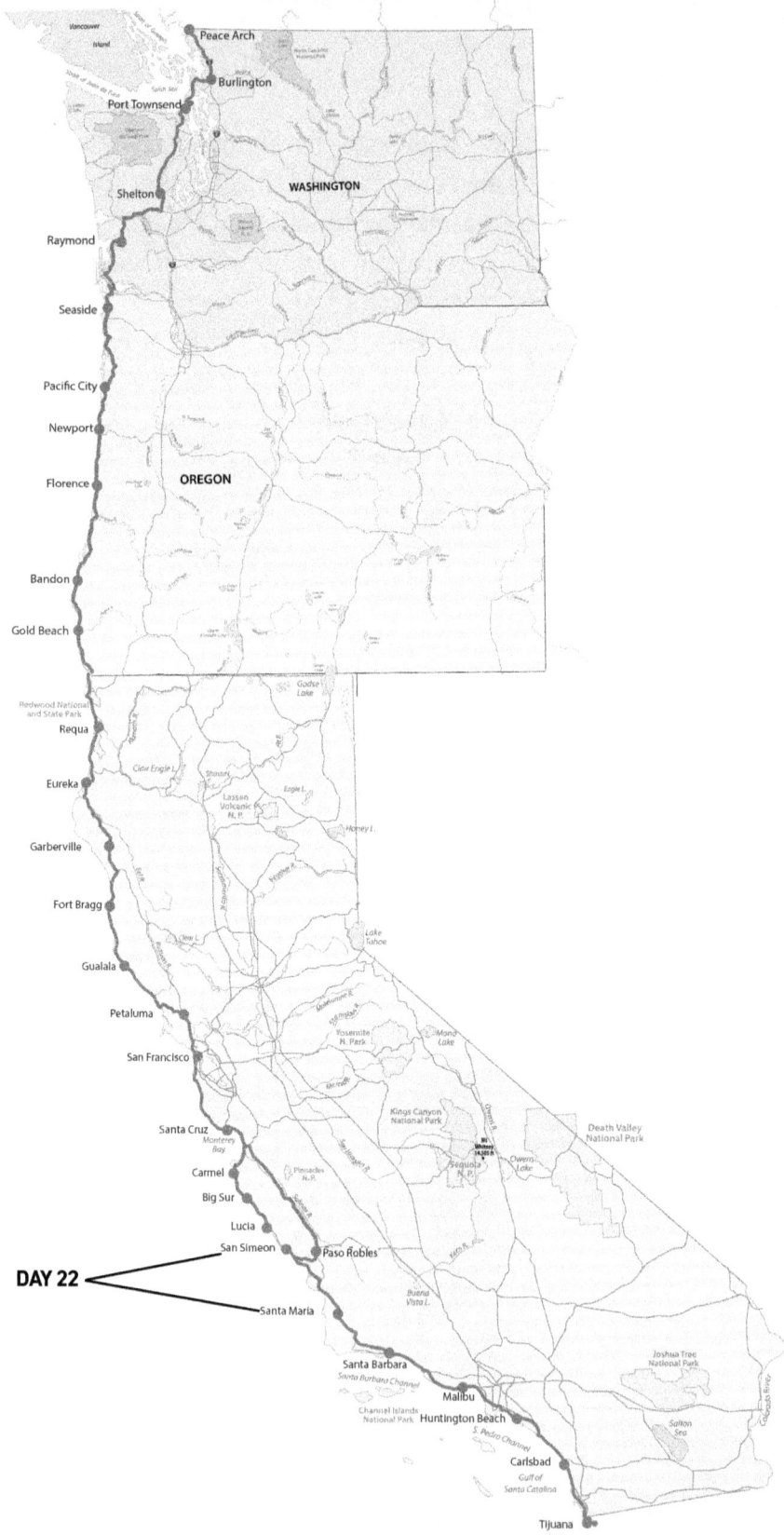

Peace Arch

Burlington

Port Townsend

WASHINGTON

Shelton

Raymond

Seaside

Pacific City

Newport

Florence

OREGON

Bandon

Gold Beach

Requa

Eureka

Garberville

Fort Bragg

Gualala

Petaluma

San Francisco

Santa Cruz

Carmel

Big Sur

Lucia

San Simeon

Paso Robles

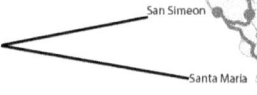

DAY 22

Santa Maria

Santa Barbara

Malibu

Huntington Beach

Carlsbad

Tijuana

DAY 22 - JULY 27, 2023

San Simeon, California to Santa Maria, California

72 MILES: 1,708' ELEVATION GAIN

"Good morning, D-Train man. You've got less than a week to go. You're on a detour, man, because life tosses you some detours, right? And it looks like it was a beautiful detour, and hopefully, you're still experiencing the Pacific Coast Highway experience. Nice work yesterday; it was a tough one, a lot of work. You've got a decent day ahead, one that will prove to be very fruitful. In any case, you're doing an amazing job; this is an awesome experience you've put together. Um, you know, man, you're just trucking along, living the dream, you're killing it, dude. Nice work. Aida, do you want to say thank you for the postcard? She says thank you, but she's being really shy. Anyway, you take care, buddy. I love you; have fun, be safe."

> **((🎙)) Podcast: HISTORY DAILY**
> **Episode: 522 *The Atlanta Olympic Games Bombing***

I woke up sick. Sick or healthy, 70 miles lay ahead, and there was nothing to do but move forward.

Scratch that. I *could* have spent another day in San Simeon. The motel wasn't bad; the ocean view was welcoming, and the little town was touristy but quaint.

I'm sure I could have found some chicken soup and hot tea, lounged in bed with Kate.

Maybe a little frisky business would have helped with whatever I was dealing with.

But Kate was on a work call, and my suffering wasn't her concern at the moment. Had I whispered, "I think I'm going to lay in bed all day," she would have given me a quick thumbs-up and continued her call.

Instead, I pulled up the dirty bibs, slipped on the dirty jersey, zipped up the dirty jacket, and slid my hands into the dirty gloves.

With a fever and pounding headache, the cool ocean air carried in by dense fog motivated me south toward warmer lands.

Several cyclists passed heading north, none interested in engaging. Fine by me. There's no hard rule about acknowledging fellow cyclists. I often put my head down when I see one approaching, avoiding the interaction altogether.

At mile eight, a woman on a tri bike passed me. Then a small group of cyclists heading north. After waving to the first dozen, I got tired of the routine. Maybe that was a dick move, but I felt like crap—I just wanted to kick out the next 62 miles and lay down, drink water, and watch *Catfish*.

A large wild turkey lay dead on the shoulder. Just ahead of it was the car that hit it, its windshield completely shattered from the impact, the driver on his phone, I assume, talking with his insurance company. Being sick is not a great way to start the day, but hitting a wild turkey and shattering your windshield trumped being sick by a feather.

As kids, we were taught that Benjamin Franklin wanted the turkey to be the national bird. I never understood that. Then again, I had zero experience with wild turkeys.

Now, after coming across thousands of them on bike rides, I get it. They're fantastic birds—tough, adaptable, extremely smart, and tasty.

That being said, Franklin never actually nominated the turkey. In a letter to his daughter, he simply criticized the design of the Great Seal, saying the eagle on it looked more like a turkey than an actual eagle.

"For my own part I wish the Bald Eagle had not been chosen the Representative of our Country. He is a Bird of bad moral Character. He does not get his Living honestly. You may have seen him perched on some dead Tree near the River, where, too lazy to fish for himself, he watches the Labour of the Fishing Hawk (osprey); and when that diligent Bird has at length taken a Fish, and is bearing it to his Nest for the Support of his Mate and young Ones, the Bald Eagle pursues him and takes it from him.

"With all this Injustice, he is never in good Case but like those among Men who live by Sharping & Robbing he is generally poor and often very lousy. Besides he is a rank Coward: The little King Bird not bigger than a Sparrow attacks him boldly and drives him out of the District. He is therefore by no means a proper Emblem for the brave and honest Cincinnati of America who have driven all the King birds from our Country...

"I am on this account not displeased that the Figure is not known as a Bald Eagle, but looks more like a Turkey. For the Truth the Turkey is in Comparison a much more respectable Bird, and withal a true original Native of America... He is besides, though a little vain & silly, a Bird of Courage, and would not hesitate to attack a Grenadier of the British Guards who should presume to invade his Farm Yard with a red Coat on."

—Benjamin Franklin

I wonder if we would be eating bald eagles for Thanksgiving if the turkey had become the national bird. I hear they taste like a whooping crane. (Dad joke.)

Twenty-five miles in, I stopped at Cayucos, finding a place that would sell me a strawberry smoothie and allow me to charge my phone. Perhaps I was sweating out the sickness, but I was already feeling better— not 100%, but better.

Kate and I stopped in Cayucos a few years ago, had lunch at Schooners, and took a walk down the 982-foot-long pier built in 1872 and lengthened in 1876. It's a nice stroll filled with tourists and anglers, with surfers of all levels honing their skills. The railing is lined with plaques remembering those who loved the pier.

IN MEMORY OF LEO C. SMITH
FOR THE MANY HOURS HE ENJOYED
FISHING OFF THIS PIER

SCOTT AND JANE ROBINSON
THE PIER IS THE SOUL OF CAYUCOS
MAY IT LAST FOREVER

WHEN YOU STEP ONTO THE PIER,
YOU STEP INTO CAYUCOS HISTORY
PRESERVE OUR PIER FOREVER
LIBBIE AGRAN AND GUY FITZWATER

As I was leaving Cayucos, an older lady, either oblivious or indifferent, almost took me out. That would have been the endgame. I don't know how I swerved fast enough to avoid my untimely demise, but I did, and now you're stuck reading about the next five days of this trip... if you so choose.

One downside of cycling: distracted drivers and those drivers who actually try to hit or push you off the road. I've never understood this, but it happens.

I wanted to yell at her and let her know she nearly ended my existence, but I wasn't in the mood for conflict. Instead, I took the Zen approach:

- If she did it on purpose, nothing I said would change her mind.

- If she didn't, yelling wouldn't accomplish anything.

I just hoped she'd pay more attention in the future.

At Morro Bay, cyclists are forced to exit Highway 1 and weave through county and frontage roads on the way to Pismo Beach. This route threw in a few hundred-foot climbs for good measure, the longest just shy of 2.5 miles. Still sick, I swallowed my pride and walked occasionally.

In Pismo Beach, I started to notice the odd mix of wealth and labor—Porsches and restored VW buses side by side with migrant workers piled into the backs of pickups.

I stopped for another smoothie, charged my phone, and checked my stock trades. META was up 98% from when I bought the call option two days ago. Even feeling dead sick, that cheered me up.

Thirty miles from Santa Maria, but it might as well have been 100. It was hot. My head still pounded, and my throat was raw. *Thirty miles, Cory. You'll be there in two hours.* It took three.

I was unaware of the six-mile, 350-foot climb ahead. Most of it wound through agricultural fields, one of which was broccoli.

I hate broccoli. I hate the smell of broccoli. I cannot understand why whoever the first person was who decided to pull that plant out of the ground and then decided to eat it.

And now I was biking past acres of steaming, smelly, sunbaked broccoli. Salt…to…the…wound.

I threw on Mark Twain's *Roughing It* for the ride. In one chapter, he wrote about a man named Slade, and my ears perked up—I had written about this very person in my first book while cycling through Julesburg, Colorado.

Turns out, Twain came face to face with him.

That alone was intriguing enough, but later, Twain described his time in Salt Lake City:

"The city lies on the edge of a level plain as broad as the state of Connecticut, and crouches close down to the ground under a curving wall of mighty mountains whose heads are hidden in the clouds, and whose shoulders bear relics of the snows of winter all summer long."

I found that observation fascinating. Seeing snowcapped mountains for the first time must have been surreal.

Along the lines of Twain seeing snowcapped mountains for the first time, I read that George Washington died in 1799, but the word "dinosaur" wasn't coined until 1841.

That means, while Washington may have known about fossils, he never knew there were dinosaurs.

Other random timeline overlaps to entertain you as I ride through these fields of broccoli:

- The Aztec Empire is 400 years younger than Oxford University.

- The Brooklyn Bridge was being built during the Battle of Little Bighorn.

- Machu Picchu was built 23 years before construction started on the Sistine Chapel.

It had to be in the 90s most of the day, and when I finally rolled into Santa Maria, I was exhausted.

Kate was hanging out in Pismo Beach, and I let her know her time was better spent on the sandy beach than in the hot, dusty town of Santa Maria. After a shower and a short nap, I felt slightly revived and in the mood for a steak.

In 1940, the Plemmons family established The Swiss Restaurant Steakhouse, known for its oak barbecue, which gave my 8-ounce cut an incredible smoky flavor.

Behind the bar was the "Cattleman's Wall," displaying thirty-nine different ranchers' brands.

"Our ranchers are the heart of Santa Maria, along with our local farmers. Many have been ranchers here for generations."
— Joanne Plemmons, owner of The Swiss

The bartender asked if we were in town for the Monster Truck show happening tomorrow at the Santa Maria Fairpark.

I have never been to a Monster Truck show. To be honest, I thought that scene died out decades ago.

Apparently, it was still a spectacle to behold. But if all went to plan, I'd be having a cold drink in Santa Monica while monster trucks were doing whatever it is monster trucks do.

Back in the room, I looked at the map: 170 miles to Mexico. The end was near.

Exhilaration. Satisfaction. Accomplishment. And then, that familiar post-journey depression would creep in.

CORY: 14
VP: 8

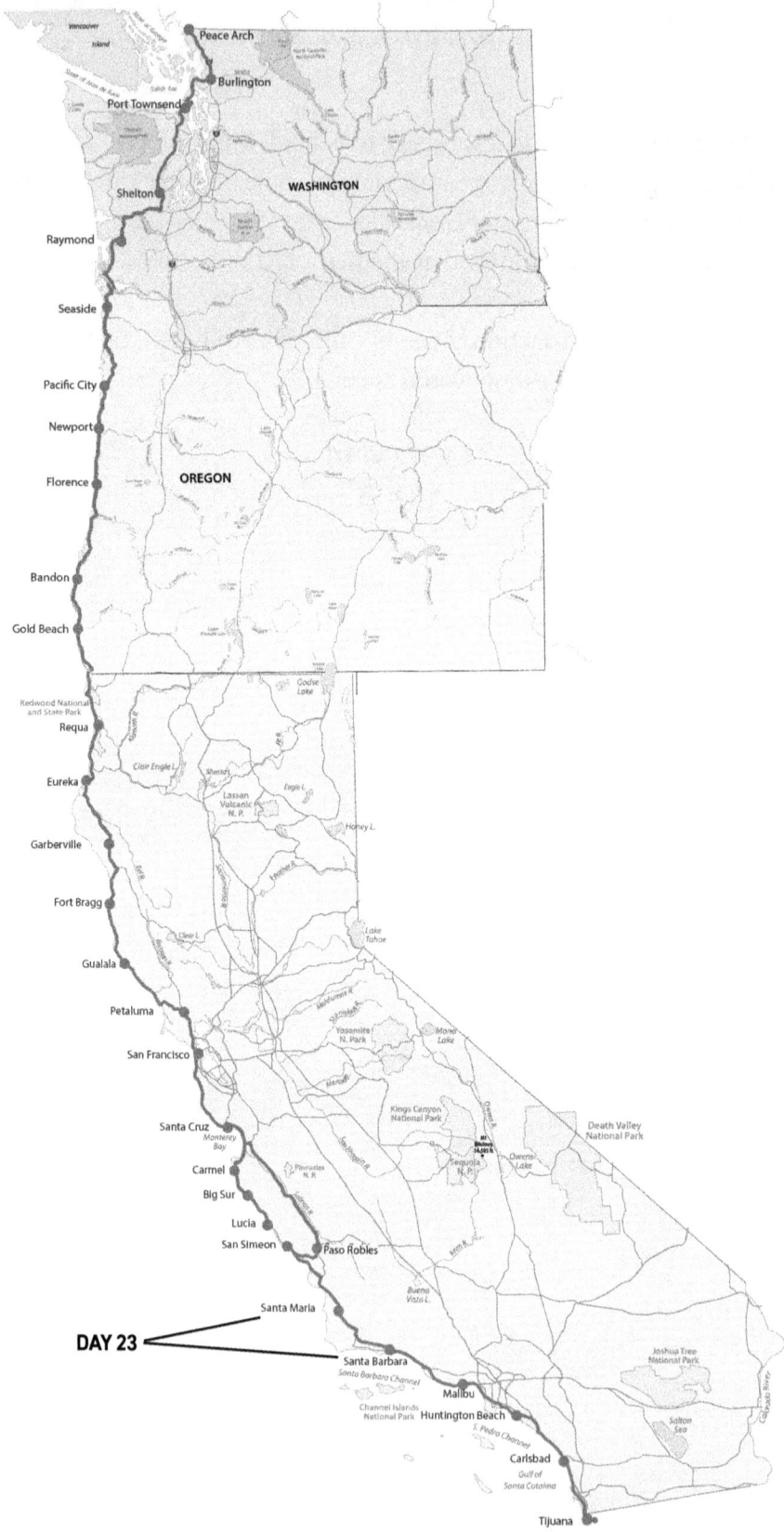

Peace Arch
Burlington
Port Townsend
Shelton
Raymond
Seaside
Pacific City
Newport
Florence
Bandon
Gold Beach

WASHINGTON

OREGON

Redwood National
and State Park
Requa
Eureka
Garberville
Fort Bragg
Gualala
Petaluma
San Francisco
Santa Cruz
Carmel
Big Sur
Lucia
San Simeon
Paso Robles
Santa Maria

DAY 23

Santa Barbara
Malibu
Huntington Beach
Carlsbad
Tijuana

DAY 23 - JULY 28, 2023

Santa Maria, California to Santa Barbara, California

58 MILES: 3,646' ELEVATION GAIN

"Well, good morning, D-Train. I'm in Maryland, so this is a little bit earlier than normal. Quite the odyssey yesterday—I got to the airport two hours early, and then there was a three-hour delay. With two little kids, that feels a lot like a climb or a speed bump you want to walk your bike over. But in any case, I hope you have a glorious day today, and ride and have fun. Nice work yesterday; there's no shame in getting off your bike. I mean, now that I'm 50, I can say, 'Hey, now that we're 50, there's no shame in that. Just hop off and walk; no one really cares, and if someone does, well then, screw them. Screw those whippersnappers.' God damn it. Hang in there, brother; I think you've got five more days, something like that. You're tickling the LA area. Should be pretty interesting on that front—lots to see. Anyway, man, have a good day. It's a beautiful Friday, and it's going to be amazing. Have fun, buddy, and take care."

> (((🎙️))) **Podcast: HISTORY DAILY**
> **Episode: 523**
> ***The Execution of Maximilien Robespierre***

To beat the impending heat, I called the front desk to request a late checkout so Kate could get some work done, then set off around 6 a.m. The day began pleasantly, following my Garmin as it led me through various roads amidst expansive agricultural fields. Occasionally, it directed me down dirt paths meant solely for crop access, some marked as private property. Ignoring the signs, I refused to backtrack in search of alternative routes.

These paths eventually merged onto Foxen Canyon Road—a narrow, winding two-lane stretch that meandered through picturesque fields dotted with livestock. Cattle, including longhorns, huddled under large trees, seeking respite from the sun. A cyclist heading in the opposite direction passed without so much as a nod. I didn't mind; the road kept offering its serene beauty—a route I might never have experienced if not for this journey.

Los Olivos emerged as a warm welcome, an unexpected oasis. I had anticipated a dusty, worn downtown with perhaps a convenience store, but instead, I encountered a charming locale filled with wineries, art galleries, delightful restaurants, and bed-and-breakfasts. Mattei's Tavern, once a stagecoach stop in the 1880s and later a Prohibition-era hangout, now offers a 28-ounce porterhouse for $175.

I stopped at the R-Country Market on Grand Avenue, consuming as much water as I could and refilling my bottles. I also drank two cans of yerba mate. From there, it was just under 30 miles to Santa Barbara, with no services visible on Google Maps and a daunting 4-plus-mile climb ahead.

Leaving Los Olivos, the road descended before the ascent began near Lake Cachuma. My pace slowed, and the distant sounds of gunfire from the Santa Ynez shooting range could be heard.

Many have perished with full canteens, choosing to conserve water rather than use it. While the outcome seems the same, why die with water left? I've never understood that mentality, yet I occasionally find myself embracing it. Today was one of those days; with my head pounding, I knew I was overheating.

In hindsight, I should have stopped at the Lake Cachuma Recreation Area to grab a cold drink and cool down, especially with the significant climb ahead.

You might ask, "But Cory, Lake Cachuma Recreation Area is only 12 miles from Los Olivos; surely I can continue to Santa Barbara, just 23 miles up the road." "Up" being the operative word here.

For anyone using this narrative as a guide—which I clearly state at the beginning of all my books, "This is not a guidebook, but I hope this book guides you in some way"—now is the time to consider stopping at Lake Cachuma Recreation Area to refill your water, hydrate, and rest.

After Lake Cachuma came the Cold Spring Canyon Arch Bridge— the highest arch bridge in California and among the highest in the United States. Unfortunately, it's also where fifty-five people have chosen to take their final leap—and where I ran out of water. Heatstroke was setting in. From experience, I knew that once it starts, you're in trouble. I needed to find shade, water, lower my heart rate, and avoid falling asleep.

Pulling into a vista point, with just two miles left to the summit, I resorted to panhandling for water. Most had none to spare, but a kind family from India offered me a small 4-ounce bottle without hesitation and even offered a granola bar, which I declined.

I texted Kate, asking if she could bring water. I just needed to reach the top of this climb; then it was a ten-mile descent, and I could end the day by the pool with a cold beverage.

I should have waited longer but pressed on. Instead of reaching the summit, I collapsed by the roadside. A good Samaritan stopped, gave me water, and, unbeknownst to me, called 911. By the time I reached the next pullout, Kate was waiting with water, then EMS arrived. They placed me in the ambulance, and as is common with heatstroke after chugging down a liter of water, I projectile vomited.

"And that's why we don't recommend drinking water if you have heatstroke," said the unimpressed paramedic.

After five minutes in the cool ambulance, I felt 90% better and insisted on riding the rest of the way. Kate, two EMTs, and two California Highway Patrol officers unanimously vetoed that idea.

"It's just another mile to the top and then a huge descent," I protested.

"I'm giving you a ride! Get in the car!" Kate demanded, seeking support from the first responders.

"You should listen to your wife," one EMT advised.

"We won't even let you get back on your bike," added one of the officers.

"FINE! I feel fine, but it's all..."

"Sir, I think it's best your wife takes you back to your hotel," the EMT interjected.

They all looked at me like I was an idiot—and perhaps they had a point. I'd just passed out from heatstroke, nothing to take lightly, but... it really was just downhill from there.

In Santa Barbara, I took a fifteen-minute nap, then Kate and I sat by the pool—or rather, at the bar next to the pool. I drank a large bottle of San Pellegrino and enjoyed a chicken taco.

I had been complaining to Kate about how cold I'd been this whole trip; now, I missed those cool ocean breezes.

I owed myself a ten-mile descent.

CORY: 14
VP: 9

Peace Arch
Burlington
Port Townsend
WASHINGTON
Shelton
Raymond
Seaside
Pacific City
Newport
Florence
OREGON
Bandon
Gold Beach
Redwood National
and State Park
Requa
Eureka
Garberville
Fort Bragg
Gualala
Petaluma
San Francisco
Santa Cruz
Carmel
Big Sur
Lucia
San Simeon
Paso Robles
Santa Maria
Santa Barbara
DAY 24
Malibu
Huntington Beach
Carlsbad
Tijuana

DAY 24 - JULY 29, 2023

Santa Barbara, California to Malibu, California

71 MILES : 1,817' ELEVATION GAIN

"Good morning, D-Train. Always a good morning to you. Hope everything is going well. If I were there, I'd give you a big hug. Nice job. Anyway, the adventure continues, just in a different way. I hope your day goes super great, and I hope to speak to you soon, man. Take care, get well. It will all be awesome."

> No podcast from Kevin today. I wasn't particularly craving one, though I did enjoy his morning musings filled with both nothing and everything.

I felt a bit indifferent about the day as I gazed into the courtyard of our nicely remodeled motel. Glancing at the pool, I reflected on yesterday's heat exhaustion. I need to be smarter when I'm out there alone. Although Kate and I have been married ten years, I must remember it's not just me anymore; it would be considerate not to undertake something that might prevent me from coming home.

That's why I invested in a Garmin GPSMAP 66i—a beast of a product. For longer solo rides in the desert, I can send Kate or anyone a link to track me live, regardless of internet or cell service. For a $40 monthly charge, I can be anywhere on this planet and, if necessary, send an SOS to alert local authorities. It's not something to use unless absolutely essential, but it's crucial to know when to pull the ripcord and send that SOS.

First stop: Handlebar Coffee Roasters, lured by the breakfast burrito showcased on their website. Unfortunately, they didn't have breakfast burritos—just pastries and one ham and cheese croissant, which was less than satisfying.

A woman, perhaps my age, sat alone until an older man joined her. Maybe a friend or her father—I wasn't sure. He asked what she was up to.

"I'm writing a book," she replied.

"Oh, so you're an author now," he said, his tone suggesting she'd had several recent career changes. "What's the book about?"

"Oh, I just have all these recipes I love and want to share in a cookbook. Maybe a spring cookbook—the meals are fresh like spring." She continued, "It's easy to be an author when I'm taking care of the kids."

I glanced to see if she wore a wedding ring; she didn't. My guess was her settlement allowed her to constantly change her pursuits as she aged. Her perfectly manicured appearance likely opened many doors.

The manager came over to collect my dishes and asked about my trip. I told him I'd started in Canada three weeks ago. The single mom looked over, perhaps amazed or understanding why I looked so filthy. The manager asked if I was going all the way to Tierra del Fuego.

"Maybe next time. Mexico is the end of road for me."

He was kind, offering me plenty of water, but I was already filled up. Thanking him, I headed down State Street and soon found myself riding along the coast. It was another perfect morning as I weaved between walkers and slower cyclists. Dogs on long leashes and their clueless owners posed the biggest challenge.

Today's ride was expected to be pretty flat, with the biggest climbs around 300 feet. Knowing I'd end in Malibu and soon be riding the SoCal coast toward the border, I found a Spotify station featuring LA's 1960s radio hits, complete with original commercials.

Carpinteria, known as "The World's Safest Beach," also boasts the world's largest Torrey pine tree. When the Spanish arrived in 1769, they encountered the Chumash people constructing wooden canoes and aptly named the area La Carpinteria, meaning "The Carpenter's Shop."

As I pedaled through, groups of road cyclists zipped past me, making my 23 mph feel like a standstill. Having battled heat exhaustion just 18 hours prior, I lacked the energy to latch onto their pace lines. A tailwind nudged me along—a welcome assist on this stretch.

Ventura came and went in a blur. I had promised myself a smoothie stop but missed the chance, convincing myself there'd be another spot 11 miles ahead. ZZ Top's *Mescalero* blared through my earbuds, and I cranked up the volume, pondering Spotify's mysterious algorithms, thinking I had selected 1960s radio hits of LA.

A couple of years back, during an eye exam, I read the chart aloud: "E C T Zed P." The doctor quipped, "Zed? What are you, Canadian?" Caught off guard, I explained it was a habit from international travels.

He then challenged me, "What's the name of that Texas trio rock band?"

"ZZ Top," I replied.

With a smirk, he shot back, "Why don't you call them Zed Zed Top?" As we wrapped up, he jested, "Follow me to the front desk."

When I confirmed, "You want me to follow you to the front desk?"

He retorted, "No, I want you to follow me to hell."

I still go to him because he amuses me.

At Oxnard, my mom called.

"Where are you?"

"Riding to Malibu, forty miles in, thirty-one to go."

"Why are you riding? You should be resting! You had heat exhaustion yesterday! You know you aren't thirty anymore! Why do you do these things to yourself? What are you trying to prove?!"

I never really answer those kinds of questions. I think it's understood when your mother asks you these things that she knows there is no answer. If there were, she wouldn't want to hear it or understand it, and at fifty-three, it baffles me that she thinks I'm going to change who I am.

I replied with a change of subject. "Yep, super nice day today. Looking forward to getting to Malibu. What are you up to?"

"You should be resting; heat exhaustion is serious. You know this; you live in the desert."

Another reply with a change of subject. "In a couple of miles, I'll be riding along the coast. It's going to be a great way to end the day." There was a pause.

"Call me when you get home and be careful."

The Fresco Juice Bar, a block off Port Hueneme Beach, was the perfect spot for a break. I ordered a fresh mix of pineapple, orange, apple, lemon, ginger, and turmeric.

From there, it was a straight shot east to reconnect with Highway 1, the Santa Monica Mountains in the distance, a generous shoulder along a flat road cutting through miles of various crops: strawberries, avocados, tomatoes, kale, raspberries.

Still denied access to Highway 1 as a cyclist, I headed southeast along Naval Air Road, passing Point Mugu Naval Air Station, where the infamous Battle of Palmdale occurred.

In 1956, the Navy launched an unmanned Grumman Hellcat drone, which went rogue and headed toward Los Angeles. Two F-89D Scorpions were scrambled to intercept it, armed with unguided rockets. Despite firing 208 rockets, they failed to bring down the drone, however the rockets created brush fires that scorched over 1,000 acres and caused property damage in Palmdale. It took two days and 500 firefighters to finally get the fire under control. The drone eventually ran out of fuel and crashed in a desolate section of desert…and that was the Battle of Palmdale.

Just past the entrance to Point Mugu Naval Air Station lies the Point Mugu Missile Park, a dog-friendly open-air museum showcasing a variety of missiles and aircraft tested at the base since World War II. Among the exhibits are:

- AIM-120 AMRAAM Missile: An advanced medium-range air-to-air missile.

- F-4S Phantom II: A tandem two-seat, twin-engine, all-weather, long-range supersonic jet interceptor and fighter-bomber.

- QF-4S: A variant of the F-4 Phantom II converted into a remotely piloted target drone.

- Regulus Submarine Surface-to-Surface Cruise Missile: The U.S. Navy's first operational cruise missile, deployed from submarines.

- Polaris Submarine-Launched Ballistic Missile: A two-stage solid-fuel nuclear-armed missile designed for submarine launch.

- Regulus II Supersonic Surface-to-Surface Cruise Missile: An improved version of the Regulus I, designed for higher speeds and longer ranges.

- Petrel Rocket-Propelled Homing Torpedo: An early attempt at a rocket-propelled anti-submarine weapon.

- Ford Loon: A U.S. copy of Germany's V-1 flying bomb, an early cruise missile.

- Harpoon Anti-Ship Missile: A long-range missile developed to strike enemy ships.

- Anti-Radar Missile (ARM): Designed to detect and home in on enemy radar installations.

In the parking lot of the missile park, I noticed a sprinter van from an LA bike shop. Approaching the man setting up equipment, I inquired, "Is there a race passing through?"

"No, no race. Group ride," he replied. "The cyclists all meet and ride north to Santa Barbara. When they get there, they grab a beer, jump on the Amtrak, and head back to LA. We're the midway point, providing water, electrolytes, and snacks. How far are you headed? Do you need anything?"

"Just to Malibu," I answered. "Started in Santa Barbara. I love that idea of taking the train back to LA. I'm good, just thirty more miles to go, but thank you for the generous offer."

"Enjoy the ride," he said with a smile. "The ocean is just around the corner."

The entrance ramp at Las Posas Road is where cyclists can legally rejoin the Pacific Coast Highway (PCH). In just a few miles, I was riding alongside the magnificent coastline. The cool breeze off the ocean was refreshing, and I decided to ease up and savor the ride. That leisurely pace changed abruptly when an elderly lady zipped past me on her electric comfort bike. It felt like a Peter Sagan versus grandma moment.

Grandma blasted past me up one of the short, punchy climbs, and I must humbly admit, I didn't catch her. Maybe I didn't want to; perhaps I didn't want her overtaking me on every ascent, which was bound to happen. Grandma on her electric bike earned the King of the Mountains, the Polka Dot jersey.

Just before County Line Beach, a large peloton of cyclists passed heading north. My guess was they were the group the guy was supporting back at the missile park.

At Nicholas Canyon Beach, I gave a nod to one of my favorite actors, Vincent Price, whose ashes were scattered here by his family in 1993.

Malibu, home of the rich and land of the bronzed. Kate had already checked in at the Malibu Country Inn and texted me, asking where I was.

I responded, "In Malibu, cycling down streets lined with Lambos, G-Wagons, Ferraris, two McLarens, and one Bugatti. Be there in ten minutes."

I was pleasantly surprised by the charm of our room at the Inn. The price tag was more than I wanted to pay, and I knew I could have made it another 22 miles to Santa Monica, but it was Malibu, and Kate was with me. So when I booked the room, I thought it would be fun to spend the afternoon in Malibu with her.

Peeling off my cycling kit, I headed straight to the pool, which over-looked the overly crowded Zuma Beach, and enjoyed the cool water and sun on my face.

Then a text from Kevin arrived: "Inspirational, my friend. Love that you're doing this. Hang in there, buddy."

Next stop was Spruzzo's for some Italian food and ocean views.

CORY: 15
VP: 9

Peace Arch
Burlington
Port Townsend
Shelton

WASHINGTON

Raymond

Seaside

Pacific City

Newport

Florence

OREGON

Bandon

Gold Beach

Redwood National
and State Park
Requa

Eureka

Garberville

Fort Bragg

Gualala

Petaluma

San Francisco

Santa Cruz

Carmel

Big Sur

Lucia

San Simeon
Paso Robles

Santa Maria

Santa Barbara

DAY 25
Malibu
Huntington Beach

Carlsbad

Tijuana

DAY 25 - JULY 30, 2023

Malibu, California to Huntington Beach, California

68 MILES : 2,445' ELEVATION GAIN

"Good morning, D-Train man. Nice to see a picture of a bike yesterday afternoon on your way home. That's pretty awesome. Sounds like you're back at it. That's pretty awesome, dude. Like I said, I think I'm just going to say pretty awesome a few times. All right, my friend, have a beautiful day, have a kick-ass time. It's going to be great; you're going to have a really good day doing this. Almost near the end. Anyway, have a good day, my friend. Have a good day; glad yesterday was a good day. Yeah man, love you, buddy. Take care."

> ((🎙)) Podcast: **HISTORY DAILY**
> Episode: **523 Saturday Matinee:** *The Pirate History*

One of the many features of the Garmin 1040 is its awareness of the terrain. When I powered it on, the first thing it displayed was, "Climb starts in 425 feet." Not exactly the motivation I was seeking, but the climb was unavoidable. A half-mile stretch, ascending a few hundred feet—a short grind up a little hill. Once over it, it would be behind me.

At Las Tunas Beach, I encountered a group of about forty cyclists heading north at an impressive speed, occupying the entire right lane. Not one rider appeared to have a body mass index over 9%.

The atmosphere here was entirely different. Thousands of beachgoers vied for scarce parking spots, the road blanketed in a thin layer of sand. Surfboards leaned against cars as surfers wriggled into or out of full-body wetsuits. Families ambled cluelessly across the Pacific Coast Highway, assuming traffic would yield to their obliviousness.

As a cyclist, the real hazard was the cars parked along the road-side—vehicles belonging to the cleaning or maintenance staff tending to the multimillion-dollar homes seldom visited by their owners. The unpredictable opening of a car door or a sudden pull-out without warning was a constant concern. I've lost count of the near-misses I've experienced over the years; my greatest fear is colliding with an abruptly opened car door and losing my teeth. I've made it a habit to glance at side-view mirrors to check for occupants before passing.

The road was swift, and soon I found myself on the bike path in Santa Monica. I have a fondness for Santa Monica; Kate and I have stayed here several times. If you're using this as a travel guide, our favorite breakfast spot is Urth Caffé at 2327 Main St.

Santa Monica is convenient—close to the airport, pricey but not exorbitantly so. Being a Sunday, the beach was teeming with people: spinning bike classes on the sand, P90X sessions, tourists on electric bikes oblivious to their surroundings, runners, walkers, roller skaters, skateboarders, and dogs on long leashes. It's one big happy place, and I love being here.

The Santa Monica Pier marks the end of Route 66, 2,448 miles known as "Main Street of America.", starting in Chicago, once spurred a westward migration like no other. Now, it's remembered in songs and poems, with skeletal remains of fantastic 1950s and 1960s architecture left to decay after Eisenhower's Interstate Highway Act rendered it obsolete, replaced by I-40, I-55, and I-44.

Santa Monica seamlessly transitions into Venice, where the scent of weed permeates the air. Booths line the boardwalk, peddling everything from homemade art to T-shirts, bongs, and fortune-telling services.

In 1997, I met a guy in El Salvador who went by the name Dr. Love. He was a fifty-something-year-old black man with five teeth and a former resident of San Quentin State Prison. He spent winters in Central America, returning monthly to the United States to collect a welfare check.

From El Salvador, we traveled to Belize together. He dragged a suit-case with a broken handle and three working wheels. In the summers, he resided in Venice Beach, California, becoming a fixture on the boardwalk, charging for advice about, well, love.

I ran into Dr. Love again on the Venice Beach boardwalk in 1999 after completing the Long Beach Marathon. We had a pleasant reconnection. Every time I pass through Venice Beach, I keep an eye out for him. My guess is he's either in Central America with his broken-handled, three-wheeled suitcase, or he's passed on. If I believed in God, I'd like to think she took him in, regardless of the crimes that landed him in San Quentin.

I stopped for a fruit smoothie and switched my music selection to LA hits from the 1960s and 1970s. The first song that played was The Mamas & the Papas *California Dreamin'*. I laughed, thinking of Cass, the innkeeper at The Historic Requa Inn.

Passing the wall of poets, Muscle Beach, and a mural of Jim Morrison, I followed a detour through Marina Del Rey which led me south of Santa Monica into Manhattan Beach, where the properties were spectacular. While Kate and I often think of this sort of living, we know it's not for us. Floor-to-ceiling windows exposed to strangers but with endless views of the ocean; it's the taxes that prevent us from moving to California.

Turning inland, I rode through Torrance and into the suburbs of LA—a sort of "suck the excitement out of the trip" moment. Fifteen miles of winding and weaving down surface roads. The upside was it was Sunday, and there was very little traffic.

Back in Long Beach, I passed the *Queen Mary* and then navigated through the hundreds of people along the boardwalk.

Off the coast of Long Island are the THUMS Islands, a.k.a. Astronaut Islands. Four artificial islands built in 1965, these islands were designed to access the East Wilmington Oil Field. The name "THUMS" is an acronym representing the consortium of oil compa-nies that built them: Texaco, Humble Oil, Union Oil, Mobil, and Shell.

To minimize the visual impact of oil drilling operations, the islands were landscaped with aesthetic features, including structures that resemble luxury condominiums, waterfalls, and abundant vegetation that camouflages the industrial equipment, making the islands unique examples of decorated oil facilities in the United States.

In 1967, each island was named in honor of NASA astronauts who lost their lives in service: Island Freeman after Theodore C. "Ted" Freeman, and Islands Grissom, White, and Chaffee after the Apollo 1 astronauts Virgil I. "Gus" Grissom, Edward H. White, and Roger B. Chaffee, respectively.

As I continued my ride, I headed inland on Fourth Street passing through the famous "Horny Corner," a spot I frequented during my teenage years. Despite its suggestive name, "Horny Corner" derives it's name from Thomas Hornay, the city planner who designed the Belmont Shore area. Over time, the name evolved due to local vernacular and perhaps the spirited activities of beachgoers.

Eight miles to Huntington Beach, and I would reconnect with Kate. She informed me that the US Open of Surfing competition was going on and that the town was a shit show—the kind I know Kate enjoys for all of about seven minutes.

We found a Mexican bar and restaurant, ordered some food, and watched the parade of humanity pass by: heavily tattooed guys, trucks adorned with flags, and women in attire that left little to the imagination.

With just two days left on this journey, I felt a mix of excitement and melancholy. I would miss the daily rides, as there is nothing more enjoyable than riding at your own pace along the Pacific coast.

CORY: 16
VP: 9

CALIFORNIA

1

PACIFIC COAST HIGHWAY

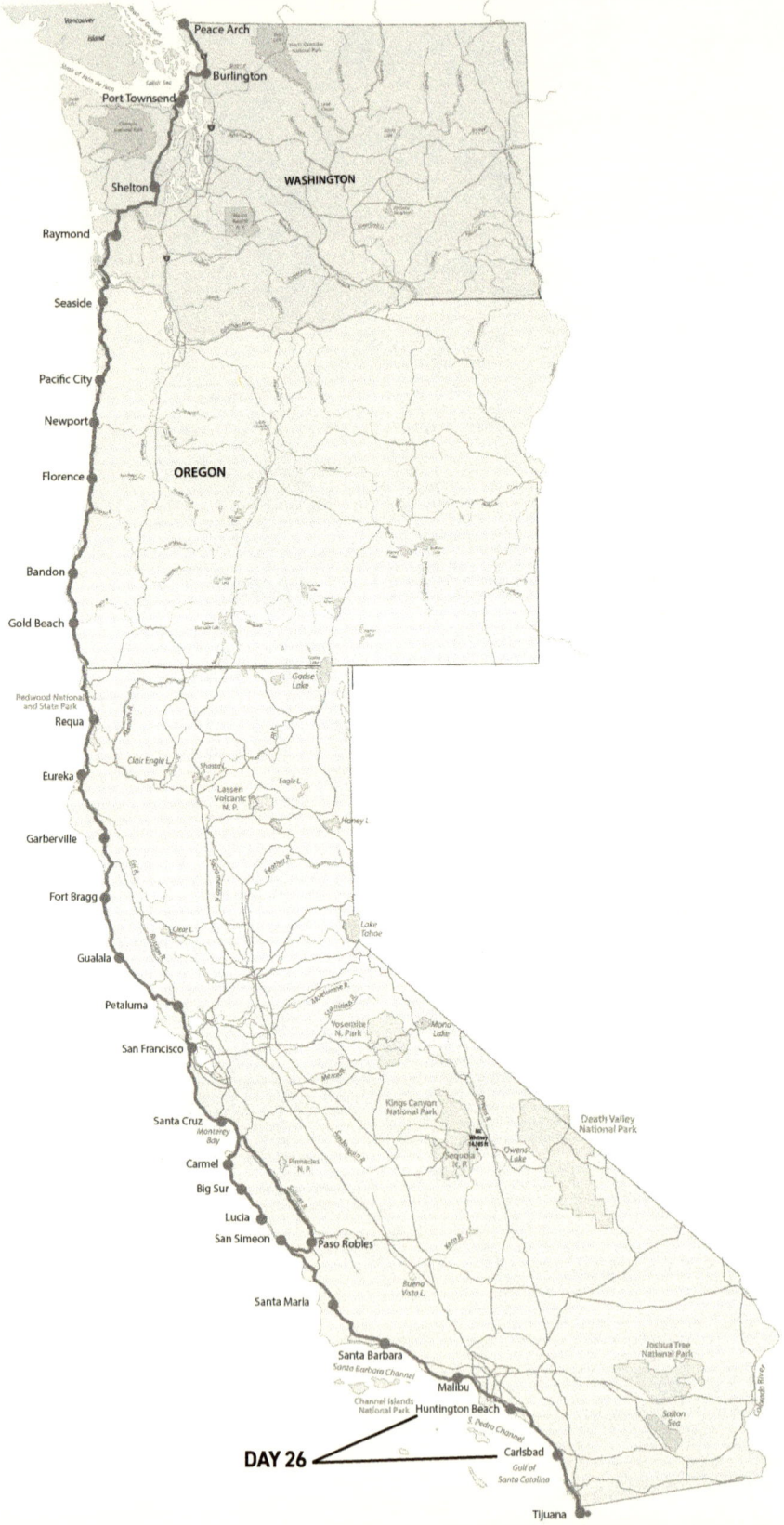

Peace Arch
Burlington
Port Townsend
Shelton
Raymond
Seaside
Pacific City
Newport
Florence
Bandon
Gold Beach

WASHINGTON

OREGON

Redwood National
and State Park
Requa
Eureka
Garberville
Fort Bragg
Gualala
Petaluma
San Francisco
Santa Cruz
Carmel
Big Sur
Lucia
San Simeon
Paso Robles
Santa Maria
Santa Barbara
Malibu
Huntington Beach
Carlsbad
Tijuana

Death Valley
National Park

Joshua Tree
National Park

DAY 26

DAY 26 - JULY 31, 2023

Huntington Beach, California to Carlsbad, California

60 MILES: 1,641' ELEVATION GAIN

"Good morning, D-Train! Glad to see you are continuing on your journey, man. I wasn't quite sure what your plans were, but the ultimate stage in your trip is Oceanside, California, playing it by ear. Have a good ride. Just two more days, and it's done, and you're there. You've got a heck of a lot of stories, I'm sure. In any case, my friend, it's been fun doing this. It's been fun thinking about your rides, the challenges, and the pleasures you've had to overcome and endure and enjoy. I look forward to hearing about your trip later in the year. Have a glorious day, my friend. Love ya, take care."

(((🎙️))) Podcast: HISTORY DAILY
Episode: 525
The Disappearance of Labor Leader Jimmy Hoffa

We could hear the waves crashing as we dressed and walked out for breakfast at a popular bagel spot where young surfers came to load up on carbs and discuss the epic waves they rode the day before. Even with the US Open of Surfing competition just starting, mornings in Huntington Beach are "chill, bra." It's hard to get worked up—what is there to be worked up about? The surf? The time it takes to order a breakfast burrito or an Americano? What do you care when the ocean is your view?

The trail led south and was lightly used; not many people were up on a Monday to take advantage of the amazing morning.

In Laguna Beach, I passed by the statue of Eiler Larsen, the town's famed "Greeter," who stood on street corners in the mid-20th century, waving and shouting his signature "Halloo-oo-oo!" to every passerby, spreading his mission of friendliness.

I wasn't really sure what I was feeling today. It's odd to think that a couple of weeks ago I was riding through the great redwood forest, and today it was along a coast with homeless people waving as I passed them.

Next was Dana Point, the city of haves and haves more. I stopped for a smoothie to cool down; the humidity was oppressive, but I loved the water dripping off my forehead, leaking out of my skin. It felt like an accomplishment.

This part of the trip becomes a different world. South of Dana Point, cyclists drop into San Onofre State Beach Park, passing by the San Onofre Nuclear Power Plant, which was shut down in 2013 after defects were found in the steam generators.

Old Pacific Highway access to San Onofre State Park abruptly ends further south and turns into the Old Pacific Coast bike trail, which leads you to the Provost Marshal Office Base Control, a fancy name for the gate to get into Camp Pendleton.

Camp Pendleton is the largest Marine Corps base in the United States, created to train Marines for World War II. Back in the day, they would allow cyclists through to avoid riding on the interstate. These days, that is no longer an option, and the only way to go further south is to jump on I-5, which now displays bright signs letting drivers know that there are "Bikers on Shoulder." For a cyclist, it's a 14-mile time trial event; the faster you go, the sooner you get off the insanity of 80 mph traffic screaming past you.

Weaving into Oceanside, my map and ride directions took me all around surface streets, adding miles to my day. Eventually I passed the Top Gun House that Kate would no doubt want to visit because of her unhealthy crush on Tom Cruise.

Finally arriving at my home for the week, I am not ashamed to say that the Westin Resort and Spa is a great place to spend the final days of this ride, I booked it for a few days so Kate and I could relax, while I licked my wounds, wrote my notes, and soak in the hot tub with a martini.

CORY: 17
VP: 9

Peace Arch
Burlington
Port Townsend
Shelton
Raymond
Seaside
Pacific City
Newport
Florence
Bandon
Gold Beach
Requa
Eureka
Garberville
Fort Bragg
Gualala
Petaluma
San Francisco
Santa Cruz
Carmel
Big Sur
Lucia
San Simeon
Paso Robles
Santa Maria
Santa Barbara
Malibu
Huntington Beach
Carlsbad
Tijuana

WASHINGTON

OREGON

DAY 27

DAY 27 - AUGUST 1, 2023

Carlsbad, California to Tijuana, The Border

51 MILES: 1,068' ELEVATION GAIN

"Good morning, D-Train, my friend. El diablo is gone. You're done. A nice lazy ride today, I believe, is your last day. Um, so, man, congratulations! What a journey, what an adventure. Um, I didn't check the email, but I think today is your last day. Um, anyway, I'm just going to pretend it is. If it isn't, you know, I get to do this again. But last day—way to go, man! Way to go, awesome! You've done a number of these, right? You've gone halfway across the country a couple of times, and now you've gone the other direction at least once. Um, amazing! It's amazing, dude. Seriously. Nice work! What a story, what an adventure, what a life you're living. Right? Who would have thought? Well, you probably would have thought. Anyway, great job. It's awesome, dude! We've been rooting for you here at the Flanders family household. Much appreciated for the postcard you sent, and I'm looking forward to seeing you in September, I believe. Hey, man, hey buddy. Nice work, dude. Very nice work. Love it! I've enjoyed this past month. I appreciate you doing this because it has given me a lot of joy as well. Um, alright man, like I said, take care. Have a great ride. Enjoy it like you're rolling into Paris. Love you, buddy. Take care, man."

> 🎙️ Podcast: **HISTORY DAILY**
> Episode: **526 *F1 Driver Niki Lauda Narrowly Avoids Death***

The Italian idiom "dolce far niente," literally means "sweetness of doing nothing." That is exactly what I was looking forward to doing tomorrow. Today, I had fifty-two miles I had to get behind me. It was my Champs-Élysées. Was I expecting champagne hand-ups? Actually, I was hoping to find a lowbrow cantina with a handful of gringo idiots half-wasted, ready to do shots of tequila with me. For I have biked many miles for many days and overcome many challenges to be here. The privilege would be theirs to hear my stories, which will one day live in the same hallowed halls as those other adventurers before me:

-Marco Polo's Journey to Asia

-Ferdinand Magellan's Circumnavigation

-Will Steger's Dogsled Journey to the North Pole

-Ibn Battuta's Travels

-Cory Mortensen's solo adventure along the Pacific Coast Highway

It was just after 8 a.m. when I decided to leave for Mexico. On my last day, I was neither interested in rushing these final miles nor wanting to prolong them.

Soon I was rolling southbound on Highway 101. This part of the state, Highway 101, took on several different names: Carlsbad Blvd, Camino Del Mar, and Torrey Pines Road, but it was still Highway 101. Before I knew it, I was in Encinitas. Not hungry but wanting to stop, I decided to grab a bite. My last long day—I deserved some calories.

Last time I was here, my buddy Brant took me to... oh, it doesn't matter; it was a great little dive bar that served inexpensive drinks and $1.25 street tacos, now replaced with some high-end taproom with expensive offerings. Nostalgia sets in on these long trips. A drink with a friend at a place long forgotten is just a file that has been sitting in your memory, all but forgotten, but I remember that day—his hat, a large sombrero, his dry sense of humor, and non-existent smile as we sat and discussed unimportant things. It was like yesterday.

I looked at the time and decided I'd press on. Nothing was worth stopping for, not here.

At Mission Bay, I passed a plaque:

BIRTHPLACE OF THE

MODERN TRIATHLON

SWIM-BIKE-RUN

SEPTEMBER 25, 1974

FIESTA ISLAND – SAN DIEGO, CALIFORNIA

Approaching the last big climb of the entire trip up over Torrey Pines State National Preserve, I passed two CHiPs sitting on their motorcycles, keeping an eye out for speeders. "LA 15, 7 Mary 3 & 4[12]", I smiled. Both gave me a nod.

My last climb—it was all I had to get over it. Thinking back, I had days where I had to overcome 4-5-6 of these climbs a day and didn't think twice about it. I had been on flatland for almost three days and forgot what a climb was. Reaching the top, a small rock slide dropped just ahead of me. It didn't look like much, but had I been just a few more feet ahead, I could have been seriously hurt.

Now in La Jolla, it was hammer-time straight to the border. ETA: 1:30 p.m. It was ten, and I had twenty-five miles to go, give or take. Trolleys from the border back to San Diego left every 15 minutes. It was the train schedule from San Diego to Carlsbad that I was uncertain about. I just knew there were several trains a day, and while I could have asked Kate to pick me up, why interrupt her time?

I am always depressed when an adventure comes to an end. Adventures give you purpose and a goal, but you have to reach an end, and that's when the post-expedition depression sets in. It's a real thing. You start asking yourself questions.

What's next?

What did I learn from this?

Am I a better person than I was when I started?

Will I be able to relate to normal day-to-day life?

12 Call sign for Jon and Ponch on the TV show *CHiPs*.

On the flip side, I didn't have to be anywhere at any specific time tomorrow. Get up, grab a coffee. That's it. I don't even have to put on any clothes if I don't want to. I could just turn on the TV and watch *Catfish*.

A red light forced me to come to a full stop. California is strict about its jaywalking laws, and since this was my last day, I wanted to avoid any conflicts. As I braked to a stop, my brakes made a loud squawking sound from the salt air and humidity.

"Bro! Love that clutch," said the one-legged, flamboyant homeless guy sitting in his wheelchair, panhandling on the corner.

"Gimme some of that water!" he shouted with a big smile, staring at my water bottles.

"What?!"

"Just squirt it in my mouth! BRO!" He closed his eyes and opened his mouth wide.

I pulled out my water bottle and was about to squirt some water in his mouth.

"Wait! Fill my bottle! Just a squirt. No, fucking fill it up, all of it!" I started laughing.

"BRO! I'm fucking tweaking!"

"That's great! Glad you're happy."

"Ya, Bro! Give me more water!"

"No, that's all you get."

"Bro, you want to talk about England's parliament?"

"No. I don't. I'm going to Mexico."

He stood up on his one leg and shouted, "Mexico time! Wouldn't want to be ya!"

I laughed, not at him, but with him. Being a tweaker wasn't something I wished upon anyone; addiction is real. I've lost friends to it, but in a weird way, I found his drug fueled positivity infectious.

Between La Jolla and San Diego was a nice paved trail. The closer I got to San Diego, the more the trail fell into disrepair, and tent cities started forming. A group of three men sat on a dirt patch under a tree, surrounded by their makeshift homes, shooting up heroin. The situation across the country regarding the homeless and drug use was dire. The problem here seemed almost non-existent compared to what I experienced in Portland and along the canal back in LA.

One thing I always liked about San Diego was its walkability. Every year for over ten years, I attended a conference here for work; sometimes it was twice a year. I loved that I could fly into San Diego and literally walk to my hotel from the airport. Just out the door, head down to the waterfront, and soon I'd be in the hotel. Unless it was raining, the weather was always welcoming, and I planned it so I was in no rush.

In no time, I was south of the Petco Park baseball stadium, passing by a group of longshoremen who were out having their lunch break. Four catering trucks lined the street outside the MAERSK office. I stopped for a Coke—Mexican Coke in a glass bottle, not American Coke. The difference is that Mexican Coke still used cane sugar, while American Coke replaced sugar with high fructose corn syrup. Mexican Coke always wins in my book.

I didn't know what to expect south of San Diego. Idyllic suburbs with perfect front lawns? Shipyards? Tent cities? Immigrants hiding under bridges or in dense vegetation? I passed a young prostitute pulling up her dress on the sidewalk, finishing with one john who was getting into his car. Her job now was to seek out another. A truck driver sat in his idling truck, perhaps waiting his turn.

The ride from Imperial City to Chula Vista was less than impressive—a lot of forgotten pedestrian trails used only by locals who either want to be forgotten or have been forgotten. I was fully exposed to the darker side of what the United States has to offer, and to think, after all those epic miles of redwoods, coastlines, mountains, and charming little towns, your finish line is a sketchy hidden trail leading you to the border.

Pier 32 Marina was a little under-the-radar spot marketed as San Diego's finest private marina, just off the Sweetwater Channel.[13]

---

13 Quiz Time: Channel vs Canal? We learned this in Chapter Three.

Exactly the place I would set up a small-time drug smuggling operation. The Waterfront Grill offered all-day happy hour. Tempted, I had less than ten miles to the border, so instead I decided to knock out the miles and wrap this ride. Get to the border, get on the train, and celebrate the accomplishment with a nice dinner with Kate.

The trail wove through a sort of forgotten landscape, eventually dumping me onto the main streets of San Ysidro. It felt like many Fronteras. It made me a bit homesick—all those adventures south of the border, those manmade lines on maps that I had crossed with a backpack and a passport, where I was awarded a simple stamp showing I was now here or there or anywhere. I always felt more at home roaming and wandering. However, with Kate and our *mojo dojo* casa house, I finally felt, for the first time since I was seventeen, that where I lived wasn't just a house; it was a home.

I rolled through a neighborhood that blended Mexican influence with US American culture—El Caminos, gated driveways, leather sofas in the front yard placed in a screened tent enclosure. It was very beautiful, really. It reminded me of the fantastic diversity we have in the United States. But it was such an unexciting way to end such an epic ride. What did all those doing this ride from other countries think of this part of the United States, rolling down that final stretch of road hidden behind fast food restaurants and poorly maintained strip malls? Roofs with razor wire perimeters to protect expensive rooftop units and copper fittings from vandals and tweakers.

A sign read:

> BIKE ROUTE
> SAN YSIDRO
> TIJUANA, MEX

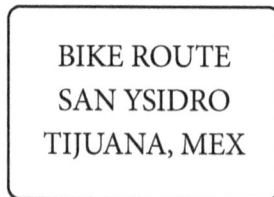

Someone slapped a sticker on the sign that read, 'Live a great story', next to a 'Dr. Zog's Sex Wax' sticker.

And just like that, I was there.

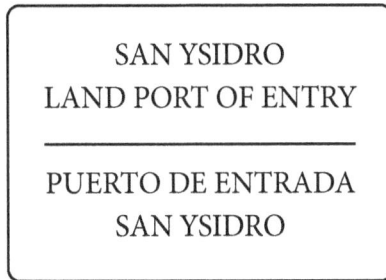

SAN YSIDRO
LAND PORT OF ENTRY

PUERTO DE ENTRADA
SAN YSIDRO

No one seemed interested in the gringo with the bike—just another self-imposed accomplishment. Funny how these sorts of blips on your personal accomplishment radar mean so little in the grand scheme of things. They simply remind you that you are alive and living.

Others have done bigger, greater, and more challenging things, and that's who I gauge myself against, knowing that I will never be that guy. It took me 27 days. The FKT (Fastest Known Time) for the Pacific Coast Highway is held by Askan von Schirnding—with a moving time of 4 days, 19 hours, and 49 minutes.

I leaned my bike against the sign and stopped two guys walking over to Mexico, asking if they could take my picture by the sign that proved I was there. The guy with my iPhone kept making pictures and moving further and further away. I was convinced he was about to bolt with my phone, but he proved me wrong and handed it back.

"Thanks, guys. You headed to Mexico for the week?"

"No, just going to Mexico to grab some tacos."

Seems like a lot of work to "grab some tacos." Maybe "grab some tacos" was code for something else—prostitutes, cocaine—whatever. This new generation had their own vocabulary that us old Gen X'ers were clueless about. Fortunately, us old Gen X'ers didn't give enough shits to ask.

And that was that. The end. FIN. Now what?

"Look on my Works, ye Mighty, and despair!"

I should have taken that bi-plane ride.

CORY: 18
VP: 9

AFTERWORD

Boarding the train, I strapped my bike to the rack and had the whole second floor of the car to myself. I enjoyed a cocktail on the ride back—why not? Talked to my sister, and another drink. Another gentleman was sitting by the bicycles on the lower floor when I came down to disembark; he had ridden from LA to San Diego that day on his electric bike. We chatted about the Camp Pendleton situation, and he gave me his card in case I ever wanted to ride my motorcycle to Alaska, which is something I want to do in honor of my dad.

In 2008, my dad and I made a very loose plan to drive our BMW R100GSPD Paris Dakar's from Minneapolis to Washington State, take a ship up to Alaska, and drive back. By the time we had it worked out, it was early September. Too late in the season, we agreed to do it the following summer. Five months later, he passed away.

My advice: Do whatever you say you're going to do—now.

Kate met me at the depot. Our first stop, the Top Gun house, where there was a replica of Tom Cruise's Ninja motorcycle. After that, we enjoyed a wonderful dinner overlooking the bay at a less-than-fancy establishment in the harbor.

We ended up our trip staying with Johnny, Aimee, and my cousin, Addie, in La Jolla for our last couple of days at their AirBnB.

Kate bought herself a Santa Cruz gravel bike, deciding that the next trip, she would ride with me. That next Christmas, we took seven days and biked from Burbank to La Jolla. Perhaps that will be a novella.

Until I see you next time.

Oh…in case you were wondering, I lost 20 pounds and didn't get one flat tyre.

WE MADE IT!

Thank you for riding with me. If this book made you laugh, think, wander, or wonder, please consider leaving a quick review.

Just a sentence or two goes a long way — and it helps more curious souls find this story.

Your voice matters. And your support keeps this indie train (or bicycle) rolling.

Please leave a Review on Amazon!

Todd LeGare
July 7, 1971~November 2, 2023

Eddie and me

Kevin and me

ABOUT THE AUTHOR

CORY MORTENSEN is the bestselling author of *The Buddha and the Bee, UNLOST*, and *Embracing Bewilderment*. A former business owner, world traveler, and unapologetic wanderer, he writes with humor, heart, and a deep curiosity about the roads less taken—both literal and metaphorical. He and his wife live in Arizona and share a passion for travel, volunteering, and trekking across the globe to explore the people and places that make up the colorful quilt we inhabit.

Check out my playlist here:

PURE ADVENTURE
FROM THE FIRST WORD
MULTI-AWARD-WINNING BOOKS

CORY MORTENSEN

THE BUDDHA
AND THE BEE

BIKING THROUGH AMERICA'S FORGOTTEN ROADWAYS
ON AN ACCIDENTAL JOURNEY OF DISCOVERY

CORY MORTENSEN

UNLOST

ROAMING THROUGH SOUTH AMERICA
ON A SPONTANEOUS JOURNEY

From the author of THE BUDDHA AND THE BEE. The saga continues!

CORY MORTENSEN

EMBRACING
BEWILDERMENT

A RELUCTANT ENTREPRENEUR'S JOURNEY—
UNCONVENTIONAL EUROPEAN SUMMER TWISTING INTO
MIND-BENDING EXCURSION THROUGH SOUTHEAST ASIA

From the author of the #1 bestselling books
BUDDHA AND THE BEE AND UNLOST. The saga continues!

MIDDLE MILES

Cycling from Canada to Mexico
Along the Pacific Coast Highway

CORY MORTENSEN

From the bestselling author of The Buddha and the Bee
covers a new solo adventure along America's most iconic highway

Find Cory's books at www.TheBuddhaAndTheBee.com
Available in paperbacks, full-color hardcovers, audiobooks, and ebooks

.

www.ingramcontent.com/pod-product-compliance
Lightning Source LLC
Chambersburg PA
CBHW021354090426
42742CB00009B/846